EMERSON AS PRIEST OF PAN

EMERSON

AS PRIEST OF PAN

A Study in the Metaphysics of Sex

ERIK INGVAR THURIN

THE REGENTS PRESS OF KANSAS
Lawrence

Library of Congress Cataloging in Publication Data
Thurin, Erik Ingvar.
Emerson as priest of Pan.
Bibliography: p.
Includes index.
1. Emerson, Ralph Waldo, 1803-1882—Criticism and
interpretation. 2. Sex in literature. 3. Polarity in
literature. 4. Love in literature. I. Title.
PS1642.S47T5   814′.3   81-4818
ISBN 0-7006-0216-X   AACR2

FOR

JAN AND ANN

CONTENTS

INTRODUCTION

In a sense this book is about Emerson's ideas about love. But it would be equally correct to say that it deals with his view of man: Any theory of man is by necessity a theory of love. Then again any theory of man must say something about the universe and man's place in it. Love, whether looked at from a Christian or a Platonistic point of view, is not merely erotic. When Plato has Socrates pray to Pan at the end of the *Phaedrus,* the recipient of his prayer is not the chaser of nymphs; it is already the All with which the Neo-Platonists liked to identify him. In the *Symposium,* another book that influenced Emerson greatly, Socrates is compared to the Great Daemon Love who fills the gap between heaven and earth, holding the whole together. In saying that his poet is "the priest of Pan," Emerson also identifies with this Socrates. There is of course also a Christian connection: His great poet is often seen as the redeemer, the mediator between man's world and God's heaven. One may say that he spent his life looking for such redeemers in literature—authors of universal autobiographies, of "bibles" that were also personal confessions. In the absence of an *oeuvre* that satisfied him entirely, Emerson had to seize the pen himself. His work contains his own dream of redemption, his own blueprint for the reconciliation of heaven and earth.

The question is: what kind of dream, what kind of reconciliation, does Emerson's work represent? This is where the idea of polarity comes in, and sex, that primordial form of polarity. Archetypally the union of the spheres is often represented in nuptial terms, as the marriage of Ouranos and Gaia; this analogy also pervades Emerson's universe, and his discussion of it. He is very much influenced not only by Platonism in a strict sense but by a broad syncretic tradition which also embraces hermetic-alchemic thought and cabalism, and in which the feminine principle tends to be associated with the earth, the male principle with heaven. Because of this connection, Emerson's view of the relation between heaven and earth cannot be properly analyzed without reference to his views on sexual polarity at the human level, and conversely one cannot discuss his views on human sexuality without reference to his ideas about heaven-earth polarity.

At neither level are we dealing with a simple pattern. The nuptial-bipolaric conception of the relation between heaven and earth—and between man and woman—is not really the dominant one in Emerson's variations on this old theme. More often than not his professed bipolaric approach yields to a monistic tendency in which the earth is assimilated rather than married to heaven. This tendency again often looks as if it were simply the reverse side of what I shall call his "dualistic" phase, in which "heaven and earth" are presented as being in conflict and bent on eliminating one another. The final tendency of both these deviations from nuptial bipolarity is the same: The earth and everything it stands for is to disappear as not of the essence. Obviously, such an attitude cannot fail to have a bearing on Emerson's view of woman, the sex which he sees as more closely associated with nature and the earth than man is.

Hell, needless to say, also enters into the picture as a universal pole. There are occasions on which Emerson seems to see woman as an instrument of the devil rather than of nature. On the whole, however, "hell" seems to bother him much less than nature and the earth. When evil is not specifically related to sinful sex, he is apt to view it in cheerfully alchemic terms, as "good in the making" or else as something not worth worrying about because it does not really exist.

Thus I shall have to paint a somewhat ambiguous picture. It will not be possible to accuse me of attributing to Emerson a system of the kind for which he himself professes such distaste. I know I am analyzing a persistent pattern in his work, rather than an explicitly stated doctrine. Accordingly, the fourteen chapters, while closely related and planned as a whole, have been made as self-contained as possible to avoid the appearance of excessive systematization.

Obviously, I do not agree with those who argue that Emerson cannot be held to any kind of consistent thoughts or opinions because of the nature of his thought and its expression. It is true that he often seems to delight in contradiction or arguing "on the other side"; his frequently desultory and rhapsodic exposition, in which the logical connection between sentences and paragraphs may be obscured, does not make the analyst's task easier; nor does his use of "indirection," and specifically of the "silences" inherent in certain types of symbolism. But Emerson is not Borges: The ideas he elaborates may not be elements of a system, but they are not merely themes of his discourse either. We shall never correctly assess his importance if we see him chiefly as "an artist who wrought in spiritual materials" (Henry James).

Even worse is the notion that Emerson is a "balanced soul" who has much to say "on both sides" and leaves it for the readers to choose between the alternatives he presents or strike their own balance. This view of Emerson, which comes close to making his attitude resemble that of the impartial newspaper editor, is an outrageous trivialization of his aim as a thinker and writer. It is patently false: He does not usually balance his exposition by arguing on both sides without dropping any hints as to where he himself stands. Nor is such a stance compatible with his philosophical position. He may like to speak about balanced views as something admirable, but his commitment to Platonic idealism prevents him from cultivating the kind of detached skepticism he attributes to Montaigne. I have already stated that he swerves from nuptial bipolarity, the most important form of balance, in his discussion of man and the universe in terms of polarity and sex.

Emerson portrays himself as "an endless seeker," but that implies that he is seeking something; he uses Proteus as an image of his poet, but the point of the myth is that Proteus can be caught and forced to tell us what he knows; again he says that he does not know exactly what sense his thought and utterance make, but he also says he does not worry much about that because he is certain that there is "a unifying tendency" which binds everything he writes together and that will be discernible at the proper distance and altitude. We should have that altitude now, almost a hundred years after his death and virtually all of his writings being available in excellent scholarly editions.

As for Emerson's method of composition, there is another side to that matter, too. If it sometimes veils his meaning, it can also reveal it. To give a few examples: What seems strange in one passage may be explained by another passage which in its turn may not be particularly clear without the other one; when he seems to argue on both sides, one may pay attention to what he says where the emphasis falls. Everything suggests that we can posit a dialectic between a desire on Emerson's part to avoid excessive clarity and an equally strong wish to reveal himself to the ideal, "intelligent" reader for whom he writes and who in the final analysis is he himself. This is true not least of the symbolism related to his use of the central idea of universal sex and polarity.

Accordingly, I hope I have been able to do justice both to the "unifying tendency" in Emerson's work and to the ambiguities that are inherent in any tendency. I might add that the ambiguities in his case are so much a part of his Platonizing philosophical tendency and so predictable that they have a consistency of their own. On the whole, his thought pattern appears surprisingly consistent when looked at in the light of his references to universal polarity and sex and his dream of redemption through the reconciliation of "heaven and earth."

The pattern I find in Emerson's thought is reflected in the general structure of my exposition, the chapter divisions. The first and last chapters (1 and 14) are of a somewhat general nature; the other twelve form four triadic parts in which I discuss a number of ways in which his view of sex and polarity affects his account of human relations and the possibility of redemption in this world. To be more specific: Chapter 1 deals with Emerson's contention that his ideal self-projection, the poet, rather than science, is able to redeem the world because he is motivated by love and marries the spheres on a nuptial basis; it is shown how this claim founders on the rock of a more dominant and more intransigent Platonistic monism whenever Emerson's argument is not set adrift by a strong undercurrent of dualism. The first triad (2, 3, and 4 in the table of contents) could be called "Heaven and Earth Compared": It purports to demonstrate the monistic tendency in Emerson's thought as it pertains to human sex and the relation between the sexes. The second triad (5, 6, and 7) does the same for the dualistic phase of his thinking: It might be called "Heaven and Earth in Conflict." These two triads belong closely together; both emphasize the tensions and difficulties besetting Emerson's thinking. The third and fourth triads are also closely related: There is ambiguity here, too, but the stress throughout is on Emerson's more or less successful attempt to solve the problem of redemption for the individual and for the species. Thus the third triad (8, 9, and 10) is about the three main directions his imagination takes in his speculation about the possibility of a nobler human society raised above considerations of sex and other earthly concerns. The fourth triad (11, 12, and 13) represents another turn of the monistic screw: It is about "internal marriage," or the heaven within. The final chapter, to avoid giving the impression that Emerson actually solved his problems once and for all, not only returns us to a somewhat more general level but focuses once more on the tension between Emerson's theoretical adherence to a bipolaric vision of the world and the actual limitations of his allegiance to it. The relation between man's mind and nature-earth forming the bipolaric point of departure in this case is filial rather than nuptial (nature-earth is the Great Mother). Following the account of the various forms of internal marriage in the fourth triad, this discussion focuses on the myth of the "balanced soul" rather than on the poet's ability to marry heaven and earth.

If the conceptual framework I am using makes it possible to demonstrate a kind of consistent ambiguity in Emerson's thought, it is also helpful in other ways. It is, for one thing, extremely versatile: There are hardly any aspects of his thought that do not come within the purview of this study. No doubt the subjects of these chapters have been chosen with a view to showing the "unifying tendency" in Emerson's writings and the ambiguities it involves, but they also represent important facets of his thinking. Indeed, I would be highly surprised if they are not of considerable general relevance.

Working on a book of this type must obviously to a large extent be its own reward, but surely the reward will be greater if

INTRODUCTION

it can be shared with others. It is my hope that this investigation will prove of interest not only to myself, and a few Emerson specialists, but to all serious students of the long cultural tradition in which Emerson in a sense occupies a strategic place. While I will not agree that he is a "balanced soul," I am willing to go along with the idea that he is a representative man. He did not produce a universal autobiography exactly, but he is representative because of the extent to which his writings reflect an important intellectual trend of the past and at the same time foreshadow some very significant phenomena to come (like, for instance, Nietzsche).

To know Emerson really is to know more than Emerson, to paraphrase what he himself says apropos of the great and representative man. One might also say that it is impossible to understand Emerson by studying him alone. This is not primarily a genetic study, but he does "stand all-related," and frequently the best way of explaining his thought—and more importantly its significance—is to use a comparative approach. What is more, much of the excitement of a prolonged involvement with Emerson definitely comes from these literary relationships, the opportunity and need to associate with the great minds with whom he saw himself identifying in love and aspiration.

Another facet of Emerson's work that is peculiarly fascinating and must be used to best advantage is its relation to his Platonic aspiration. His idealism was not mere theorizing: To him as to Thoreau, it involved a serious, almost existential struggle to rise in the scale of being. Some critics complain about the difficulty they experience in bridging the gap between "the live man" and his "phantom" or "dream" image of himself. But this is missing the point in the sense that he himself found it difficult to bridge the gap between what he preferred to see as his mundane self and his ideal or angelic self, and always resented this fact. In analyzing Emerson's idea of man in the context of his extended autobiography, we must never forget the distinction between the thinker and his thought. But we must also remember that his ideal vision of man and himself is very much part of the live Emerson and that he himself felt that over the years he was slowly, much too slowly, in his own person bending the real in the direction of what he thought of as the ideal. In some respects he actually did not have to do much bending; there are cases in which his personal experience colors his view of the ideal. In short, if we want to understand what Emerson is all about, it is as important to note the auto-biographical dimension of his thought about man as it is to relate it to the intellectual history of the world.

KEY TO PARENTHETICAL REFERENCES

CEC   *The Correspondence of Emerson and Carlyle,* ed. Joseph Slater (New York, 1965).

CEG   *The Correspondence of Ralph Waldo Emerson and Hermann Grimm,* ed. F. W. Holls (Boston, 1903).

CSE   *A Correspondence between John Sterling and Ralph Waldo Emerson,* ed. E. W. Emerson (Boston, 1897).

E   Ralph Waldo Emerson, *Essays* and *Essays: Second Series* (Boston, 1841–1844; facsimile rpt., Columbus, Ohio, 1969).

EL   *The Early Lectures of Ralph Waldo Emerson,* ed. S. E. Whicher, R. E. Spiller, and W. E. Williams, 3 vols. (Cambridge, Mass., 1961–1972).

G   Ralph Waldo Emerson, Preface to Saadi's *Gulistan or Rose Garden,* trans. Francis Gladwin (Boston, 1865).

J   *The Journals of Ralph Waldo Emerson,* ed. E. W. Emerson and W. E. Forbes, 10 vols. (Boston, 1909–1914).

JN   *The Journals and Miscellaneous Notebooks of Ralph Waldo Emerson,* ed. W. G. Gilman et al., 14 vols. to date (Cambridge, Mass., 1960–1978).

L   *The Letters of Ralph Waldo Emerson,* ed. Ralph Rusk, 6 vols. (New York, 1939).

LF   *Letters from Ralph Waldo Emerson to a Friend,* ed. C. E. Norton (Boston, 1899).

KEY TO PARENTHETICAL REFERENCES

M   Ralph Waldo Emerson, "Visits to Concord," in *Memoirs of Margaret Fuller Ossoli*, 2 vols. (Boston, 1851), I.199–316.

P   Ralph Waldo Emerson, *Poems* (Boston: Ticknor and Fields, 1860).

RW   *The Works of Ralph Waldo Emerson*, ed. J. E. Cabot, 14 vols. (Boston, 1883–1887).

UW   *Uncollected Writings: Essays, Address, Poems, Reviews and Letters by Ralph Waldo Emerson*, ed. Charles Bigelow (New York, 1912).

W   *The Complete Works of Ralph Waldo Emerson*, ed. E. W. Emerson, 12 vols. (Boston, 1903–1904).

Note: Since virtually all of Emerson's poetry is printed in the ninth volume of the Centenary edition of the *Complete Works* (W) and can easily be found in the index to that volume, page references to the poems are given only when a poem is not included there, or is relatively long, or is not identified by name. Quotations from the *Journals and Miscellaneous Notebooks* (JN) have been simplified, in that words and phrases deleted by Emerson in the process of writing have been ignored in the interest of readability.

1

SYMBOLISM AND SCIENCE: EMERSON'S POET AS RECONCILER AND REDEEMER

Emerson did not always see a contradiction between the poet's attitude toward nature and the scientist's. During his visit to the Jardin des Plantes in 1833, he was impressed by certain exhibits which had been arranged in such a way as to suggest a continuum between man and the lower forms of life—that is, the unity of man and nature. It was "a beautiful collection," he notes, and made him feel "as calm and genial as a bridegroom" (JN.IV.199). This is certainly a poetic approach to nature, and yet it is followed by the statement that the experience also made him want to become a naturalist.

In the portion of the early lecture called "The Uses of Natural History" based on this entry (EL.I.8), the reference to bridegrooms has been dropped, however. Possibly the author felt it was too personal. There is every reason to believe that his imagination on that memorable day in Paris was stimulated not only by the scientific collections he was viewing but also by the memory of his first wife. He had recently been celebrating the beauty of nature as a reflection of her beauty in "Thine Eyes Still Shined" and other poems, and another journal entry (JN.V.212) suggests that "calm and genial" is how he himself felt when he was wedded to Ellen Tucker. On the other hand, he may also have wanted to dissociate his poetic self from the naturalists for purely ideological reasons.

In "The Uses of Natural History" he already seems preoccupied with the conflict between the aims and claims of the poet and those of the scientist. This conflict was to become a leitmotif in his later writings, including the lecture entitled "Poetry and Imagination," written almost forty years later, where he nevertheless still speaks about "the mysterious relation" that nature bears to man's experience and says that "The lover sees reminders of his mistress in every beautiful object" (W.VIII.9–11).

The conflict in question bears upon a central problem in Emerson's thinking: the modalities of man's redemption. His poet becomes the redeemer of man because his love of nature brings man and nature together again, overcoming the old divorce. This theme, like the celebration of nature as a reflection of the beloved woman, is as such a commonplace in Romantic poetry; on one occasion Emerson quotes a passage in Wordsworth's "The Recluse" according to which everyday life will be restored to a paradiselike state on the day when we are again "wedded to this goodly Universe / In love and holy passion" (EL.II.273).

In the words of Novalis, the German poet-mystic to whom Carlyle drew Emerson's attention, man is the messiah as well as the groom of nature. The idea in this case is that man-the-poet by showing the "consanguinity" (W.I.63) of nature liberates and redeems her from the isolation imposed upon her by various modes of dualistic thinking, including the radical dualism of science. The process can be considered nuptial and bipolaric in the sense that man in rendering nature this service also finds his own status in the universe clarified and his spiritual energies enhanced; in fact, if it had not been for the favors that nature in her turn bestows on her redeemer, he would not be able to do much for her or his fellow-men. Significantly, "The Poet," where the poet's mission is defined as the redemption of the natural man, is one of the places where Emerson most forcefully uses the nuptial approach to nature, insisting that the poet must leave the company of men and for a long time lie "close hid" with her because, as he puts it, "This is the screen and sheath in which Pan has protected his well-beloved flower" (W.III.41–42).

In an important variation of the idea that man-the-poet is the lover of nature, he becomes the *sine qua non* of the marriage of heaven and earth (his mind being of heaven and his body of the earth). The two images are sometimes used conjointly, as in the passage in *Nature* where Emerson adopts another Romantic cliché, the notion that man's salvation hangs not on the advances of a new scientific spirit but on his return to an earlier, childlike state associated with a lost Eden. In this perspective, "The lover of nature is he whose inward and outward senses are still truly adjusted to each other; who has retained the spirit of infancy even into the era of manhood" (W.I.9). In the same passage it is intimated that if a man achieves this feat "his intercourse with heaven and earth becomes part of his daily food." This is another way of saying that the poet, as the chief representative of man, is "the public child of earth and sky" (W.IX.47), which again is the same thing as seeing him as the seal of the archetypal marriage of Ouranos and Gaia, the bond which holds the two spheres together.

The common denominator of Emerson's various nuptial conceptions of the poet is the idea—again rather unscientific—that man, and especially the poet, is at the very center and core of the universe. This assumption—stated explicitly in *Nature,* "The Poet," and many other places—is very versatile. One of its most striking metaphorical expressions is the suggestion that the poet is not so much a token of the love of heaven and earth as the very copula which holds them together *in coitu,* as it were. In a *Dial* article Emerson writes quite graphically: "The poet, like the electric rod, must reach from a point nearer the sky than all surrounding objects, down into the earth, and into the dark wet soil, or neither is of use" (W.XII.366). In other cases, his use of the old assumption that man is "the point wherein matter and spirit meet and marry" (JN.I.187) conjures up visions of man's brain as a kind of cross-roads inn where heaven and earth may have their rendezvous and embrace, thanks to the offices of the poet. The poet, in this perspective, becomes the go-between or "match-maker" (JN.XIV.355), whose act of seeing a possible marriage of a natural phenomenon and an eternal truth is at the same time its performance.

In a letter to Lydia Jackson, who was to become his second wife, Emerson describes himself not as a naturalist but as a poet-seer of this kind—as "a perceiver and dear lover of the harmonies that are in the soul and in matter" (L.I.435). The poet apparently derives great pleasure from seeing things fall into place: "The poet knows the missing link by the joy it gives," says his portrayer in "Poetry and Imagination," with a punning allusion both to the "marriages" seen by the poet and to the theory of evolution which presumes to prove the unity of man and nature (W.VIII.10). In the same text it is suggested that the poet keeps his eyes riveted on the horizon, the line along which heaven and earth are joined: "The poet sees the horizon, and the shores of matter lying on the sky, the interaction of the elements" (W.VIII.41).

However, it is time to say that such suggestions of a peculiarly erotic imagination are not the only indications of the gulf dividing Emerson's poet and the naturalists. The whole issue is complicated by the circumstance that he is even more apt to argue the idea that the poet unites heaven and earth in a manner contradicting both his nuptial approach to the question and the viewpoint of science. I am referring to the monistic phase of his thought, in which the earthly pole tends to be assimilated by heaven and in the process voided of its own substance. This tendency is closely linked to the Platonistic version of Emerson's theory of poetic symbolism, which is based on the assumption that the phenomena of this world are mere mirror images of their equivalents in the spiritual realm and therefore have no value beyond their symbolic function.

Perhaps such a devaluation of the earthly world is more or less inevitable at the level of a technical discussion of its symbolic function; after all, symbols are always inferior to that which they symbolize. But Emerson frequently takes a similarly unflattering view of the earth even when the mirrorlike correspondences that make poetic symbolism possible are not technically involved. Thus he finds occasion to argue that Goethe failed to become the redeemer of man's mind because he was too willing to regard earthly life as an eminently worthwhile affair that does not leave much to wish for in the next, unless it be more of the same (W.XII.330–333). Even Wordsworth is criticized for suggesting in his "Intimations of Immortality" that earthly life has its own beauty and satisfactions: "The world is very empty," says Emerson, "and is indebted to this gilding, exalting soul for all its pride. 'Earth fills her lap with splendors' not her own" (W.II.147).

This monistic view, alien to science *and* humanism, suggests an apocalyptic idea of man's redemption rather than a merely millennial dream of a terrestrial paradise of the kind reflected in

Wordsworth's lines about the wedding of man and nature. No doubt Emerson himself sometimes took a conservative view of the matter in speculating about the poet's ability to bring about a change in human affairs through an adroit use of the symbolic correspondences between heaven and earth, but from the beginning of his career (when his hopes of this order were strongest) one also finds explicit prophecies of a frankly apocalyptic transformation of the human condition.[1] Thus "The Uses of Natural History" contains a quotation from Coleridge: "For all that meets the bodily sense I deem / Symbolical, one mighty alphabet / For infant minds." A clear suggestion that nature has a merely temporary function, this passage from "The Destiny of Nations" prepares the reader for the author's own subsequent hints that the external universe may eventually disappear "when its whole sense has been comprehended and engraved forever in the eternal thoughts of the human mind" (EL.I.24–26).

It may seem difficult to find a nuptial image for this conception of man's redemption, unless it be the old one-person marriage in which the wife is virtually annexed and assimilated to the husband. However, Emerson sometimes does resort to more or less nuptial language even when he expresses a view of the relation between man and nature which is ultimately monistic because it reduces nature to a mere object or instrument, a belonging of man's. In *Nature,* for instance, he suggests that nature is at best "thoroughly mediate" and "made to serve," and that it receives the "dominion" of man "as meekly as the ass on which the Savior rode" (W.I.40). This may look like a peculiar version of man-the-poet as the messiah of nature, but it is perfectly compatible with another statement Emerson makes in *Nature*—that the place of nature in her marriage with man is under man.

Whether couched in erotic terms or not, the idea of man's "dominion" over nature must be called aggressive as well as contemptuous, and thereby hangs the tale of another complication affecting Emerson's discussion of the relation between man and nature. He denies in *Nature* that he shares the hostility to nature which he here attributes to Plotinus and Michelangelo. However, many of his phrasings, especially in the section called "Idealism," suggest that he sometimes regards nature as a somewhat intractable and even inimical entity that is to be forcibly "degraded" into an object and then assimilated into the mind of man. As so often happens in the writings of his chief philosophical authorities, the ancient Platonists, the monism of *Nature* in some degree looks like an expedient therapy for a dualistic fear of the natural state of man. Although the author argues that scientists also know how to suck all life and substance out of nature-matter and leave it "an outcast corpse" (W.I.56), this fear, needless to say, is different from the radical dualism which in a sense forms the metaphysical basis of science since Descartes.

The contradiction between the ultimately monistic view of nature, with its dualistic overtones, and the image of the poet marrying a love-sick heaven to a love-sick earth is fairly obvious. It affects Emerson's discussion of poetic symbol-making at the technical level of correspondences as well as at the more general level of the poet's alleged ability to redeem nature and man. Emerson's ability to ignore this discrepancy must be called one of the most intriguing problems that the student of his poetic theory and practice has to confront.[2] He is obviously not incapable of seeing it; indeed, he comes close to putting his finger on it in a passage in *Nature* where he discusses the tension between what he calls "the ideal theory"—that is, the notion that the external world is only an illustration of the human mind—and "the popular faith," or the belief that this world actually exists and is as solid as it seems. The latter position seems in line with the lyrically nuptial approach to nature which Emerson sometimes attributes to the poet, and yet "the ideal theory" is the technical basis for his theory of poetic symbolism. As he himself suggests, the two positions are incompatible.

In pursuing the question of why Emerson chooses not to face this contradiction squarely in his discussion of the poet, we again come across the problem concerning his relation to the naturalists and science in general. It is more than a coincidence that nuptial imagery and stress on the importance of love are apt to appear in his more critical comments on science, which also claims to be able to improve the condition of man. To put it differently, one reason why Emerson uses nuptial imagery as much as he does and closes his eyes to its logical incompatibility with his monistic conception of the "union" of heaven and earth is that he sees science, not Platonism, as the chief threat to the claims of his poet. Science,

Emerson feels, ought to be put in its place: Analysis is not enough; the analyst-scientist must be complemented by and indeed made subordinate to the lover-poet (EL.I.81).

In a limited sense this is what happened to the scientist in Emerson. No doubt he seriously desired to become a naturalist during his 1833 visit to the Jardin des Plantes. It is as if the young man, after losing his first wife and resigning from the ministry, were contemplating at the same time a new career and a new kind of "marriage" for himself. However, it was not meant to be. He did begin to lecture on science-related topics after his return to the States, and although his first fervor soon cooled off, he always continued to take a keen interest in the *results* of scientific research. But the patient *methods* of science were not for him: To the end of his life, he was to prefer those of the poet, to whom the world is always "virgin soil," and who can be defined as "a true recommencer, or Adam in the garden again" (W.VIII.31).[3]

The most remarkable aspect, perhaps, of Emerson's running controversy with science is the polemic use this post-Christian Platonist makes of the idea that the poet loves both the parties he joins in marriage and that this is what makes him morally superior and hence a greater benefactor to man than the scientist, sometimes represented as a cold-blooded dissector whose foremost instrument is the knife. This view is present already in "The Naturalist" (1835), where Emerson concedes that some of the great naturalists of the past—like Cuvier and Linnaeus—were inspired by a genuine "love of the whole" (of the particular as well as the general), but only to express the more forcefully his skepticism concerning the hordes of naturalists of his own day (EL.I.79–80).

In *Nature,* where the marriage of poetry and natural history is seen as the road to redemption, "love" is said to be as important as "perception," and the "patient naturalists" who "freeze their objects under the wintry light of the understanding" represent the fallen state of man (W.I.74). This is also the point driven home with great eloquence in "Blight," where Emerson uses the word "know" in an almost Biblical sense when he says that the young naturalists who invade his woods "love not the flower they pluck, and know it not"—and then goes on to paint a distressing picture of how the earth is becoming increasingly frigid and "the rich results of the divine consents / Of man and earth, of world beloved and lover / The nectar and ambrosia, are withheld" (W.IX.140–141).

No doubt Emerson was sincere in his fear for the future of mankind, but there is reason to believe that the virulence of the attack, as well as the references to sexual union and offspring, is caused in part at least by an unhappy feeling that poetry, from the standpoint of science, is little more than fantasy and dream. The problem could only be compounded by the circumstance that this view was not confined to the scientific community: Schelling, a philosopher who otherwise shows great respect for poetry and was sometimes accused of being a poet, concedes that the poet joins the universal and the particular in a union which does not objectively take place—that is, he does not perceive the laws that govern the universe in themselves but only through a symbolic medium. Among German Romantic poets with whom Emerson acquired some familiarity, Novalis unabashedly characterizes the world of the poet as dream and fairy tale, and Jean-Paul suggests that dreaming is unvoluntary poetry. They could of course still find the poet capable of a higher—or deeper—truth than science, but to Emerson this view was not entirely satisfactory, at least not as long as he attached serious millennial or apocalyptic hopes to the symbol-making of his poet.

Apparently feeling that it is on this side he is most vulnerable in his lover's quarrel with science, Emerson spends much energy defending the poet against the charge of being a vendor of dreams. In *Nature,* for instance, he finds it imperative to argue that not only the poet but man is an "analogist," and that the analogies he perceives, far from being "the dream of a few poets here and there," are "constant" and "pervade nature" (W.I.27). Clearly, he still believed at the time that the phenomena of the earth correspond to those of heaven on a one-to-one basis according to a fixed divine plan. He was also capitalizing on the authority of Guillaume Oegger, who holds that the correspondences in question are the tools of God in teaching and communicating with man.[4] This notion enables Emerson to affirm that the relation between the two poles of the universe which inspires the poet "stands in the will of God and is so free to be known by all men," i.e., that poetry is also an exact science and can therefore be a powerful weapon "in the arsenal of power" (W.I.34–35).

Actually, we are here, too, dealing with a pattern of great durability. In some respects Emerson's attitude hardly changed even after he discovered the subjective nature of poetic symbolism, that is, the polyvalence of natural objects and the "fluxional" quality of the symbolic connections to which they give rise (W.III.34): In a relatively late poem, the poet still rides to power "Horsed on the Proteus" (W.IX.288). By the same token, Emerson did not necessarily feel compelled to recant entirely because geology and the study of the slow processes of evolutionary change made a millennial revolution in human affairs through the offices of the poet seem less likely. He appears to concede a great deal to the scientific view of these matters in "Fate," but in the end he still comes out on the side of "Freedom" (W.VI.3–49). In a slightly later journal entry, he notes that he can see beforehand that he will not believe in "the Geologies," the earth-bound sciences (JN.XIII.51).

Emerson did change his position somewhat, of course. He became more prone to view redemption as a more personal and also as a less definitive affair, something not unlike the freedom for which a man will have to fight all his life in order to keep it. But here, too, the poet is opposed to the scientist. Whereas the poet remains the redeemed man as well as the redeemer, the scientist is still seen as the epitome of man unredeemed and in need of poetry (JN.XIII.261). During one of his many later journal meditations on this theme, Emerson notes that "these geologies, chemistries, astronomies, sciences leave us where they found us" (JN. XIII.412). He uses the same phrase in discussing Goethe's shortcomings as a redeemer of the human mind: A man like him "should not have left the world where he found it."

On other occasions, Goethe appears in a better light, as when Emerson says in "Poetry and Imagination" that "science does not know its debt to imagination" and that Goethe was in a position to give hints to science. In the same essay, he suggests that fields like geometry, chemistry, and hydraulics are "secondary science" and exist mainly to furnish "rhymes" for "the truer logician," the poet. Here, again, man's redemption emerges as the final goal to which science remains blind: "I honor the naturalist; I honor the geometer, but he has before him higher power and happiness than he knows" (W.VIII.10–56).

In this later period, too, the nuptial conception of poetic symbolism is in evidence without being clearly distinguished from the "Platonic" view which Emerson once contrasts with "the so-called scientific" tendency, always "negative and noxious" (JN. XIII.356). In "Poetry and Imagination," where the defense of poetry against the pretensions of science can be called the leitmotif, he suggests that even if the nuptial relation to heaven and earth is not objectively present in the sense of being discernible to all men, genius is still able to "rightly say the banns" (W.VIII.47). However, this language is contradicted by the earlier, persistently Oeggerian statements to the effect that the world is "an immense picture-book" and that God himself (unlike science) "does not speak prose, but communicates with us by hints, omens, inference and dark resemblances in objects lying all around us" (W.VIII. 9–12).

In a sense, then, Emerson's battle with science only exacerbates the conflict between his Platonism and the frequently nuptial approach of his poet. However, this does not mean that his intermittent stress on bipolarity should be seen as sheer rhetoric or merely a convenient tool to clobber science with. The beauty and "consanguinity" of nature is felt by most men, and by Emerson more than by most men. There can be no doubt that he loved nature and the earth in his own way. If some of the individual phenomena which make up the whole of nature, like snakes and rats, were not attractive, he could still reap satisfaction from seeing what he construed as the illuminating symbolic connection between such earthbound creatures and the higher world of moral and intellectual thought.

One can even say that Emerson's readiness to appreciate the "lower" realm and marry it to the higher was enhanced by his reading of Greek philosophy. He was not entirely wrong in regarding Platonic idealism as a lesser threat than science to his view of the poet as the reconciler of earth and heaven: Plato himself had natural feelings about the beauty of the sensible world, including the beauty of humans; in fact, he was even willing to admire the celebrator of this world, Homer, provided the *Iliad* and the *Odyssey* were not introduced into his Ideal State. There is also a certain ambiguity in some of his mythic statements, as when he says that the Great Daemon Love not only fills "the whole space" between heaven and earth but prevents the two parts of the universe from falling apart. This sounds like an allusion to the marriage of Ouranos and Gaia and suggests the desirability of keeping it intact. So does Plotinus' way of representing intellect as recumbent on the *anima mundi* or sensible world sometimes referred to as "the Mother."

It is true that this scheme still leaves Plotinus' highest hypostasis, the One, out of touch with the *anima mundi*. It is also true that Plotinus' gospel of love, like Plato's fable about the Great Daemon, formally provides only for upward love and aspiration on the part of the individual seeking reunion with the One; as for the One, it needs nothing and loves nothing below itself. However, the One is occasionally referred to as "the Father," and the dance of the creation round its creator is sometimes discussed in terms of a father-daughter relationship, an image implying some kind of mutual affection. Furthermore, although the Bible alone unequivocally makes God's love for his creation an example for man and discusses it in clearly nuptial terms, Proclus, in whom Emerson was very much interested, does take a step toward reconciling his master's philosophy with Judeo-Christian doctrine in this respect.

Besides, the limited role of true bipolarity in the Platonistic discussions of these matters was to some extent obscured by Emerson's selective approach to this school. Although thoroughly impressed with authors like Plotinus and Proclus, he was as impatient with their elaborate dialectical structures as he was with the methods of science. His pantheism represents a simplification of these systems which through a shift of emphasis tends to make the monistic position more organic and more agreeable to man's natural feeling about the world he inhabits: Instead of carrying the idea that matter is "the end or last issue of spirit" (W.I.34) to the point of seeing it as "dead Mind" (W.XII.17), the pantheist in Emerson may focus his attention on the notion that the divine effluvium after all does reach everywhere and thus can be said to permeate the universe. Such a faith does not leave God "out" of him (W.I.63). On the contrary, it legitimizes the kind of homage to the "consanguinity" of nature that Emerson found in Wordsworth's early poem "Tintern Abbey." He has been accused of fixing himself forever in this posture, and it is true that if his poet is "the priest of Pan" (W.II.39), it is largely because of the attraction that this way of thinking exerted on him.[5]

Strictly speaking, Emerson's brand of pantheism does not in itself do much for bipolarity of the kind on which his theory of redemption through poetic symbolism is supposed to be based. It acquits the individual soul willing to embrace the earth as well as heaven of the sin of loving what is really unworthy of its love, but the perspective is still monistic and the love a kind of self-love, subject and object being essentially the same and the opposition between heaven and earth obscured along with the distinction between hypostases. On the other hand, one might say that the obfuscation of this issue is advantageous to a philosopher in Emerson's situation in that it throws a veil over the conflict between bipolarity and monism which otherwise might stare him in the face. Pantheism à la "Tintern Abbey" is a pleasant invitation to vague and comforting thinking about love and bipolarity on a universal scale. Emerson is sometimes able to combine a pantheistic vision of the world not only with Proclus' idea of a love traversing the universe in both directions but also with Empedocles' conception of love as the constitutive cosmic force and the related hermetic-alchemic notions about a love cementing the whole in all directions. Such influences explain poems like "Cupido" ("The solid, solid universe / Is pervious to love; / With bandaged eyes he never errs, / Around, below, above") and "Beauty" ("He saw strong Eros struggling through, / To sun the dark and solve the curse, / And beam to the bounds of the universe").

The hermetic-alchemic school of thought in itself must have encouraged Emerson to ignore the contradiction between his doctrine of mirrorlike correspondences and the more nuptial view of poetic symbolism which helped him defend the office of the poet against the claims of science. Empedocles also stresses the importance of similarity in spite of the bipolarity suggested by his erotic view of the universe, but even though his thought appealed to Emerson, it has come down to us in a rather fragmentary state. Hermetic-alchemic doctrine, by contrast, is extremely well documented and has the further advantage of a syncretic alliance with various forms of Platonism, ancient and modern. Emerson absorbed elements of it at an early age through the works of seventeenth-century authors like Cudworth, Browne, Henry More,

Donne, Herbert, and Milton. This influence was mightily reinforced by the vogue alchemic-hermetic thought enjoyed during the Romantic period.

The image of the mirror is used to explain the relation between heaven and earth in *Hermes Trismegistus: The Divine Pymander,* of which Emerson acquired a copy in 1842.[6] Yet alchemy, supposedly founded by Hermes, stresses the nuptial analogy to the point of making sexual polarity seem just as important as the heaven-earth axis: The *Ars Chymica,* a body of authoritative alchemic writings, states categorically that woman is "the earth of man" ("terra hominis") and man "the heaven of woman" ("coelum feminae"). In fact, some of their *coniunctiones*—including those of the sun and the moon and the outdoors and the house, which Emerson uses in *Nature*—are not as clearly in line with the heaven-earth axis as with the idea of universal sexual polarity. The connection with the heaven-earth opposition is usually there if one looks for it—the opposition of the sun and the moon, for instance, can be seen as a variation of the sun-earth *coniunctio*—but the vagueness helps further obfuscate the contradiction between his two conceptions of the poet's "marriage" of heaven and earth.[7]

With respect to the conflict between the lover-poet and the dissector-scientist, Emerson profited from the ideas of the German Romantic philosophers who attempted to update Neo-Platonic thought by stressing the hermetic-alchemic strand of the syncretic tradition. To the Germans, the alchemic-hermetic vision of a world held together by a union of opposites conceived of in analogy with sexual polarity seemed not only more in accordance with man's natural feelings about nature but also more "organic" and hence truer than the mechanistic world-view of Newton or the radical dualism of Descartes. In the same spirit, Emerson denounces the "surgical" approach of modern metaphysics (W.XII.14) and declares that "whosoever shall enunciate the law . . . embracing mind and matter diminishes Newton" (JN.XI.235).

In "Beauty," chemistry is compared rather unfavorably with alchemy, and the reference is clearly to Emerson's by then somewhat faded dream of a millennial revolution in which the poet was to play a leading role: "Chemistry," he says, "takes to pieces, but it does not construct." Alchemy, on the other hand, "which sought to transmute one element into another, to prolong life, to

13

arm with power,—that was in the right direction" (W.VI.282). On the whole, the pseudoscientific claims of alchemy, couched in nuptial language, appealed to his imagination: Not only does his poet also produce "gold" through his poetic marriages of heaven and earth—even his conception of the poet as a redeemer bringing "the Age of Gold again" (W.III.87), which he never entirely gave up in spite of the retrenchments forced by science, is matched by the historical dimension of hermetic-alchemic thought with its clearly messianic overtones. As a member of the Homeric chain beginning with Hermes Trismegistus and picking up Proclus on the way, the great man of this school is also a uniter of heaven and earth, or male and female, and in this capacity he is prophetic of the saving *rebis,* or Philosophers' Stone.

As mentioned, Emerson does not entirely reject science, but prefers to subordinate its findings to those of the trouvère. It ought to be added that he finds it easier to render science serviceable in this manner when he does not respect the line between science and alchemy too scrupulously. Thus he is capable of saying in "Poetry and Imagination" that the poet is inspired by "real rhymes" furnished by science, namely, "the correspondences of parts in Nature, —acid and alkali, body and mind, man and maid, character and history, action and reaction," all the way "up to the primeval apophthegm that 'there is nothing on earth which is not in the heavens in a heavenly form, and nothing in the heavens which is not on the earth in an earthly form'" (W.VIII.48–49). The heaven-earth axis may seem somewhat obscured in these examples, but the male-female analogy is clear, although Emerson has juggled the order in which the two married opposites are listed. Even the opposition between "character" and "history" is supposed to be thought of in these terms, witness a passage in "Character" (W.III.97).

Two series of opposite pairs in "Compensation" (W.II.96–97) also chart the universe along these lines. Emerson's main inspiration in this case probably is not the Pythagorean table commonly referred to as "Alcmaeon's decade."[8] In the first series, "rhymes" like inspiration-expiration and systole-diastole, also found in "Poetry and Imagination" (W.VIII.46), suggest the influence of Goethe's updating of alchemy.[9] The erotic analogy which goes with this orientation is also much stronger than in the ancient table. It is in fact insistent enough to make a Victorian lady blush, at least in the second series: "Spirit, matter; man, woman; subjective, objective; in, out; upper, under; motion, rest; yea, nay."

The idea of universal sex does not seem to have bothered Emerson as such (cf.JN.IX.375). On the contrary, the universalization of the theme appears to have had a reassuring effect on him. So does the authority of science when allied to hermetic-alchemic thought in this manner; in spite of his general defensiveness, he does not hesitate to invoke it when he sees fit. He is somewhat cautious in "Love" as he elaborates the idea that "the power of love is indeed the great poem of nature" with allusions to Linnaeus as well as to Goethe's *Elective Affinities:* "The dualism which in human nature makes sex," he says, "in organic matter strives and works in polarity, showing itself in elective affinities, in explosion, in flame, in new products" (EL.III.52). But he clearly lets himself go in describing how the same "dualism" (here another word for bipolarity) works in the vegetative kingdom. Here "it solemnizes in the springtime the marriage of plants with the splendid bridal apparel of these sons and daughters of beauty, in whose sibylline leaves we read the approach of man."

However, this enthusiasm fades very quickly at the approach of man—when Emerson has to discuss the specifically sexual relations of real "sons and daughters of beauty." In "Woman" (1855), he hails Swedenborg, who as a mystical author draws on hermetic-alchemic lore, as "a sublime genius who gave a scientific exposition of the part played severally by man and woman in the world, and showed the difference of sex to run through nature and through thought" (W.XI.415–416). But there is no sign in this address or elsewhere that he shares Swedenborg's desire to marry men and women on a permanent basis. In fact, even in "Love" (the lecture) there is a strong emphasis on the idea that man and wife operate "severally" in what he calls "the real marriage" and that their ultimate destiny is the flight of the alone to the Alone, everything else being mere side show. Here we are again confronted with the kind of dualistic fears which Platonizing philosopher-poets so easily couch in strictly monistic terms—this time at the human level.

The monistic tendency is also noticeable in Emerson's more philosophical analyses of the roles which men and women are "severally" assigned in this world. Even in texts like "Woman" and "Love" one detects a tendency to void the feminine principle of substance in analogy with the treatment the earthly pole of existence suffers at the hands of the Platonists. This is not the place to pursue this matter in depth, but the phenomenon has an obvious bearing on our final assessment of Emerson's defense of the poet as the reconciler of heaven and earth, and I shall therefore give one example of how the analogy operates. Consider once more the archetypal and hermetic-alchemic opposition of sun and moon: In Book Eight of *Paradise Lost,* Milton speaks of these celestial bodies as "the two great Sexes which animate the world," and yet the reader of this work is never allowed to forget that the moon—Eve—is the lesser light and borrows whatever light she has from the sun—Adam. Emerson follows this pattern fairly closely in his own way. Not only does he often use the sun and moon as symbols of the sexes—he repeatedly states that the wife reflects the wisdom of her husband (W.IV.26 and W.XI.406–407).

Another reason for bringing this matter up at this point is that the conception of the feminine or wifely function as a mirror-like reflection of a male or husbandly reality tends to render the phenomenon of woman not only unsubstantial but dreamlike in character. In a section of "Friendship," friends of either sex are dismissed as strictly speaking phenomenal and shining with "a faint moon-like ray" (W.II.197); but as the image suggests, this aspect of the objectification of the external world is also an aspect of its feminization. Nor does this objectification-feminization stop at persons; ultimately it embraces and engulfs the whole sensible world as "otherness." This view also needs to be examined for its effect on Emerson's defense of the poet as the reconciler of heaven and earth: It must be said that he is not always cautiously mindful of the need to avoid giving the scientists and other skeptics a chance to dismiss the poet as a dreamer.

Significantly, Emerson's subject-object dialectic owes as much to the Hindus as to Parmenides and Heraclitus, or Fichte. In a journal note (echoed at the beginning of "The Natural History of Intellect"), Emerson has this to say about the task of the poet: "As Vishnu in the Vedas pursues Maya in all forms; when, to avoid him, she changes herself into a cow, then he into a bull; she into a doe, he into a buck; she into a mare, he into a stallion; she into a hen, he into a cock, and so forth; so our metaphysics should be able to follow the flying force through all transformations, and name the new pair, identical through all variety" (JN.XI.417). This concept of the poet's universe may seem erotic enough, but as Emerson specifies in another place, the object of Vishnu's supposedly amorous pursuit, as the god's "illusory energy," is really only "one of his principal attributes" (W.VII.172). In other words, the earthly-feminine side of existence identified as "Maya" is the subject's dream and illusion.

One suspects that a poet who actually attempted to emulate Vishnu in his role as the wooer of Maya would soon find his subjective self adrift in a Calderonian dream world. Emerson does complain fairly often both in his journals (e.g., JN.VII.499) and in his essays (for instance, in "Experience") that life is illusory and dreamlike. If he does not specifically blame such feelings of malaise on his poetic activities, it is probably due to the fact that he to some extent could count them among the inevitable pains of unrenewed and skeptical moments—the Platonists expressly compare the uninitiated life to vain dreaming.

Emerson is by no means entirely unaware that the world of his poet-redeemer sometimes resembles a dream, especially in terms of his revised theory of poetic symbolism, according to which the marriages seen by the poet are not "constant" and fixed by the will of God but fugacious and subject to instant divorce like the loves celebrated in his revised version of Swedenborg's doctrine of heavenly marriage. However, even when he discusses the activities of the poet in the light of his later view of poetic symbolism, he does not seem particularly worried by the ironic analogy between this dream and that of the skeptic. On the contrary, he shows a marked tendency to praise the Protean and dreamlike character of poetic symbolism—whenever the focus is not on the respective merits of the poet and the scientist. Thus "the convertibility of every thing into every other thing" is in *The Conduct of Life* seen as the supreme mark of the poetic imagination (W.VI.304). The passage contains a reference to fairy tales, but the power in question obviously also fits spontaneous dreaming, as well as the tendency of alchemy, which Emerson, as mentioned, praises for its ability to "transmute one thing into another." As for the unions of subject and object that are a conspicuous feature in his own updating of alchemy, he specifically notes in "Demonology" that they are easily accomplished in his own dreams (W.X.7–8). "Brahma" and certain portions of "Woodnotes" look like celebrations of this theme.

It would not be correct to construe such passages as indirect and intermittent concessions on Emerson's part that science was right after all or that experience itself taught him that the analogies of the poet were not much more than the dreams of the poet. It is better to say that he, on revising his theory of poetic symbolism, was content to fall back to some extent on the conviction of Novalis and many other leading Romantic poets that the world of the poet, while subjective, is nevertheless truer than those seen by the scientists and other skeptics. Moreover, by falling in line in this respect, Emerson gained—and immediately availed himself of—the opportunity to integrate his new view of symbolism with his ever-increasing conviction that nothing is true except in transition and that "the only way in which we can be just, is by giving ourselves the lie" (W.III.245).

Besides—and this is perhaps the most remarkable instance of Emerson's ability to have it both ways—there is the lesson he learned from the number symbolism of the Pythagoreans. Their school, as shown by "Alcmaeon's decade," also represents a vision of the world that in spite of some dualistic overtones can be viewed as bipolaric and, in part at least, inspired by natural sexual polarity. It is true that Emerson's great interest in Pythagoras and the Pythagoreans (between whom he could hardly be expected to distinguish very rigorously) may partly have been based on a misunderstanding: Apparently viewing one of the polaric pairs in the decade ("limited" and "unlimited") as synonymous with "visible" and "invisible," he mistakenly felt that Pythagoras saw the relation between the physical and spiritual realms in the same light as Plato. But his association of Pythagoras and Plato is correct in the sense that this pre-Socratic did initiate a mathematization of the world which fascinated the aging author of the *Timaeus,* and one can also see why Emerson should view this element in Pythagoreanism as support for the rather large claims that he continued to make for the poet: Here was inherent polarity with nuptial overtones—suggested, for instance, by the difference in pitch between male and female voices—and yet so pure and ghostly that it can be expressed in numbers, indeed with mathematical exactitude. A universe reduced to music and song—what an answer to science.

SYMBOLISM AND SCIENCE

Emerson lived to find this view of the matter reinforced by modern science itself. A passage in "Poetry and Imagination" (W.VIII.4–5) shows that he by the early seventies felt that science had begun to vindicate his poet by delineating a universe that was no less ghostly than that of poetic symbolism. However, already at the beginning of his career, in "The Uses of Natural History," he speaks of a "harmony" or "undersong" pealing from the facts uncovered by natural science, a song to which the naturalists themselves are deaf but which the poet's ear is quick to catch. Only one scientist, the one who was also a symbolist, Swedenborg, is credited with having heard the song and shown how "creative force, like a musical composer, goes on unweariedly repeating a simple air or theme, now high, now low, in solo, in chorus, ten thousand times reverberated, till it fills earth and heaven with the chant" (W.IV.109).

Emerson achieves further integration through references to Pan in texts where the order of the universe is described as music. Such references add an erotic note at the same time as this note is kept suitably vague since the god whom the poet is supposed to serve, if a symbol of the procreative urge in the universe, is even more an image of the divinity posited by pantheistic monism. Emerson seems to have found pantheism and Pythagoreanism as compatible as pantheism and hermetic-alchemic thought, no doubt encouraged in this respect by the circumstance that Pythagoras was sometimes believed to have invented the theory of the harmony of the spheres. In "The Natural History of Intellect," where Pan is defined as "the All," Emerson recounts the old myth according to which the pipes of this god "make the music of the spheres, which, because it sounds eternally, is not heard at all by the dull, but only by the mind" (W.XII.36). Pan is referred to as the choregus of the universe in poems like "Pan," the epigraph to "The Poet," "The Harp," and "Woodnotes."

It is most convenient, however, to end this examination of Emerson's vindication of the poet by looking at "Merlin." In this poem, Pan is not mentioned, but the musical structure of the world is an important theme. Moreover, "Merlin" offers an opportunity to sum up my previous discussion of his ideas about the marriage of heaven and earth and at the same time relate them to his interest in magic, as well to a somewhat different kind of marriage which he most willingly performs.

In "Merlin," the famed Celtic sorcerer is described as a poet whose "mighty line / Extremes of nature reconciled" (W.IX.122). One realizes that these extremes are not heaven and earth when one finds his Muse portrayed as a "Bird that from the nadir's floor / To the zenith's top can soar." Obviously, Emerson has a Blakean marriage of heaven and hell in mind. As the second section opens, one may still get the impression that he is about to produce "the great poem of nature" and show "the difference of sex to run through nature and through thought." But instead the Pythagorean opposition between even and odd is here applied to the reconciliation of just and unjust, and alchemy turns out to be the art of turning evil into good. There is no reference to the union of heaven and earth, and as for the marriage of male and female, it remains illusory on the whole, in spite of the Schellingian-Boehmean allusion to the barrenness of a single sex. Even the idea that a creative genius marries the two sexes in his brain is expressed only through a vague allusion to the fertility of mated thoughts. What is more, the stress on identity rather than the union of opposites implicit in the characterization of polarity as "rhyme" is followed up in the series of examples of mated pairs given to illustrate the alleged onmipresence of sex and marriage: twin stars, twin leaves, the two feet of a body, thoughts "Perfect-paired as eagle's wings." The insistence on the "married sides" of the body in particular calls to mind not the marriage of male and female but the Aristophanic fable in Plato's *Symposium* according to which "the best men," as halves of originally male "wholes," are yearning for reunion with their severed and identical other half.

Perhaps the substitution of identity and similarity for true nuptial bipolarity does not in itself imply a low opinion of the feminine principle: Affinity and likeness are sometimes stressed in discussions of heterosexual love. But one should note the extraordinary emphasis on masculine power that goes hand in glove with the celebration of poetic magic in the first section of "Merlin." The author's association of poetic power with magic, also noticeable in "Poetry and Imagination" (W.VIII.43), is not just another illustration of his distrust in the methods of science; it undercuts the justification of this distrust—the idea that the scientist does not

have the love of nature which allegedly makes the poet the redeemer of man and nature. As Désirée Hirst has pointed out, the
fascination with magic and power for its own sake and regardless
of conventional morality is usually coupled with contempt for
nature and the feminine principle.[10] Such contempt was not particularly characteristic of Emerson as a private citizen: Not only
is his love of nature raised above all doubt—he married twice, and
some of his best friends were women. But a certain disregard for
nature and woman is definitely an important facet of the philosophy expounded in his published works. Moreover, this strain in
his thinking, with its undercurrent of sexual dualism, is much more
in line with his commitment to Platonic idealism than the nuptial
approach he so often attributes to his poet.

2

SEXUAL POLARITY AND SEXUAL POLITICS: EMERSON AND THE EMANCIPATION OF WOMEN

The concept of polarity is as important in what has recently been called "sexual politics" as in Emerson's contributions to the metaphysics of sex.[1] Moreover, the two subjects are closely related. Not a few of the archetypal or hermetic-alchemic polarizations which figure in Emerson's discussion of the poet's marriage of "heaven and earth" (such as active and passive, the outdoors and the house, intellect and emotion) have a bearing on the question regarding woman's place in the universe obvious enough to make them suspicious to many feminists. Theoretically, one might imagine a set of bipolaric opposites suggesting that men and women complement and balance each other on a basis of natural equality; in fact, Emerson sometimes seems to envisage something of that order. Yet in a society in which men traditionally dominate, at least outwardly, the equation is easily undone by value judgments giving greater weight to the male side. The active then takes precedence over the passive principle, the house yields to the outdoors, and affection takes a back seat to intellect. This happens quite frequently in Emerson's works.

Before discussing Emerson's performance from this point of view in any detail, it is worth pointing out that some progressive women among his contemporaries—like Margaret Fuller in America and Elizabeth Barrett Browning in England—were already inclined to see the definition of male and female in terms of polaric oppositions as exaggerated and misleading. They did not exactly reject the idea that woman represents the heart while man stands for intellect—to mention again what is perhaps the most central polarization of this kind—but they felt that both sexes really have, or should have, a large share of both. The complete and fully developed individual, male or female, is in their view androgynous.[2]

This theory, which had been quite popular among the German Romantics, represents an updating of the old hermetic doctrine according to which man's redemption hinges on the return of the original, angelic Adam. Instead of the image of a hermaphroditic Adam who can be restored by returning the rib out of which Eve was made to its original place, Fuller and those who thought like her favored twin but separate images like Minerva and Apollo: The goddess presumably combines a woman's heart with a man's mind while the god somehow reconciles a man's mind with a woman's heart.

Undeniably, Apollo and Minerva are excellent images of a diviner humanity in which woman is raised to man's level not by courtesy but through a sharing of power. But this does not mean that everybody who was familiar with this theory adopted it as readily as Margaret Fuller. Emerson, like many other male intellectuals of his time, clearly found the idea of female androgynes somewhat repugnant.

Emerson is also among those male thinkers who take a dim view of the more extreme position according to which there are no significant intellectual or emotional differences between the sexes, only role-conditioning imposed by society. In this view, frequently expressed long before the publication of Mill's essay *On the Subjection of Women,* the traditional bipolaric oppositions are—so far as human psychology is concerned—replaced by a kind of radical sexual monism. Equality, the crucial issue in sexual politics, is achieved not through a rapprochement but through a complete assimilation of both sexes to a unified image of man.

It is true that Emerson is fascinated by the *capostite* of radical sexual monism, Plato's outline of the Ideal State. But then Plato can hardly be said to be entirely sincere in having Socrates argue that there is no essential difference between the mental equipment of men and women and that women therefore may assume the same political functions as men. The circumstance that he so quickly adds that women have the same abilities in a lesser degree than men suggests that most of his androgynous guardians will be male. *The Republic* is an attempt to sketch a way of restoring man to "his first and best state" so far as this can be done by purely political means, and Plato solves the problem posed by the existence of woman by making her a kind of honorary man. However, in the *Timaeus,* the companion volume in which man's salvation is discussed from a more metaphysical point of view, he explains that the ideal state of man was lost through the fall into sexual differentiation and even—in a passage that distressed Margaret Fuller as much as *The Republic* encouraged her—that women represent a fallen state of man.[3]

The Republic is of course the classic illustration of the close connection between sexual politics and the metaphysics of sex. On the whole, the essentially monistic viewpoint of Plato and his followers has had a profound impact on the discussion of woman's place in the modern world. The influence goes in both directions: Radical thinkers willing to ignore the fact that the author of *The Republic* assimilates woman to man may claim his as an ally in their fight for sexual equality. Traditionalists starting out with the assumption that men and women are roughly complementary in a bipolaric fashion—although not necessarily on a basis of equality—may be inspired by his theory of more and less to organize their sets of bipolaric oppositions in such a way that their tendency is ultimately compatible with sexual monism. Emerson's works illustrate how short the road from bipolarity to monism is, once the idea of equality has been abandoned.

The closer look at Emerson's "sexual politics" I am proposing, while no doubt a worthwhile end in itself, can therefore also serve the purpose of studying the specifically monistic tendency in his discussion of the proper relation between man and woman. Such a perspective offers a convenient way of isolating, as it were, the conflict between the monistic strain in his thinking and the nuptial and bipolaric approach which he so often claims for his poet: The dualistic fear of sex and the sex which frequently appears to underlie expressions of sexual monism of the Platonic-Christian type is not likely to obtrude itself when the focus is on the social and political aspects of sex, i.e., on the question of equality.

My selection of texts is predicated on this concern. There is a sense in which all or most of Emerson's work might be considered relevant. The monistic tendency in his view of the sexes weaves in and out of his paragraphs, but it is rarely totally absent in any lecture, essay, or poem of any length; if nothing else, a tendency to ignore the possibility that there might be some women among his readers, very noticeable in some essays and lectures, could be construed as "political." Nevertheless I shall focus the discussion on a few texts in which Emerson deliberately sets out to compare the two sexes with explicit or implicit reference to the woman question as it was put in his day.

If one applies this principle, the choice is actually quite narrow. Even the texts in which one would expect some comment on the women's movement, or generally on the role of women in society, often entirely ignore this problem. For instance, the listing of "Rights of Women" as part of a "fruitful crop of social reforms," in the introductory lecture to "The Present Age" (EL.III.196), shows that Emerson was not unaware of this problem at the opening of the fifth decade of the century—he did, in fact, discuss the series in some letters to Margaret Fuller during the time of preparation. But other than this brief reference, which may have been a gesture in her direction, the rights of women are not mentioned in any of the lectures that make up this series, not even in the one entitled "Reform." Only as the pressure on him to say something on the subject mounted, did he on some rare occasions condescend to abandon his lofty philosophical point of view and momentarily descend into the political arena. "Politics," an essay published the same year as Fuller's *Woman in the Nineteenth Century,* still centers on the evolution of "the wise man," whose relations with other men are "angelic" (W.III.216), but unlike the lecture of the same name in the series called "The Present Age" it contains some fleeting references to the existence of woman. Another essay in that volume, "Manners," features a comment on the women's movement sustained enough to offer a foothold for analysis. It is one of the texts I use here. Another one is "Woman," the address which he was asked to deliver at the Boston Women's Convention of 1855, perhaps because of his quondam association with Fuller and his friendship with Lucretia Mott, the collaborator of Elizabeth Stanton at Seneca Falls.

To these two texts I want to add the lecture entitled "Love," first delivered in 1838 as part of a series called "Human Life." It does not specifically offer any comments on the woman question, but must nevertheless be considered a *de facto* political statement because of the prescriptive spirit in which the roles of man and wife are discussed and because Elizabeth Peabody liked it so much that she decided to use it in her girls' school. An analysis of certain portions of this lecture will not only demonstrate how modest the expectations of intellectual women could be in Emerson's time, but will also help us see how little his opinions on these matters changed over the years.

In "Love," composed at a time when Emerson still appears to have been relatively satisfied with his own marriage, the section of greatest interest from our present point of view is the one that was dropped in the essay which he later published under the same title. It begins with what amounts to a table of opposite pairs which can be related both to the previous, rather lyrical discussion of universal polarity and sex (also omitted in the essay) and to the subsequent analysis of the proper relations of man and wife. Not least the suggestion that "marriage unites the severed halves and joins characters which are complements to each other" (EL.III.62) seems to promise a balanced and bipolaric account of these relations. However, the discussion that follows is something less than that.

The leading complementary polarity adduced, apart from the opposition of the outdoors and the house, is clearly "Intellect" and "Love." This may at first sight seem flattering enough to woman and the feminine principle, given the title of the lecture. But soon afterwards "Love" is reduced to "affection"—a sentiment which obviously is much more homely and personal and has nothing to do with high Platonic love and aspiration—while "Intellect," which is associated with the higher Platonic realms, remains unchanged on the masculine side. The suggestion that there is "always" affection in woman, whereas man excels in understanding, only underlines the idea that she is not his intellectual equal in this world.

Even little things, like the distribution of capital letters, are telling in this context: "Intellect" and "Love" are both capitalized, but when Emerson goes on to speak of the "objects" of these attributes, "Truth" (the object of "Intellect") is capitalized, while "goodness" (the object of "Love") is not. This can only suggest that the "goodness" he is referring to is not of the transcendent kind, although "Truth" obviously is. The significance of these minutiae is heightened by the circumstance that the opposition of man's love of "Reality" to woman's love of "order" seems to point forward to the later suggestion that woman's "taste and love of order" tend to degenerate "into a trivial tyranny"; it certainly does not indicate that she is enamored of cosmic order and harmony. It is true that "power" and "grace," another pair of opposites, are both in the lower case, but here the salient fact is that whereas "power," one of the most conspicuous attributes of Emerson's God, is associated with man, woman is not associated with beauty, another divine attribute of which he has much to say in this lecture. "Grace"—in the sense in which the word is used here—is a rather mundane thing which is never attributed to the Godhead, and the introduction of this term at this point must perforce be related to the suggestion that "man goes abroad into the world and works and acquires," while "woman stays at home to make the house beautiful."

Emerson does say at the end of the paragraph that there is "somewhat sacred and oracular and nearer to the Divinity" in woman's affection. However, this statement may not be such a great compliment to woman from his point of view. It is in part a bow to woman's traditional religious submissiveness, but the phrasing—especially the word "oracular"—also calls to mind Pythia, Apollo's priestess at Delphi, who, supposedly a mere mouthpiece of the god, pronounced words of wisdom that she did not understand. As Emerson follows up this point in the next paragraph, he stresses the idea that women, unlike men, arrive at the right "sentiment" not through conscious mental effort but through a mysterious passive inspiration.

This inspiration is hardly considered on a par with that of Emerson's poet, always thought of as male. Nor can it really be said that he is here anticipating the later Victorian conception of the wife as the savior of her rough mate. He notes that woman even "in very unfriendly condition" is found to be "the spontaneous adviser of noble courses," but the theme is dropped as soon as it is introduced; there is no attempt to apply the idea to the more friendly conditions of his own time. It is true that he also says that man and woman in addition to their respective strong points have "corresponding weakness and temptations," and that these "find their fortress in the other." But the reader may well wonder how woman, even with the virtuous inclination attributed to her, could possibly become the fortifier of the man who "mighty in his faculties and resources, impelled ever to action and experiments, makes experiment of the bad as well as of the good": She is portrayed as essentially weak not only through the manner in which the force of man is stressed but also through insistent references to her susceptibility to anguish, suffering, and tears.

By the same token, the suggestion that man and woman must "balance and redress each other" is not followed by an elaboration of this theme but rather by an enumeration of the negative traits in the wife that the man has to learn to put up with: "The man must not be offended at the superflous, supererogatory order and nicety of the housewife," but should "bear with little extremities and flourishes of a quality that makes comfort for all the senses throughout his house." This administration to the comfort of the senses, through dust-gathering and other earth-bound activities, is said to be compensated for by a precious "sensibility" which "gives the person who hath it, an universal life, and mirrors all nature in her face." However, especially in this context, such a phrasing also seems to stress the lower half of the universe and nature (the two words are here synonymous) and fails to lift woman in a convincing manner from nature-earth and the *mundus sensibilis*. Besides, there is a hint that all wives do not possess this sensibility, and this point is reinforced by the next paragraph, where Emerson —apparently discarding the idea of mutual balancing and redressing—describes "the rare women that charm us" and details the things women must not do if they want to qualify for that category.

Thus it seems fair to say that Emerson is here moving away from the "perfect equality" which he in another part of the lecture (EL.III.55) says that love "delights in." Indeed, if woman is made to represent less transcendent qualities than man, if she is to suppress more of herself and in the process adjust to the needs and desires of man, one may reasonably conclude that he is here allowing himself to be influenced not only by ordinary feelings of male supremacy but by the monistic current of the philosophical tradition within which he operates.

More specifically, the goal of the mutual adjustments recommended in "Love" is not the development of a Minerva-Apollo type of androgynous human completeness. Emerson gets close to the idea for a while as he stresses the independence both man and wife are supposed to gain by learning from each other—the emergence of "the real marriage" in which the nuptial bond has been loosened (EL.III.66). But "the real marriage" is clearly viewed as the point at which one's final and cosmic destiny should become one's major concern, and it is emphasized at the end of the lecture that the individual must subordinate the emotions to the intellect if that destiny is to be properly fulfilled. This—in view of the way in which the natural differences between man and woman are defined—suggests that the ideal candidate for union with the One, if at all androgynous, will be so on a male basis. Indeed, the cosmic prospects of woman seem somewhat dim in this light, and Emerson does not seem particularly interested in her case from this point of view.

A similar subordination of the emotions to what Emerson sees as essentially masculine attributes is also conspicuous in his outline of the somewhat androgynous gentleman ideal in "Manners": "Manhood first, and then gentleness" (W.III.123). This outline is the main thing in the essay, and the discussion of woman's place appears toward the end, as a kind of afterthought. The author introduces the subject by defining the respective spheres of man and woman in terms of archetypal oppositions: "The open air and the fields, the street and public chambers, are the places where Man executes his will; let him yield or divide the sceptre at the door of the house" (W.III.149). This formula suggests not only that man should rule outside of the home but also that he may opt to exercise his will in the latter place, too, provided that he there shares his power with the wife. As it stands, it seems to reflect a view of woman's place conservative enough for a Pericles to have accepted it. Emerson is not eager to confer equality upon woman but, if anything, seems ready to subordinate her to man as he subordinates the affections to intellect and other qualities he considers male.

Subsequently, the logical connection between Emerson's sentences is not always so clear, but some points are indisputable. First of all, one notes that the specific reference to the question concerning the emancipation of women is preceded by the suggestion that American political and other institutions have been friendly to them and that as a result "a chief felicity of this country" is that "it excels in women." Such a fortunate situation does not seem to call for reforms. There is also a suggestion that women's alleged tendency to excel has caused "a certain awkward consciousness of inferiority in the men" which "may give rise to the new chivalry in behalf of Woman's Rights," but this way of putting it appears to ignore the women's movement as such and must be linked to the subsequent hint that the fuss over the status of woman is mainly the result of agitation on the part of chivalrous but misguided male thinkers and politicians: "Certainly let her be as much better placed in the laws and in social reforms as the most zealous reformer can ask, but I confide so entirely in her inspiring and musical nature, that I believe only herself can show us how she is to be served."

Nevertheless this part of "Manners" can to some extent be seen as Emerson's immediate answer to certain ideas expressed by his feminist friend Margaret Fuller not only in *Woman in the Nineteenth Century* but also in earlier *Dial* articles, and in conversation. Such a link is indicated by the provenance of some of the expressions of his own chivalry in behalf of woman, like the suggestion that "the wonderful generosity of her sentiments raises her at times into heroical and godlike regions," or the statement that woman "by the firmness with which she treads her upward path . . . convinces the coarsest calculators that another road exists than that which their feet know." In a journal entry from 1843 (JN.VIII.368–369), these very phrases are used with reference to Fuller, with whom he had just had a conversation which left him with high—though rather ephemeral—hopes concerning her and other women's ability to "soar."

Here again, what strikes one is that Emerson is not content to suggest that even women like Fuller shine mainly through sentiment and a kind of religious fervor, but goes on to describe an entirely different type of woman, indicating his preference for such women by dwelling on it at much greater length. "But besides those who make good in our imagination the place of muses and

Delphic Sibyls," he says, "are there not women who fill our vase with wine and roses to the brim, so that the wine runs over and fills the house with perfume," women who "inspire us with courtesy" and "unloose our tongues," women in whose company "our walls of habitual reserve vanished." These are the women about whom poetry is written, and also the women who make men feel that they are back in paradise: "We were children playing with children in a wide field of flowers. Steep us, we cried, in these influences, for days, for weeks, and we shall be sunny poets and will write out in many-colored words the romance that you are."

This is apparently the type of woman Emerson really finds musical and inspiring, the kind who should be consulted about the true needs and aspirations of her sex. It is therefore interesting to note the sensual character of this effusion. He does not entirely confine this woman to the sensual sphere, but she has no intellectual pretensions and is ruled by her emotions. She is "perfect in her own nature," although the bias of that nature "was not to thought, but to sympathy."

The whole passage is so uncharacteristic of Emerson that it can be explained only in terms of his political-philosophical controversy with Fuller. But in spite of the references to a beauty celebrated by some Persian poet, it also echoes a personal experience that made a deep impression on him. In fact, he is using this very experience in his oblique answer to Fuller. When he speaks about how perfect "Persian Lilla" was in her own nature, he is actually paraphrasing the loving but condescending manner in which Milton describes Eve to the visiting Angel in Book Eight of *Paradise Lost,* but significantly he had previously resorted to that paraphrase in a journal comment on Anna Barker, an overwhelmingly attractive but not very intellectual young woman introduced to him by Fuller (JN.VII.260). This cross-reference hardly loses in interest because Fuller, identifying with Madame de Staël, the only woman mentioned in "Manners" besides "Persian Lilla," affected to see Barker as her "Recamier" (M.I.283-284).

Although polemic and uncharacteristic of Emerson (who apparently was not steeped long enough in Barker's influence), the passage just analyzed nevertheless confirms and reinforces the conclusions I drew on the basis of his early lecture on love. What we are dealing with here is not after all a chivalry or woman-worship of the Victorian type, but something more feudal, as suggested both by the intrusion of the names of medieval Persian poets and by the allusion to Milton. In spite of the suggestion that Lilla-Barker is "perfect in her own nature," we are far from anything resembling the idea of equality between the sexes, and the tendency to bar woman from the intellectual sphere, the one which to Emerson is closest to the ultimate reality, is philosophically speaking a step in the direction of sexual monism.

It remains to examine Emerson's posture in "Woman," which was published more than ten years after "Manners." This text is of crucial importance in determining the extent to which he actually allowed the monistic bent of his philosophical idealism to influence his public comments on the women's movement. It is easily his most sustained effort to deal with a question of which he himself says by way of introduction that "none is more seriously interesting to every healthful and thoughtful mind" (W.XI.405). Given the fact that he was fifty-two at the time of its composition, it should also represent his mature and more or less final position on the subject. Finally, it ought to reflect the most positive and liberal attitude of which he was capable at the time, since he had to read it to the delegates of a women's convention.

The tone in which Emerson explains the nature of woman to the ladies attending the Boston convention *is* friendly, and some of his specifically political statements are remarkably liberal for the time. However, this aspect of the address is not likely to impress the modern reader as strongly as the tension between these positive statements and a different, rather negative attitude to the women's movement and generally to the idea that woman can and ought to do as much as man in all walks of life. This attitude is expressed not only in a number of conservative political suggestions showing that the speaker was more of a product of his time than he always liked to think, but also and above all in the philosophical rationale for these suggestions, given in explicit and implicit polarizations of the natures of man and woman. The result is contradiction rather than balance—an argument which goes two ways in the manner which D. H. Lawrence thought typical of some other American authors.[4]

It would not be accurate to say that the liberalism is all on the surface and that Emerson's more conservative feelings on the subject are conveyed to the listener or reader only through an undercurrent of meaning; they are actually fairly obvious. Yet as so often when Emerson feels that the "prejudices" of his audience preclude an entirely frank statement of his position, he sometimes chooses indirect means of expressing himself—through underlying archetypal or hermetic patterns of imagery and through literary allusion. Also, his prose tends to become even more rhapsodic and *discousue* than his famous theory of composition requires. Not only are the transitions sometimes unclear—it is not always apparent at first sight what he considers hypothetical and what is supposed to be fact, what is his own opinion and what is a view he disapproves of or states objectively as one held by many.

This again is not to say that Emerson emerges as a hypocrite in "Woman." The peculiar quality of his exposition in this address may be attributed to the bewilderment of a man who has not made up his mind and is torn between conflicting impulses, or perhaps rather to the difficult situation of a lecturer who suddenly finds himself in a situation which he has long tried to avoid—that of saying something polite and nice to the assembled representatives of a movement which in many ways runs counter not only to his ingrained masculine beliefs but also to his philosophical convictions—both reflected in journal notes on which he is heavily dependent.

One illustration of the double vision resulting from this dilemma is the epigraph to Emerson's address, which is taken from Patmore's *The Angel in the House* (1854):

Lo, when the Lord made North and South,
And sun and moon ordainèd he,
Forth bringing each by word of mouth
In order of its dignity,
Did man from the crude clay express
By sequence, and, all else decreed,
He formed the woman; nor might less
Than Sabbath such a work succeed.

This vindication of the superiority of woman must be called a rather strained interpretation of the passage in Genesis according to which God created woman as a kind of afterthought, noting that man needed a companion—a companion soon demoted to servant. One can also say that the passage quoted by Emerson,

like the whole of *The Angel in the House,* is an expression of the
"parasitic" forms of gallantry which in the words of the Prince
in Tennyson's *The Princess* seem to raise woman up but in reality
"drag her down."

Another example of how the argument in "Woman" tends to
go in two directions is afforded by Emerson's use of Tennyson. The
address actually contains an allusion to *The Princess,* published
in 1847, shortly before Emerson met the author during his second
visit to England. But Emerson does not adduce the Englishman
as a liberal authority on the woman question; he chooses to lump
him with Aristophanes, Rabelais, Mohammed, and other authors
who in his opinion charge woman "with temperament" and maintain that "women have not a sufficient moral and intellectual force
to control the perturbations of their physical structure." These
authors, says Emerson sarcastically, draw "a morbid anatomy" and
"such a satire as might be written on the tenants of a hospital or
an asylum for idiots" (W.XI.417). It is of course hard to recognize
Tennyson's attitude in this characterization; perhaps Emerson only
remembered the views of Ida's father, which reflect the harsh
polarizations of a feudal and patriarchal society:

> Man for the field and woman for the hearth;
> Man for the sword, and for the needle she;
> Man with the head, and woman with the heart;
> Man to command, and woman to obey;
> All else confusion.

But what is really curious is the way in which the attitude Emerson supposedly is criticizing begins to take over in his own exposition before the end of the paragraph. Through an intriguing
shift of focus, he ends up arguing that "the affection of woman"
is *also* needed in the world, and this statement introduces another
paragraph in which he suddenly exclaims, apparently with reference to the views he has just denounced, "But for the general
charge: no doubt it is well founded." He then goes on to argue
that women *are* victims of temperament and never "unhindered
by any influence of constitution," as many men allegedly are.

This is not the only contradiction in the address with respect
to the role of body chemistry and the emotions in the lives of
women. At the beginning of "Woman," Emerson objects, apropos
of Plato's suggestion that "women are the same as men in faculty,

only less in degree," that "the general voice of mankind has agreed that they have their own strength" (W.XI.406). But this seeming vindication of bipolaric equality between the sexes is followed somewhat anticlimactically by the statement that "women are strong by sentiment," and that "the same mental height which their husbands attain by toil, they attain by sympathy with their husbands."

Moreover, this polarization of the sexes in terms of intellect and emotion, which we have already found in "Love" (the lecture) and in "Manners," is reinforced by suggestions like "Man is the will, and Woman the sentiment" and "In this ship of humanity, Will is the rudder, and Sentiment the sail." This may seem less harsh than the statement of Ida's father, and perhaps even compatible with the idea of bipolaric equality—to the extent that the sail, although it must obey the rudder, can nevertheless be seen as equally important to progress. But Emerson goes on to argue not only that woman is incapable of steering but also that things which do not pertain to "the life of the affections"—like, for instance, the arts and trades—are seldom "a primary object" to her. Because they exist only in relation to man—to some man— they will quit anything "for a suitable marriage." Here one glimpses the Old Testament view of woman as companion-servant.

In this context, Emerson applauds the readiness for self-sacrifice and self-effacement which he finds in women—what he sees as their eagerness to "lose themselves . . . in the glory of their husbands and children." He is particularly impressed with Mrs. Lucy Hutchinson, who in her biography of her late husband sees herself as nothing but "his pale shade." In this case the monistic tendency shines through quite clearly.

This is not all. By another sudden turnabout, Emerson reverts to "Plato's opinion," noting that "it is true that, up to recent times, in no art or science, nor in painting, poetry or music, have they produced a master-piece." He does offer past restrictions on education and lack of equal opportunity as an excuse, but nevertheless tends to rub the matter in. Nor is the balance really redressed by the subsequent statement that women shine "in an art which is better than painting, poetry, music, or architecture,—better than botany, geology, or any science; namely, Conversation." It is debatable whether women are really "the civilizers of mankind" thanks to this art and the "social influence" which promotes it. Moreover, the suggestion suffers from the circumstance that Emerson mentions "The best intercourse between men in old Athens" (as well as in London and Boston) as support for the idea that this pastime is "the last flower of civilization." He knew as well as anybody that this form of intercourse was indeed "between men" in the mother of the arts and sciences, where women, as indicated by Plato's *Symposium*, were barred even from discussions of the nature of love.

Plainly the word "civilization" is used in a very restricted sense in this area of "Woman." Take the suggestion that women "finish society, manners, language": It is followed by statements like "Form and ceremony are their realm" and "They embellish trifles." There is a rather obvious relation between such observations and Emerson's conviction, also expressed in the early lecture on love, that women are confined by their very nature to a narrow sphere within the realm of events and circumstance. The concomitant suggestion that women are likeable because they are "so finished" sounds almost like a pun in this context; it certainly reminds one of the personal "perfection" of "Persian Lilla," charming but quite circumscribed as to her intellectual horizons. On the whole, the matter of women's social influence is tied to their alleged "relative" nature; it is suggested that they need the trappings of form and ceremony to appear to any kind of advantage and that it is in this sense that they are "always making the civilization which they require."

Even more significantly, perhaps, Emerson—after speaking with quite uncharacteristic enthusiasm about decorum, dances, flowers, forms, as the "homes and attendants" of women—turns to arguing that "there is no gift of Nature without some drawback," and that there is a "penalty" on the "exquisite structure" of women. It has made them "More vulnerable, more infirm, more mortal than men" (W.XI.412). In this very context, their physiological makeup is also said to make them victims of illusions: "They emit from their pores a colored atmosphere, one would say, wave upon wave of rosy light, in which they walk evermore, and see all objects through this warm-tinted mist that envelops them." Emerson adds a few words about the dialectical status of "the passion of love," so important to women. Though beautiful, he says, "it is profane to that which follows it." In fact, all of the affections which seem to loom so large in the lives of women "are only introductory to that which is beyond, and to that which is sublime."

Later on, Emerson notes: "Nature's end, of maternity for twenty years, was of so supreme importance that it was to be secured at all events, even to the sacrifice of the highest beauty" (W.XI.418)—an even clearer suggestion that woman, at least during her fertile years, is not likely to soar into the realm of intellectual beauty. He does not exactly deny woman access to that which is sublime, but as in the lecture on love he contrives to find her sublimity, too, in the lower and misty realm of the emotions, and specifically in the area of religion. Moreover, in mentioning again her traditional role as sibyl, he stresses even more than in the lecture her ability to fulfill that beautiful role even among nations in which her position is otherwise lowly and "the laws resist the education and emancipation of women." In fact, he suggests that they owe their "power of divination" to "their social position" as much as to "their nature." In a very similar way he stresses the point that if women tend to attain a greater "religious height" than men, they owe this in part at least to their "sequestration from affairs and from the injury to the moral sense which affairs often inflict" (W.XI.414).

Even more striking is the emphasis on "humility" (a word derived from "humus," Latin for "earth") in this context: "We men have no right to say it," says Emerson, "but the omnipotence of Eve is in humility" (W.XI.413). He then quotes two lines from the *Divine Comedy* which portray the Virgin Mother as "Created beings all in lowliness / Surpassing, as in height above them all," adding that the author of *Paradise Lost* shares this vision of Dante's and that the "victory" of Griselda, in "The Clerke's Tale," is "her supreme humility." Surely the reference to the story of Griselda, that caricature of wifely obedience—Chaucer himself does not think women should follow her example—is surprising in an address read to the delegates of a women's convention. The same thing must be said about the mention of Milton's "vision" of Eve. Book Four of *Paradise Lost* contains a passage, also long admired by Emerson, which expressly denies that Eve is the equal of Adam and underlines that while "His fair large front and eye declared absolute rule," Eve's countenance implies "subjection." If this is not the passage Emerson has in mind in "Woman," there is another one in the same book where Eve addresses her husband with all desirable humility:

> My Author and Disposer, what thou bidst
> Unargu'd I obey; so God ordains,
> God is thy Law, thou mine; to know no more
> Is womans happiest knowledge and her praise.

Emerson does not entirely circumvent the question of equality in his address. But in this respect, too, one notes a certain tendency to tie the discussion to the idea that woman's nature is predominantly emotional. He begins by dwelling on the prominent role played by women in certain nonconforming religious societies, like the Shakers, and ends by suggesting that the doctrine of Swedenborg marks the most important step on the road toward equality between the sexes since the completion of the "hôtel" where Madame de Rambouillet presided over conversation (W.XI.415–416). Those among his listeners who had read his recently published essay on Swedenborg may have found a certain irony in the circumstance that Swedenborg's conception of heavenly love, which Emerson converts into a theory of conversation, is based on the Paulinian-Miltonic idea that woman is essentially a learner and lover of man's wisdom.

After adding that woman has acquired "a feeling of public duty and an added self-respect" by being enlisted in the Abolitionist movement, Emerson proceeds to a more specific discussion of "the new attitude of Woman; urging by argument and by association, her rights of all kinds,—in short to one half of the world." At first blush this passage sounds almost breath-takingly liberal, but one soon finds that the speaker has no intention of joining her in urging these rights. He does take up a number of objections to the women's movement, presumably to demolish them, but he has a way not only of granting them equal time, but also—as in the case of the opinions he at this very point attributes to Aristophanes, Rabelais, and Tennyson—of ending up on the side of the skeptics.

Following his references to the physiological obstacles which do work against "the new claims," Emerson dwells on the opinion of "well-meaning persons" who, without denying the "mathematical justice" of these claims, yet feel that "the best women do not wish these things" and that "they are asked for by people who intellectually seek them, but who have not the support or sympathy of the truest women" (W.XI.418–419). Emerson does not explicitly identify himself as one of the "well-meaning persons," and he expresses a certain sympathy for the intellectual women who in his opinion out of bitterness and frustration have given up all hopes of being "polished and fashioned into beauty" and therefore feel they have nothing to lose by resorting to abrasive measures. Nevertheless, one cannot help seeing in this distinction between two types of women an echo of the discussion in "Manners" involving Margaret Fuller and Anna Barker. Nor is one surprised, after the following, rather liberal-sounding discussion of the suffrage question, to find Emerson stating, this time clearly on his own behalf, that he does not think that it "yet appears that women wish this equal share in public affairs" (W.XI.423–424).

Emerson adds that it nevertheless is "they and not we that are to determine it." But this remark again reminds one of "Manners," where he tells zealous reformers that woman herself is best able to show us how she should be served. So does the suggestion that women ought to be allowed to "make their way by the upper road." The "upper" road, it is intimated, is spontaneity coupled with contemplation and prayer: "I need not repeat it to you—your own solitude will suggest it—that a masculine woman is not strong, but a lady is. The loneliest thought, the purest prayer, is rushing to be the history of a thousand years."

In the final paragraphs, which are of crucial importance since they contain the rhetorical climax, the prescriptive tendency takes over completely, and it turns out to be of a somewhat conservative nature. Reform would not be needed, says Emerson, if we could only have "the true woman, the adorner, the hospitable, the religious heart"; such a woman "moulds the lawgiver and writes the law" because "Every woman being the wife or the daughter of a man,—wife, daughter, sister, mother, of a man, she can never be very far from his ear, never not of his counsel, if she has really something to urge that is good in itself and agreeable to nature." This effectively puts woman back in the house, as the natural place for her to be—possibly with a needle in her hand. But Emerson does not stop there. In discussing the most suitable way for woman to find her happiness, he notes: "Woman should find in man her guardian. Silently she looks for that, and when she finds that he

is not, as she instantly does, she betakes herself to her own de-
fences, and does the best she can. But when he is her guardian,
fulfilled with all nobleness, knows and accepts his duties as her
brother, all goes well for both." Here we are again confronted
with a version of the feudal idea that man should command and
woman obey. It is gentle, but also condescending, and the same
thing can be said about the brief final paragraph in which Emerson,
after noting that "the new movement is only a tide shared by the
spirits of man and woman," dismisses his audience on the optimistic note that they can "proceed in the faith that whatever the
woman's heart is prompted to desire, the man's mind is simultaneously prompted to accomplish."

To sum up, it is questionable whether Emerson's views on the
women's movement became significantly more liberal in the years
we have covered. In a sense, the final paragraphs of "Woman"
make him sound even more conservative than Plato, who after all
assumes that some women may be qualified to be guardians in his
State, in spite of the general inferiority of the sex. On the whole,
he is not more conservative than Plato, of course. On the contrary,
it is a strict construction of Platonic doctrine that often willy-nilly
causes him to push the idea that woman is more vulnerable and
mortal than man beyond the point where the slide toward sexual
monism begins. By no coincidence, his advocating of male guard-
ianship irresistibly calls to mind the passage in the *Phaedrus* which
impressed both him and Plotinus so much—the one in which Plato
says, "Every soul plays a guardian attention to that which is in-
animate" (JN.VII.547).

3

THE MAN OF BEAUTY AND WOMAN'S BEAUTY: AN ASPECT OF EMERSON'S AESTHETICS

Even in eras when she was socially subordinate to man, the beauty of woman has usually been a favorite topic with poets, unless they were beholden to Plato, that is. The Platonist pursues beauty as single-mindedly as the troubadour, but his orientation nevertheless tends to be different, for he is supposed to be interested in mortal beauty only as a phenomenon which may help his soul grow wings and soar in the direction of what alone is truly beautiful—that is, ideal and heavenly beauty. Plato himself does not find woman's beauty as useful as that of young men from this point of view, apparently because he thought it was too closely associated with the life of the senses and the need to propagate the species.[1] A few of the poets affected by his philosophy have more or less successfully tried to update it and find a more honorable place for woman in the Platonistic scheme. What does Emerson, who in "The Poet" defines his ideal ego as "the man of beauty" (W.III.4), have to say on this subject?

Emerson would be much easier to deal with, and also much less interesting, if it could simply be assumed that he was characterized by an insensitivity to feminine beauty matching the way in which it is treated in the Platonic dialogues he cherished so much. Fortunately, there is no more reason to make such an as-

43

sumption than there is to think that he was insensitive to the beauty of nature of which he also speaks slightingly on occasion. He had been proud of the fragile beauty of Ellen, his first wife, and it is clear that he was impressed, perhaps troubled, by the personal attractiveness of Anna Barker, the friend of Margaret Fuller and later the wife of his friend Samuel Ward.

On the other hand, there can be no doubt that Emerson allowed himself to be deeply influenced by Platonic idealism in his philosophical treatment of feminine beauty and tended to associate it with the earth rather than with heaven. To some extent he consciously projects the image of a man torn between his appreciation of female charm and respect for the philosophy which tells him that he must not succumb to it. In "Nominalist and Realist," for instance, he speaks of how a pretty girl, "a genuine creature of the fair earth," is capable not only of "making the commonest offices beautiful," but of quenching, for the moment at least, the "running fire of sarcasm" he usually directs "at ignorance and the life of the senses," thus "insinuating a treachery and contempt for all we had so long loved and wrought in ourselves and others" (W.III.246). Another passage worth noting is the journal entry in which he comments on his repeated viewing of the Venus de' Medici in Florence in 1833: "I reserve my admiration as much as I can; I make a continual effort not to be pleased except by that which ought to please *me*" (JN.IV.169).

In the latter case it is of course difficult to draw the line between the influence of Platonic idealism and Victorian prudishness reinforced by lingering traces of Puritan morality: A formidable array of religious and philosophical obstacles made it difficult for Emerson to adopt an unreservedly admiring attitude to feminine beauty. In fact, it often made it difficult for him to maintain the somewhat contemptuous view of feminine beauty which is consistent with his philosophical monism. Not seldom he betrays the kind of dualistic fear of female attractions which one sometimes encounters in Christian references to them and which can also be found in the writings of Plato. The two views are so intimately related that one can say that they are separate only as the two sides of a coin are separate. Nevertheless it is not only possible but convenient to examine one side at a time. I shall here concentrate as much as possible on Emerson's monistic approach to this problem.

THE MAN OF BEAUTY AND WOMAN'S BEAUTY

Needless to say, there were also intellectual and sentimental forces at work in Emerson's time and place that encouraged him to take a more positive view of woman's beauty. One thinks in particular of the so-called "woman worship," the tendency to view her not as the temptress but as the savior of her rough mate. It should be noted, however, that these forces did not necessarily impel him to celebrate the beauty of woman in terms of bipolaric opposition of heaven and earth—that is, to freely express his admiration of woman *qua* woman. The use of monistic imagery to exorcise dualistic apprehensions is very obvious when he in a letter refers to Anna Barker as "Angelina" (L.II.338).

Platonism itself offers a certain foothold for maneuvers of this kind. Plato tolerates and encourages the love of the personal beauty of boys and young men to the extent that it is understood that this beauty is only a reflection of ideal and universal beauty, and Emerson makes various attempts to enlarge the category of persons who can be used as a first step in the dialectic ascent to include beautiful women. Thus he sometimes implies that the beauty of Anna Barker is universal rather than personal, and therefore uplifting—and harmless. In one case (L.II.306), one perceives a note of domestic as well as philosophical prudence: Emerson is giving Margaret Fuller permission to bring Anna to his house, and apparently it is important to make it clear to everybody, including Lidian, no doubt, that a beauty like hers, while it cannot be "possessed" by anybody, can be enjoyed by all. On another occasion, Helen of Troy, to whom he once compares Anna, is adduced as an example of the kind of beauty that "draws all eyes and hearts into a feeling not of the desire of appropriation but somewhat far higher" (EL.II.276 and JN.VIII.176).

Emerson himself does not always seem entirely convinced by this kind of reasoning, and one can see why. After all, the author of the *Symposium* has Pausanias dwell on the idea that the celestial Aphrodite inspiring spiritual creativity, far from being the common concern of all mankind, is accessible only to the few. There is definitely something that invites disbelief when Emerson categorically states in "Love" that a man who sees a beautiful woman "runs to her and finds the highest joy in contemplating the form, movement and intelligence of this person, because it suggests to him the presence of that which indeed is within the beauty, and the cause of the beauty" (W.II.181). Sexuality and the "mundane" Aphrodite are not gotten rid of that easily.

Plato's insistent suggestions that feminine beauty is inferior to boyish beauty as food for heavenly love is closely related to—indeed in part predicated on—the idea that what he sees as the more strongly sexual nature of woman's constitution, her heavy physiological and psychological involvement in the reproductive process, prevents her from seeking the higher, ennobling kind of beauty even to the extent men do. Thus Emerson is closer to his chief philosophical authority in the area of "Woman" where he not only says that women are more "personal" and more influenced by their "physical structure" than men but remarks, "Nature's end, of maternity for twenty years, was of so supreme importance that it was to be secured at all events, even to the sacrifice of the highest beauty" (W.XI.418).

In "Worship," this rather different monistic approach to the beauty associated with the feminine principle—it consists in seeing it as inherently inferior and not very closely related to the Deity—is applied to a more or less Christian context. Emerson here takes issue with what he calls "Chaucer's extraordinary confusion of heaven and earth" in his portrayal of Dido (W.VI.207):

> She was so fair,
> So young, so lusty, with her eyen glad,
> That if that God that heaven and earth made
> Would have a love for beauty and goodness,
> And womanhede, truth, and seemliness,
> Whom should he loven but this lady sweet?
> There n'is no woman to him half so meet.

The contemptuous view of "womanhede" implied in this criticism of Chaucer is underlined by the circumstance that Emerson, after branding the quoted lines as an illustration of medieval grossness, goes on to speak of "the religions of men" in his own age as "either childish and insignificant or unmanly and effeminating."

Anna Barker did not entirely escape having her beauty assessed in these terms as well. In a journal entry dating from the time of their first acquaintance, one can see Emerson struggling against the overwhelming impact of her beauty by telling himself: "She is not an intellectual beauty . . . the predominating character of her nature is not thought but emotion or sympathy, and of course she is not of my class, does not resemble the women whom I have most admired and loved, but she is so perfect in her own nature as to meet these by the fulness of her heart" (JN.VII.260). It appears that Anna did not possess the intellectual brilliance of certain women in Emerson's acquaintance, like his aunt Mary Moody Emerson or Sarah Bradford Ripley (women not noted for physical beauty). It is therefore understandable that Margaret Fuller should have seen Anna as her "Recamier," while she herself identified with de Staël, the famous intellectual who was so fond of this merely beautiful woman, and that Emerson should end up looking at the association of the two beauties as his own (J.IX.549). In moods less appreciative of fullness of heart, he may well have agreed with the Duchess d'Abrantes, whose dismissal of the beauty of Madame Récamier and other women like her as an empty façade he quotes at considerable length in a notebook (JN.VI.327).

A good place to study this whole syndrome is the essay entitled "Beauty" (1860). This text contains statements that at first sight would seem highly complimentary to woman. Emerson notes, for instance, that according to Mohammed, God gave "two thirds of all beauty" to woman; again he dwells on the allegedly universal appeal of famous beauties like Helen of Troy and Pauline de Viguier (W.VI.296–297). However, there is something ambiguous about examples like these. He himself notes that when Pauline showed herself on her balcony, as she was compelled to do twice a week, "the crowd was dangerous to life": This suggests an audience motivated by the vulgar Venus rather than by the exclusive love of intellectual beauty. It also fits the fatal character of Helen's beauty, which was indeed dangerous to life. In her case, there is a further ambiguity in the circumstance that she was something of a slut even in her own eyes and was spared after the fall of Troy only because Menelaos could not withstand the apparently universal appeal of her left breast. As for Mohammed, finally, he may have appreciated feminine beauty, but one aspect of this appreciation is his decision to veil it. No matter what interpretation one puts on this act, it does not suggest that the prophet thought that great personal beauty is "universal" and ought to be enjoyed by everybody.

Such an array of examples suggesting the opposite of what Emerson supposedly wants to say can be imputed either to carelessness or to a subconscious ambivalence. In neither case can one say that he is trying very hard to strike a balance between a bipolaric vision of the universe which would do full justice to the beauty of woman and the earth as well as to heaven. The over-all impression created by the essay is that the author sees the praise of feminine beauty as a necessary formality, a concession to popular prejudice that must be made before a more philosophical note can be struck.

Thus the suggestion that beauty "reaches its height in woman" is less significant in an analysis of the argument of "Beauty" than the implied contention that woman's beauty appeals primarily, or too often, to the senses and actually has little to do with "that haughty force of beauty, *'vis superba formae,'* which the poets praise" (W.VI.305). This implication is present not only in the obvious application of the warnings against a low and popular Venus to which the passion inspired by *vis superba formae* is clearly opposed (cf. JN.IX.16), but also in the way in which the author dwells on the transitory character of personal beauty: "The radiance of the human form, though sometimes astonishing, is only a burst of beauty for a few years or a few months at the perfection of youth, and in most, rapidly declines." This statement has been traced to a journal quotation from a certain *Manual of Artistic Anatomy* declaring, "There is a burst of beauty in woman, at puberty, at times, astonishing to all beholders," but lasting for a very short time, sometimes "only a few months." For good measure, Emerson adds that "a pear is only in perfection for about ten minutes" (JN.XIII.98).

Even without access to this kind of background, the reader is apt to guess that it is primarily the feminine variety Emerson has in mind when he dismisses external beauty as superficial and ephemeral. After making his bow to feminine beauty, he somewhat anticlimactically turns around and argues that after all it is not beauty that inspires "the highest passion," but "expression." This trait is said to "degrade" beauty just as he elsewhere (W.I.57–58) says that spirit degrades matter, and there are indications that the examples of "expression" he has in mind are chiefly masculine: "If command, eloquence, art or invention exist in the most deformed person, all the accidents that displease, please, and raise esteem and wonder higher" (W.VI.299–301). Moreover, this allusion to Socratic ugliness is fully in harmony with the tone of the first part of the essay, which is also a hymn not so much to beauty in general as to heroism and manhood, things based on beauty of soul in Emerson's Platonistic perspective.

It would not be entirely correct to say that the Platonists are Emerson's sole inspiration in this respect. When he says at the end of "The Eye and the Ear" that the man whose spiritual senses have been cleared and purified will "see beauty that is to be desired where others see no form or comeliness," he seems to be alluding to the passage in Isaiah that so often has been seen as a prophecy of Jesus Christ (EL.II.277). A similar note is struck at the beginning of the "Divinity School Address," where "A more secret, sweet, and overpowering beauty" is said to appear to man "when his heart and mind open to the sentiment of virtue" (W.I.120). It is tempting to relate this sentence to the reference in the last paragraph of the same address to "that supreme Beauty which ravished the souls of those Eastern men, and chiefly of those Hebrews." However, such references to the Bible do not in any way contradict his Platonistic assumptions, and are usually accompanied by entirely orthodox statements, including Greek themes: In the "Divinity School Address," for instance, he notes, after complaining that the preachers of his time shear Jesus "of the locks of beauty and the attributes of heaven," that "when I see a majestic Epaminondas, or Washington; when I see among my contemporaries a true orator, an upright judge, a dear friend; when I vibrate to the melody and fancy of a poem; I see beauty that is to be desired" (W.I.133).

Plato and the Greeks are certainly the supreme authority in the section of *Nature* which deals with beauty (W.I.15–24). Emerson notes, "Even the corpse has its own beauty," but there is no suggestion that women are beautiful; as a matter of fact, there is no hint that they exist, except in the reference to "the high and divine beauty which can be loved without effeminacy." This beauty, we are told, must have a "spiritual" element in it and is found only "in combination with the human will": An act of heroism confers an extra splendor on the natural setting where it occurs, as when Leonidas and his hundred "martyrs" spent a whole day dying at Thermopylae. The significance of such passages flows from the circumstance that not only "spirit" but the open air and will-power are associated with the masculine principle in Emerson's works in accordance with archetypally established patterns.

There is also the beauty of the ephebes, praised by some Greek authors as insistently as that of great ladies by the courtly poets of later times. As Emerson knew, Leonidas had not a few of them with him at Thermopylae, and while there is no explicit reference to them in *Nature,* his journals from this time contain statements like: "We admire the Greek in an American plough boy often" (JN.V.199). In "Friendship," he expresses a preference for the company of ploughboys (W.II.205).

Such passages are not unlike the references to "tan-faced" prairie-boys and male companionship in the open air that one finds in Whitman. Whether the latter was influenced by his "master" in this respect is hard to determine, but Emerson certainly found inspiration in the work of his pupil: It is after studying the first edition of *Leaves of Grass* (1855) with its frontispiece picture of the author looking like a young man living in the open air that Emerson writes in his journal: "Give me the out-of-door thoughts of sound men,—the thoughts, all fresh, blooming, whiskered and with the tan on" (J.VIII.532).

Here we are of course moving away from the Greeks, although not necessarily from the Platonists (one notes the emphasis on "thoughts" in the last quotation). Incidentally, Emerson was at this time readying *English Traits* for publication. In this book, uplifting beauty becomes closely tied to the Nordic race. The beauty of "both branches of the Scandinavian race"—that is, the English and the Norse—is extolled and related to both spiritual values and life in the open air. After suggesting that the women of this race are not noted for beauty, Emerson dwells on the idea that "the bronze monuments of crusaders lying cross-legged in the Temple Church at London . . . are of the same type as the best youthful heads of men now in England;—please by beauty of the same character . . . and mainly by that uncorrupt youth in the face of manhood, which is daily seen in the streets of London" (W.V.66).

This lyrical account of the personal beauty of the male members of the blond and blue-eyed race, which continues for three paragraphs, should be compared with the outdoor-indoor symbolism in a poem called "Romany Girl":

THE MAN OF BEAUTY AND WOMAN'S BEAUTY

> The fair moon mounts, and aye the flame
> Of Gypsy beauty blazes higher.
> Pale Northern girls! You scorn our race;
> You captives of your air-tight halls,
> Wear out indoors your sickly days,
> But leave us the horizon walls.

At first sight this may look like a hymn to the beauty of gypsy
women, but one soon perceives that this theme is only one side of
the argument and not necessarily the most important one: Many
readers are apt to be more impressed by the attack on New England
womanhood, the kind of woman Emerson was surrounded by in
Concord and Boston. These women are portrayed as dwelling
indoors, and at least in this sense "Romany Girl" cannot really be
said to contradict his general position, which is that the beauty
found out-of-doors is superior to that found indoors, or in the
women's quarters.

This archetypal opposition sometimes combines with that of
heaven and earth in another scheme used by Emerson to discount
feminine beauty as illusory. In a way this scheme is similar to
the theory of "cristallisation" set forth by Stendhal in *De l'amour*,
according to which the lover projects his personal ideal on the
beloved person. However, Emerson is not as even-handed as the
Frenchman, but is mainly interested in arguing that the man
projects his ideas of perfection on the woman he falls in love with
in an act of wishful thinking. In a late journal description of this
process, the lover is compared to the sun and the sky, the beloved
woman to the earth: "The maiden has no guess what the youth
sees in her. It is not in her, but in his eyes, which rain on her the
hints of form and grace of Eden; as the Sun, deluging the landscape with his beams, makes the world he smiles upon" (W.VI.430).
Emerson also makes the point that the male lover does not understand the treacherous process but foolishly imagines that heavenly
beauty is descending on *him*: "We know what madness belongs
to love,—what power to paint a vile object in hues of heaven"
(W.VI.41).

The importance of this negative theory of feminine beauty in
Emerson's thinking is further underlined by a number of other
versions of the same idea. In a journal passage, he notes that individual beauty is due to the action of the sun itself, or of other

radiant objects of a nonpersonal nature; the example given is: "The cheek of the maiden would be pale but for the sun and wind or for the glitter of the lighted and decorated hall filled with other beauty reflecting rays on her" (JN.V.225–226). In "Illusions," too, it is suggested that a woman's beauty may come from anywhere, except from herself. It is true that Emerson seems to be generalizing about both sexes when he says, "There is the illusion of love, which attributes to the beloved person all which that person shares with his or her family, sex, age, or condition, nay, with the human mind itself." However, he adds: " 'Tis these which the lover loves, and Anna Matilda gets the credit of them" (W.VI.319). Even the Romantic distinction between "fancy" and "imagination," the former function seen as superficial, the latter as central, can serve in this context, as shown by a passage in "Poetry and Imagination." Here, too, Emerson may sound objective when he describes fancy as "a play as with dolls and puppets which we choose to call men and women." But he says this only after noting, by way of a concrete example, that "the lover is rightly said to fancy the hair, eyes, complexion of the maid" (W.VIII.28–29).

Much of the significance of passages like these comes from the fact that Emerson never suggests with equal explicitness that there is something illusory about the physical appeal of men. With respect to them he remains fairly close to the spirit of the *Phaedrus,* the dialogue in which Plato in an entirely positive vein and without suggesting that there is anything illusory about the process says that the lover projects his inner vision of perfection on his beloved. There are not a few passages in which he projects his own image of ideal beauty on male individuals, although the desire to mold the persons in question in this image is not always present for the simple reason that the persons he admired were often older than he.

The case of Edward Everett is particularly interesting in that it shows how early Emerson's Platonism came to him. According to Cabot, Emerson's admiration for this classics professor was "so great as to subject him to the ridicule of his more prosy classmates."[2] In the journal one reads that Everett "had a radiant beauty of person, of a classic style, a heavy large eye, marble lids which gave the impression of mass which the slightness of his form needed, sculptured lips, a voice of such rich tones, such precise and perfect utterance that although slightly nasal it was the most mellow and beautiful and correct of all the instruments of the time." Furthermore, "This eminently beautiful person was followed like an Apollo from church to church wherever the fame that he would preach led, by all the most cultivated and intelligent youths with grateful admiration" (JN.VIII.268 and 270).

If Emerson in his youthful admiration for Everett seems not unlike what Plato in the *Phaedrus* calls a "follower of Apollo," he is more like a "follower of Zeus" in his much later worship of Edward Taylor (Melville's "Father Mapple"). What most impressed him about this preacher was what he in his journal describes as an Olympian presence which made everybody feel diminished and yet not resentful of this feeling (JN.VII.360). On the other hand, the same entry contains a kind of rapprochement between the two kinds of Romantic idolatry in that Taylor is said to be "more beautiful than the Amore Greco"; the reference here is to a statue portraying a youthful beauty associated with Apollo and the ephebe.

One may of course wonder why Emerson would want to mention this sculpture in this context—even in the privacy of his journal—since "Greek love" is a byword for "boy-love." But Emerson's works present many problems of this kind, so many, in fact, that they shed a somewhat ironic light on his insistent vindication of the "innocence" of his ideal self-projection, the Poet. The effect produced is in a sense the opposite of the impression created by Socrates' way of confessing that he is enamored of this or that handsome young man. Whereas a reading of works like the *Phaedrus* and the *Symposium* is likely to result in a growing conviction that Socrates is innocent of sensuality, the reader of Emerson, if at all attentive to this aspect of his utterance, may well end up telling himself: If this is innocence, it is indeed a "formidable innocence" (W.IX.51).

The point must not be exaggerated. But such passages should not be ignored either, or shrugged off as a cultural rather than a personal thing. Emerson is clearly at one with Plato in the latter's assumption that the admiration of male beauty stands a better chance of remaining Platonic than the passion aroused by feminine beauty, and this may be enough to explain his tendency to use male examples of physical beauty, as well as the restrictions he imposes on himself in dealing with the same phenomenon in women. However, it also appears that he, as if to compensate for his restraint with regard to woman's beauty, sometimes allows himself more latitude in describing masculine beauty than his master does and requires him to do. The circumstance that the words "whiskered and with the tan on" have been erased in the previously quoted journal note about the thoughts of outdoor men is one indication that he occasionally thought so himself.

In view of Emerson's tendency to express himself obliquely and by "indirection," it is important, in examining this aspect of his aesthetics, to look at his relation to some of his chief modern authorities on beauty. One name he invokes more than once is that of Winckelmann. In "Books," he recommends the *History of Ancient Art* by this author, explaining that "Winckelmann, a Greek born out of due time, has become essential to an intimate knowledge of the Attic genius" (W.VII.202). In "Beauty," he notes that while others in the eighteenth century labored to develop modern science and its "post-mortem" dissection of nature, Winckelmann opened up the study of beauty as a study of life. At the same time, Emerson suggests that we can all follow in his steps; no books or laboratories are needed. Both teachers and subjects "are always near us," nor do things like "Knowledge of men, knowledge of manners, the power of form and our sensibility to personal influence" ever go out of fashion (W.VI.286). In spite of a fleeting reference to "the beauty of schoolgirls" in the follow-up paragraph, the emphasis, as in the remainder of the essay, is clearly on the male form and influence; the initial or topic sentence itself suggests as much: "No object really influences us but man, and man only in his superiorities." This bias is also hard to miss in the area of "Behavior" which contains a reference to Winckelmann; one notes in particular the author's fascination with the aquiline nose of Julius Caesar and "the military eye" which may confront him at any time in the street (W.VI.181).

In "Art," a similar tendency is related to the lesson Emerson learned from the Prussian art historian, even though he is not explicitly mentioned and the argument is in part based on other premises: In deploring that the artists of his own time had severed the study of art from the study of life and thus deprived it of its organic roots—its basis in religion and love—the author roundly dismisses what he somewhat ambiguously calls "ideal sculpture" in favor of the art gallery he has in the "public assembly" and the infinite variety of "this living man" (W.II.357). Somewhat later, the suggestion that "a great man is a new statue in every attitude and action" is matched by the statement that "a beautiful woman is a picture which drives all beholders nobly mad." But apart from this passage, which incidentally seems to relegate distinction in women to a lower plane than that of moral or spiritual greatness in men, feminine beauty is not mentioned in this essay; the stress is on the attractions of superior men. Thus the public assembly is said to teach us that Homer was right in portraying all men as giants; the *Transfiguration* of Raphael is praised for its "calm benignant beauty" and the sublimity of the face of Jesus, but also and above all for its lifelike quality: "It seems almost to call you by name," and looking at it is said to be like meeting a friend. In short, the central idea is that life can be just as "lyric" as a work of art or a poem, and the essay can be said to indicate that Winckelmann's writings had a liberating and encouraging influence on the Emerson who would cast lyrical glances about him in streets and public places (JN.V.247 and W.I.84–85); they helped him become the prophet as well as an early admirer of Whitman.

The irony of Emerson's enthusiasm for the gospel of Winckelmann is that the latter, while prone to dwell on the abstract idea of beauty, was really, to quote Wellek, "quite remote from all that": Both as a man and a writer, he appears to have been deeply influenced by sensualism; his approach to Greek statues was sensual, even sexual, and with respect to them, as well as in his private life, he favored masculine beauty.[3] This is not to say that Emerson was also "remote from all that," but the affinity he perceived between himself and Winckelmann can be seen as one more indication that the sensual man is more alive in him than either he or his critics are generally willing to admit.

Emerson's own fascination with the manly form is also reflected in his reaction to Michelangelo, the great artist who was also a poet. Unlike Winckelmann, Michelangelo was not to Emerson an authority on the superiority of living sculpture—he says that this artist was dissatisfied with "Grace in living form except in rarest instances" (EL.I.110). Nevertheless, a similarly ironic discrepancy arises in this case, not least between Emerson's stressing of the idea that Michelangelo was a pure Platonist "contemplating ever with love the idea of absolute beauty" and the refusal on the part of not a few competent scholars to believe that all of his relationships with handsome young "Apollos" were entirely Platonic.[4] The only plausible explanation of Emerson's failure to take account of certain ambiguities in Michelangelo's sonnets is that he used a bowdlerized edition of them and actually believed, at least until he read Grimm's book about the artist (CEG.59), that they were all addressed to Vittoria Colonna.[5] Such an explanation also enables us to assume that he was not aware that the artist in one poem calls Vittoria "a man in a woman." On the other hand, one does not see any reason why he should not have noticed that Michelangelo in another case dismisses woman's beauty as "dissimil' troppo"—that is, too different from the kind of beauty which is apt to inspire a lofty and elevating love in a masculine heart.[6]

Emerson did of course have access to Michelangelo's paintings and sculptures in more or less unadulterated form. Here the problem is not whether they are all "innocent," as he says they are, but whether they and his own comments on them are compatible with the conventional view that beauty reaches its height in woman, which as mentioned, he sometimes echoes. It is well known that this artist pushed his preference for the male form to the point of using male models even when he was painting women. One must perforce agree, in principle at least, with John Addington Symonds when he says that Michelangelo "emerges as a mighty master who was dominated by the vision of male beauty, and who saw the female mainly through the fascination of the other sex."[7] What is more, Emerson also notes this, although he is not equally explicit: In the journal for 1839, he says, "The genius of Michel aims at Strength in all figures, not in gods and prophets alone, but in women and in children" (JN.VII.278). Years later, in "Power," this orientation earns Michelangelo (and Cellini) the epithet "masculine" (W.VI.74), and yet later, in *Society and Solitude,* Emerson suggests that "Michel Angelo's head is full of masculine and gigantic figures as gods walking, which make him savage until his furious chisel can render them into marble" (W.VII.326–327).

Michelangelo's concentration on the nude male form did not cause Emerson to express the kind of misgivings reflected in his comments on the Venus de' Medici. In his lecture, he dwells on the pleasure he derives from "that cartoon of the soldiers coming out of the bath and arming themselves" (an incident in the Pisan War) and shares the artist's scorn for those who wanted to clothe the "terrific prophets and angels" of the *Last Judgment* (EL.108–111). Indeed, he ties this bias in Michelangelo's selection of motifs to what he sees as the latter's stress on the analogy between "the finite form and the infinite inhabitant"—his perception of the divine dimension of humanity. It is safe to assume that it is this vision, Michelangelo's idea of man, that Emerson is referring to when he tells Lydia Jackson, to whom he was then engaged, that he is going to pay her a visit on a certain day provided he can "attain unto the Idea of that man" by the deadline he had set for himself in his work on the lecture on his favorite artist (L.I.435).

The lecture also shows in considerable detail what Emerson came up with in this respect—the idea that the secret of Michelangelo's greatness is his ability to see human grandeur and beauty as symbolic of the superhuman. In this regard, he says, Michelangelo represents the acme of the anthropomorphic tendency in Western art—i.e., he is even more significant than the Greeks.[8] Nevertheless, Jove and Apollo stand out among the examples of the artist's works which make us feel "that we are greater than we know."

The goddesses are not entirely ignored in this context. Emerson also says that Goethe suggests that he who has not seen the Juno at the Rondanini Palace "is but half himself." However, this attempt to balance his statement suffers somewhat from the circumstance that the Rondanini sculpture which Goethe comments on in his *Italienische Reise* is not a Juno but a Medusa, as pointed out in a note to the *Early Lectures* (EL.I.104). Nor can the abundant use of phrases like "the human figure," "human clay," and "human nature" in this part of the lecture alter the impression that the word "human" here, as in the lecture on Milton, comes very close to meaning "manly."

The fact that the images of Jove and Apollo are stressed by Emerson in this context is significant in the sense that these gods are the most important among the models of divine beauty between which the lover can choose in molding his beloved in his own ideal image, according to the *Phaedrus*. By no coincidence, the link between art and Platonic love implicit in Emerson's choice of examples can also be glimpsed in Plotinus' tractate "The Intellectual Beauty," where Phidias' Jove, for which the artist had no mortal model, is mentioned as an illustration of the idea that the artist imposes his inner and personal but yet divinely inspired vision of beauty on his block of marble. Michelangelo himself on occasion seems to take this view of the matter, and it therefore does not seem unreasonable to argue, as Charles Seymour has done, that the *David*, which Emerson saw standing "in the open air" in 1833, is the young Michelangelo's ideal self-portrait in these very terms.[9]

On at least one occasion—in "A Sonnet by Michel Angelo Buonarotti"—Emerson endorses the modified version of Plotinus' theory preferred by the Christian in Michelangelo, which emphasizes the idea that the artist does not, properly speaking, "create beauty" but serves as an instrument in disengaging or liberating a form that the Creator has confined in his material (W.IX.298). But he clearly favors the more sanguine view of the matter and tends to attribute it to his favorite artist in spite of the latter's religious scruples. He can do so with relative ease because the distinction between the Creator of the universe and the artistic creator is obscured when Jehovah is replaced by an "Over-Soul" who is the "original" self of all souls, witness the allusion to Michelangelo in "The Problem" (W.IX.6).

That is not all: The main reason why I am dwelling on this facet of Emerson's relation to Michelangelo is that he uses the image of the sculptor to clarify the creative activities of his ideal alter ego in "The Poet." While arguing the superiority of artistic creativity over biological reproduction, he here tells the story of the genesis of a marble sculpture of "a beautiful youth, Phosphorus, whose aspect is such that it is said all persons who look on it become silent" (W.III.24). There seems to be an allusion to the idea that the sculptor only acts as the midwife of forms imprisoned in his material in the suggestion that this sculpture illustrates "the new type which things themselves take when liberated." But the idea that "Phosphorus" is a case of self-expression is clearly present in the statement that the sculptor strove to express his own feeling of happiness and its cause in the only way in which it could be done, by indirection. Moreover, it is in this sense that "the poet also resigns himself to his mood."

This might be called the story of Pygmalion with a difference, and it is illustrative of Emerson's own use of indirection—as well as of his personal desire to unite the sculptor and the poet as he thought Michelangelo did—that there should be a journal entry from 1842 (JN.VIII.316) showing that the artist whom he claims to have known in "younger days" is none other than himself: Waking up and going to the window before daybreak one morning, he was filled with a feeling of great tranquillity and satisfaction, and when he tried to express it he found that he had "cut out a Hesperus in marble" (Hesperus is Venus as the Evening Star, Phosphorus the same planet in the morning). The "stone" out of which he had formed this "figure of a youth" seemed to him "porous to love and truth," but characteristically he immediately adds that he should not let his thought dwell on this image but transcend it, remembering the fugitive and merely vehicular nature of all symbols. Here speaks the Platonist in him who also prevents him from alluding to the existence of woman, let alone woman's beauty, in "The Poet."

4

A TRAGIC VISION: EMERSON'S "HOUSE OF PAIN" REVISITED

Perhaps nothing brings out more clearly the strain of sexual monism in Emerson's thought than his tendency to view woman as a tragic phenomenon based on the idea—also advocated by Plato—that her powers are not essentially different but less than man's. He speaks in *Representative Men* of "the yawning gulf between the ambition of man and his power of performance, between the demand and supply of power . . . which makes the tragedy of all souls" (W.IV.183), but neither there nor elsewhere is there any indication that he thinks men are as tragic as women from this point of view. On the contrary, he habitually associates power with the male principle. In the early lecture on love, for instance, power is the male attribute opposed to female "grace" (EL.III.62). In view of his equally strong inclination to associate the masculine rather than the feminine principle with heaven and intellect, it also seems significant that he in "The History of Intellect" defines heaven as "the added sense of power" (W.XII.46).

Inspired by another phrase which appears in this text, Sherman Paul has used the concept of the horizontal-vertical diagram to illustrate what he sees as the most notable tendency in Emerson's thinking, the upward and heavenly thrust of his love and aspiration—his "angle of vision" (W.XII.10). According to Paul, this diagram also fits Emerson's "distinction between masculine and feminine powers," the vertical line representing man's soaring ability, the horizontal one the more earth-bound strength of woman.[1] However, the statements he adduces to show that Emerson attributes "horizontal" powers to woman are not particularly well chosen: He does say that "to create is the proof of a divine presence" (JN.V.341) and also that man is creative and woman receptive (JN.V.195), but the latter passage is aimed at explaining what he sees as the creative impotence of the typical American artist of his time by defining him as "a vase to receive and not a fountain to impart *character*"; it does not in any way suggest the existence of specifically feminine powers of equal importance to the creative process. In some other discussions of the creative mind (e.g., JN.XIV.277), Emerson significantly equates "eunuchs and women."

Emerson's *oeuvre* does contain some statements which are perfectly in line with the archetypal and bipolaric vision of heavenly rain falling on a receptive and fertile earth. But in these cases he is always discussing the marriage of heaven and earth in very general terms. With respect to the creative capabilities of women, he seems more interested in an image which he came across in the Confucian *Shih Ching*: " 'When a daughter is born,' said the Sheking, 'she sleeps on the ground, she is clothed with a wrapper, she plays with a tile, she is incapable either of evil or of good' " (JN.IV.300). The quotation follows the remark, "The condition of young women even the most favored excites sometimes a profound pity"; and the attempt to show that this is not necessarily true— the reference to "the rare women that charm us" because they do have a happy constitution which makes up for the humblest circumstances—suffers from the very fact that they are considered exceptional. The image of woman as a helpless and harmless child perfectly fits his monistic view of the sexes. The struggle between his unconscious fascination with it and his conscious need to reject it is also reflected in other passages where he quotes this Confucian ode (EL.I.280 and W.XI.414–415).

For rather similar reasons, Emerson also tends to associate woman with old age and death. "Old Age" contains an epigram according to which "Age, like woman, requires fit surroundings" (W.VII.320). In "Fate," it is suggested that even the stoutest revolutionary will contract something of woman's nature along with gout and palsy as he "begins to die" (W.VI.13). The same Platonic-archetypal polarization of male and female is behind the blunt statement in "Woman" that women are "more infirm, more vulner-able, more mortal, than men" (W.XI.412).

In a sense, Emerson's "perfect Adam" (W.IX.283) is above all an ideal of adult health: It is through a healthy mind in a healthy body that we are to gain the power that will enable us to stand up to Fate. It is therefore also worth noting that he feels that women in particular fall woefully short of this ideal and are par-ticularly aware of the fact: "Almost every woman described to you by woman presents a tragic idea and not an idea of well-being" (JN.VII.56). On another occasion, he notes, "Sanity is very rare: every man almost and every woman has a dash of madness" (JN.VII.44). The difference he sees between men and women may seem slight in this case, but is actually very significant: All men may not be healthy and sane, but the poet, or ideal man, is by definition "the healthy man," as well as "the manly man" (W.-VIII.26).

This view of woman is definitely linked to her physical con-stitution and the effect that it allegedly has on her angle of vision. Specifically, we are here faced with Emerson's adherence to the age-old belief that man stands for intellect, woman for affection. Here, too, the distinction is obviously thought of as less than absolute: If affection "makes the basis of the nature of Woman," men are nice enough to recognize "its occasional claims on them" (EL.II.281). On the other hand, intellect as such "is entirely void of affection," and Emerson does not waver in his belief that the exalted region which it represents is the only one that is really worthy of man. In this context he tends to associate mental health with the "dry light" that Heraclitus thinks "makes the best souls," opposing it to the "moist and colored mists" of the affections which allegedly make it difficult to see our true heaven (EL.II.249). Emer-son does not in this particular passage relate this distinction to the difference between the sexes. But in "Love," an elaboration of the idea that woman represents the emotions and man intellect pre-cedes the final passage in which he speaks of "the moments when the affections rule and absorb the man" as morbid interludes when our happiness is in jeopardy because it is dependent on another person: "In health the mind is presently seen again—its overarching vault, bright with galaxies of fires, and the warm loves and fears that swept over us as clouds must lose their finite character and blend with God to attain their perfection" (EL.III.67). Similar cloud-and-heat imagery occurs in a journal entry beginning with a quotation of Plato's suggestion that women are "the same as men in faculty, only less" and stating again that "few" women are sane: "They emit a coloured atmosphere, one would say, floods upon floods of coloured light, in which they walk evermore, and see all objects through this warm tinted mist which envelopes them" (JN.XI.444–445).

When this journal note was used in "Woman," the statement about the rarity of sanity among women was dropped, but Emerson does not fail to allude to the "tragedies" which are likely to befall them because of the capacity for love and passion which he sees as their greatest gift (W.XI.412). This is the theme Byron dwells on in *Don Juan*. But Emerson also sees women as "victims of temperament" in another sense: On the same page, he notes that "the passion of love," while beautiful, is "profane to that which follows," and this statement is followed a few paragraphs later by the suggestion that the demands of nature, "motherhood for twenty years," rob women of "the highest beauty." Such a view makes woman seem like a tragic phenomenon not only because of the importance traditionally attached to personal beauty in women, but also and more importantly for what it suggests concerning her ability to acquire beauty of soul through dialectic soaring. Emerson often expresses the opinion that marriage is more of an obstacle than a help to those who want to grow spiritually and rise in the scale of being, and that this is particularly true of women, because their physiological liabilities make them overemphasize the importance of this circumstance. In "Domestic Life," for instance, where he takes both sexes to task for their "low" aims, women, not men, are seen as excessively preoccupied with things like love and marriage: "It is pitiful," he says, to "date and measure all the facts and sequel of an unfolding life from such a youthful and generally inconsiderate period as the age of courtship and marriage" (W.VII.123–124).

Actually, Emerson is torn between pity and disapproval confronted with this spectacle. On the one hand, one finds him noting with surprise what he sees as the strange attachment of even the finest women—who should know better—to the institution of marriage: "They are all hysterical," he says in a comment on Margaret Fuller's journals which also contains references to rosy mist: "The unlooked for trait in all these journals to me is the Woman, poor woman. . . . She is bewailing her virginity and languishing for a husband" (JN.XI.500). On the other hand, he sometimes feels that what he considers the basic constitutional difference between men and women makes it seem cruel to insist on manly self-sufficiency "in conversing with a lady": There is something "tragic" even about the fine women "who have had genius and cultivation" if they have not "been wives" (JN.V.410). This statement is based on the conviction that no woman ever had enough genius and culture to compensate for the loss of husband and children, the things which her "relative" nature requires above all. Ostensibly, he attempts to refute the idea that women have to feel inherently inferior with respect to cultural creativity, but the suggestion that they should not despair just because no woman so far—not even Sappho or Madame de Staël—has proved able to "satisfy the imagination and the serene Themis" only makes their situation seem more hopeless. Significantly, he ends this meditation on the potential of women by dwelling on the proneness to tears he has noticed in the most favored of young maidens and which makes it look as if grief is their "native element."

No wonder, then, if the minstrel handling the wind-harp in one of Emerson's poems, is said to know "the law of Night and Day, / And the heart of girl and boy, / The tragic and the gay" (W.IX.237). This series of parallel oppositions sums up something essential in Emerson's view of woman. Nor is there any dearth of other hermetic or archetypal polarizations that tend to confirm the idea that woman's is a tragic existence devoted to suffering. There is, for instance, the distinction between "passive" and "active," with which Emerson was familiar not only from his schoolboy study of the *genera verbi*, but from Cudworth and Schelling. He seems to have been intrigued by the latter's elaboration of this distinction in terms of a divine "doer" and an earthly "sufferer," the former obviously associated with the masculine, the latter with the feminine principle (JN.V.337). The original and literal meaning of the word "passion" being "suffering" (as in "the passion of Christ"), this universal polaric dichotomy fits the notion that woman's susceptibility to "the passion of love" is tragic because it is, strictly speaking, a mode of suffering—of suffering things to happen to one even though they may not really be in one's best interest.

"The Tragic" begins with what might well be an unconscious allusion to the archetypal opposition of male and female in terms of the open air and the house, especially as the general argument is also easy to relate to Schelling's dichotomy of the world in terms of the doer and the sufferer: "He has seen but half the universe who never has been shown the house of Pain" (W.XII.405). In this part of the essay, Emerson begins by dialectically acknowledging that there seems to be such a thing as pain, but he soon turns to expounding a view of suffering in accordance with his monistic view of evil as something merely phenomenal. The word "passion" does not fail to appear in this context: "For all melancholy, as all passion, belongs to the exterior life" (W.XII.413). This statement is significant because "exterior life" obviously means everything that is earthly and bodily and hence superficial, a mere "garment," in Emerson's philosophical perspective. Thomas Taylor, his cicerone in Platonic lore, specifically argues that suffering is superficial and of the body, in a long note to his translation of the *Timaeus*.

Even more striking is the celebration of the idea that "all sorrow dwells in a low region" to which Emerson proceeds in "The Tragic" (W.XII.410). Anatomically speaking, the reference is to the entrails, or perhaps rather to the midriff, which happens to be the part of the body which Plato in the *Timaeus* compares to the women's quarters in a house. Like Plato, Emerson opposes this part to the head, the seat of intellect. At the end of "The Tragic," intellect is characterized as "a consoler, which delights in detaching or putting an interval between a man and his fortune and so converts the sufferer into a spectacle and his pain into poetry." In terms of the opposition of high and low, the sphere of the intellect is the "region whereunto these passionate clouds of sorrow cannot rise"—a distinction which seems calculated to remind us once more that he habitually sees misty and earthbound emotion as a feminine attribute, opposing it to man's clear and soaring mind.

The idea that pain is superficial and dissolves when one's eye-beam is sufficiently erect is actually the basis of an explicit criticism of another aspect of woman's capacity—or appetite—for suffering. Emerson also says in "The Tragic" that "the horrors of 'the middle passage' " which make "a tender American girl" doubt the Divine Providence as she reads about them are only apparent: These "crucifixions" do not come to such as her, and to "the obtuse and barbarous" to which they do come "they are not horrid, but only a little worse than the old sufferings" (W.XII.415).

It is true that Emerson occasionally bows to female intervention on behalf of the slaves, but his principal tendency is to see compassion as simply another form of passion, of suffering; from a philosophical point of view he is as little impressed with it in women as he is in the case of the suffering Christ inflicted upon himself out of a downward and visceral love. In "Courage," scholars and thinkers are criticized for their "effeminate habit" of losing heart at the sights of evils that will not disturb "a healthy mind." Here, too, the impression given is that tragedy can on the whole be abolished or relegated to the plane of aesthetics if only the woman in us can be brought under control (W.VII.275–276).

Emerson does not invariably see woman and the feminine principle in so somber a light. There are occasions on which he argues "on the other side." Once—after a visit by the Goethe-enthusiast Margaret Fuller—he even commends Goethe for the portraits of women he has drawn in *Wilhelm Meister,* finding them not only very respectful to woman but remarkably "hopeful" (JN.VII.10). However, such notes are luxuries he can indulge in only at the expense of his Platonistic philosophy. Moreover, when he argues on the other side, he usually strikes one as a man who is trying hard and yet not quite succeeding in convincing himself that the female sex is doing all right. Take again the case of Margaret Fuller; fresh from a conversation with her in 1843 he notes in his journal: "For me today, Woman is not a degraded person with duties forgotten, but a docile daughter of God with her face heavenward and endeavouring to hear the divine word and convey it to me" (JN.VIII.372). The use of the word "endeavouring" here is not calculated to suggest that woman is actually successful in this respect. Moreover, the insertion of a modifier like "today" indicates that Emerson himself is aware that this has not always been his position. Nor will it be his typical stance in the future, witness his final verdict on Fuller in a journal entry from 1850 prompted by his reading of Fuller's letters to Caroline Sturgis. He likes them, he says, but "they are tainted with a female mysticism which to me appears so merely an affair of constitution that it claims no more respect or reliance than the charity or patriotism of a man who has just dined well and *feels good.*" The problem with "our noble Margaret" is that "her personal feeling colours all her judgments," and that her hearer "is long imposed upon" because of the "precise and glittering nomenclature" in which she wraps the "merely sensuous and subjective objects" with which she is concerned (JN.XI.293).

On other occasions, Emerson's intermittent effort to convince himself that woman's situation is not entirely hopeless seems to be predicated on the idea that wifehood annexes most women to a man in a kind of reintegration of the original Adam: "A man pities a woman, but his wife does not excite pity any more than himself. He reckons her fortunate in being his. In the whole then no woman is pitiable" (JN.VI.188). If the logic seems to break down in the final sentence, this only shows just how hard Emerson is trying.

The logic is impeccable in another journal entry, where Emerson in substance bases his optimism on the fact that men and women after all belong to the same species and often enough are blood-relatives. "It is folly," he says, "to imagine there can be anything very bad in the position of woman compared with that of man, at any time; for since every woman is a man's daughter and every man is a woman's son, every woman is too near to man, was too recently a man, than that possibly any wide disparity can be" (JN.VIII.411).

A magic formula with which Emerson arms himself in this context is: "The girl is the least part of herself." The phrase is sometimes quoted in the English of Landor's *Imaginary Conversations* (e.g., JN.IV.44), sometimes directly from Ovid's *Remedia Amoris: "Minima pars sui puella"* (JN.XIII.390). Ovid's point is simply that what we love in a woman is mostly an illusion due to cosmetics and other artifices, an idea which itself is close enough to Emerson's more monistic view of woman. In the second of the cited instances, he notes, as a kind of gloss on the Ovidian sentence, that "they who are not substance have need of the compensation of costume." But his fascination with this dictum is due in part to the fact that it can be used—with a characteristic Emersonian twist

—to express the idea that woman's *femininity* is not an essential part of her, an idea which so far as he is concerned vastly improves her situation. As a woman she may on the whole be less divine than man, but nevertheless "God is in the girl. That is the reason why fools can be so beloved by sages, that, under all the corsets and infirmities, is life, and the revelation of Reason and of Conscience" (JN.VIII.367).

Sometimes Emerson's desire to take a more optimistic view of woman is expressed indirectly, as an impulse to *save* her reflecting a belief that she is not beyond salvation, that biology is not destiny: "I thought again today how much it needs to preach the doctrine of Being against Seeming. Especially to young women the tendency . . . is almost irresistible in favor of preferring appearances" (JN. V.380). And a few days later: "I scarce ever see young women who are not remarkably attractive without a wish an impulse to preach to them the doctrine of character. . . . Could once their eye be turned on the beauty of being as it outshines the beauty of seeming, they would be saved" (JN.V.389). However, here, too, the wording suggests that the chances of changing their angle of vision are slim; one is reminded of the blunt suggestion in *The Conduct of Life* that "women, more than all, are the element and kingdom of illusion." In this case, he chooses to express his pity in these terms: "And how dare anyone, if he could, pluck away the *coulisses*, stage effects and ceremonies, by which they live? Too pathetic, too pitiable, is the region of affection, and its atmosphere always liable to *mirage*" (W.VI.315–323).

Occasionally, the pity is replaced by impatience: "The Indian Squaw with a decisive hat has saved herself a world of vexation. The tragedy of our women begins with the bonnet. . . . Put on the squaw's man's hat, and you amputate so much misery" (JN.XI.145). Especially in view of the situation of women under the tepees— not exactly one of equality—this can hardly be seen as a serious call for social reform. The word "decisive" is quite obviously a pun on the etymological meaning of the word: It is related to the Latin verb "decido," which means about the same thing as "amputate"—Emerson is sarcastically suggesting that the state of women would improve drastically if their femininity, or at least everything the bonnet stands for, could be eliminated in one swift action.

In other cases, Emerson does seem to think that society rather than the physiological makeup of woman is to blame for their sorry state. In a journal entry from 1845, he even offers an economical explanation according to which marriage is a form of prostitution into which women are pressed because they do not have access to professional careers: "In our civilization her position is often pathetic, what is she not expected to suffer for some invitation to strawberries and cream." However, the last sentence of this entry suggests, somewhat ironically, that the biological constitution of women is at the root of the problem after all: "Mercifully their eyes are holden that they cannot see" (JN.IX.108). As early as 1834, Emerson had expressed the opinion that women are not so unfortunate after all because their physical organization prevents them from realizing their situation: Corinne, the heroine of a novel by Madame de Staël, is "a true representation of the tragedy of woman which yet (thanks to the mysterious compensation which nature has provided) they rarely feel" (JN.IV.260).   .

No doubt Emerson himself was not always fully aware of how tragic the situation of woman actually is in terms of his views. Even the circumstance that much of his commenting on her psychological and metaphysical status is confined to his journals does not have to be construed as self-conscious self-censuring. Moreover, his failure to include in his published works an explicit statement of the logical conclusions of his views on woman and the destiny of man has caused his critics to maintain a deplorable silence concerning the limits which mark his philosophical optimism in this respect. Any failure to take these things into account will necessarily in some measure distort his vision.

Newton Arvin's now classical article, "The House of Pain: Emerson and the Tragic Sense," can serve to illustrate this point.[2] Arvin argues not only that Emerson's optimism is worthy of our respect because it did not really come easily to him, but also that he sometimes goes "beyond Tragedy" by overcoming the opposition between optimism and pessimism, in the process displaying "religious courage" in the Kierkegaardian sense. In this context, Arvin introduces an interesting version of the familiar dichotomy between active and passive, between the doer and the sufferer: "I have said that his thought—or better his feelings—moves back and forth between a trusting passiveness and an energetic activism; and for the most part this is true. But there are moments in his work when the dichotomy between the passive and the active is transcended, and what he expresses is a spiritual experience that partakes of both—an experience of such intensity, yet such calm, that neither of the words, 'active' or 'passive,' quite does justice to it."

There is no explicit reference to the sexual aspect of the dichotomy here; more specifically, Arvin does not try to do for Emerson what G. Wilson Knight does for Hamlet in a rather similar argument—attribute androgyny to him.[3] Yet one cannot help noting that one such "moment" is the passage in "The Problem" where Michelangelo is described as "the passive master" who has no choice but to conceive and gestate his masterpieces under the pressure and influence of the Over-Soul—an imaginative statement of the idea that the great artist is androgynous (W.IX.8). Thus Arvin's vindication of Emerson's thinking from this point of view leads us to the latter's own image of the self-sufficient man of genius and more particularly to his stated feeling that such a man, by the very fact that he unites the qualities of both sexes, does not need a woman to complement his being as much as other men do (JN.VIII.175)—a timid way of saying that woman is tragically inessential so far as great men are concerned.

A similarly ironic effect is produced by the circumstance that Arvin chooses to illustrate his thesis by adducing the following passage from "The Method of Nature" (W.I.194):

> We ought to celebrate this hour by expressions of manly joy. Not thanks, not prayer seem quite the highest or truest name for our communication with the infinite,— but glad and conspiring reception,—reception that becomes giving in its turn, as the receiver is only the All-Giver in part and in infancy. I cannot,—nor can any man,—speak precisely of things so sublime, but it seems to me the wit of man, his strength, his grace, his tendency, his art, is the grace and the presence of God. It is beyond explanation. When all is said and done, the rapt saint is found the only logician. Not exhortation, not argument becomes our lips, but paeans of joy and praise.

It is in passages like these, and especially in the use of the word "praise," says Arvin, that we find "the quintessential Emerson," and "unless we have deafened ourselves to any other tones than those of anguish and despair, we should still know to be inspirited by everything in his writings that this word symbolizes." Perhaps so, but what Emerson says here will seem much more likely to cheer a manly heart than a woman's, if one considers the implications of a phrase like "manly joy," the incantatory use of the masculine pronoun, and the human attributes and achievements singled out as signs of the presence of God.

Explaining what he means by "the All-giver . . . in infancy," Emerson says—in a later passage not quoted by Arvin—that "the intellect still asks that a man be born," because "there is no man; there hath never been." In this perspective, too, woman seems tragically irrelevant. Not only is "Intellect" primarily a masculine attribute to him, the opposite of "sentiment," which he sees as the chief attribute of woman; the frequent use of phrases like "a man" and "no man" throughout the essay points in the same direction: Whenever Emerson prophetically discusses the long-range prospects of man, he makes it clear that he feels that "man is manly," to quote from Melville's *Battle-Pieces*. In "The Sphinx," he speaks of "The fate of the man-child, / The meaning of man" and makes Mother Nature refer twice to her "boy." In "The Song of Nature," where he bewails the fact that "the man-child is still unborn" in spite of all her "labor," all the approximations of "a man" cited are masculine.

The climactic last words of "The Method of Nature," to which Emerson's view of man as the God to come is closely related, perfectly fit this pattern: If the future course and final goal of history is summed up in the phrase "through universal love to universal power"—where does that leave woman? It would be wrong to say that the sentiment Emerson so often associates with woman is here reduced to a mere means to an end. The love he is speaking of is upward Platonic love and aspiration, and ordinary love (whether charity or passion) has nothing to do with it. But if the goal of humanity is absolute and divine power, it would seem that woman is expendable in terms of Emerson's own estimate of her powers.

Perhaps the analogy between Emerson's view of the powers of woman and his view of the blacks shows better than anything else what the logical conclusion concerning the future of woman is in terms of his vision of the goal of history. Virtually all relevant statements in Emerson's works suggest that he was convinced that the black man was also a tragic phenomenon because his powers were inferior to those of the white man. Moreover, it is quite striking how the polarizations to which he resorts in his discussions of these matters call to mind his analyses of the difference between male and female. He is not entirely responsible for this coincidence, of course: Archetypal polarities are involved here; one notes, for instance, that a series like the already quoted one involving day and night, boy and girl, gay and tragic, fits the opposition of white and black as well as that of male and female. By the same token, the opposition of the doer and the sufferer reappears in the white man and the black slave. In fact, even the idea of a fall as explanation of the servitude of the black man—echoing the explanation of Eve's—is present in the biblical story about the curse placed on the descendants of Ham. Thus Emerson is operating within a well-established tradition when he writes (more charitably than when he denies the horrors of "the middle passage"): "The Whole History of the negro is tragedy. By what accursed violation did they first exist that they should suffer always?" (JN.VII.58). Even when he tries to see the situation of the black man in a less somber light, polarizations reminiscent of the archetypal male-female oppositions may surface. On one occasion he compares the black man to "a rich cedar swamp," thus tying him not only to the earth but to humidity (the emotions) and a luxuriant but somewhat vegetating life (EL.III.371).

Based on such assumptions, Emerson tends to take a dim view of the prospects of the black race. In a journal note from 1840 (where he sees the black man not as the consequence of ancestral sin but as a kind of "fossil" formation), he says, "It is plain that so inferior a race must perish shortly like the poor Indians" (JN.VII.393). The implication is that nature will prove the shrewdest Abolitionist; as for the reasons why the black man has not disappeared long ago, Emerson's guess is that he might be needed to teach "this generation" pity (perhaps in the absence of a cathartic drama). In spite of his suspicious attitude toward the Abolitionists, he obviously never supported the cause of slavery; on the contrary, he opposed the Fugitive Slave Law in 1850 and was all for John Brown in 1859. But even emancipation must have seemed like a somewhat academic question to anyone who did not see the black race as a viable one, and it is indicative of his readiness to insist on logical conclusions in this case that he never seems to have lastingly and consistently changed his mind on that issue. He may waver on occasion, as in "Emancipation in the British West Indies" (1844), where the appearance of a Toussaint makes him leave the question open, noting that whites and blacks, men and women, will be saved not by compassionate reformers, but, if at all, by their own power (W.XI.144–145). There is also the "Boston Hymn" of 1863, in which he wishes the black race good luck in the chivalrous tone a man might use in speaking to a woman who insists on going her own way. Yet in 1856 he notes in the chapter called "Race" in *English Traits* that "race in the negro is of appalling importance" (W.V.48), and journal passages from that time suggest that the blacks are headed for the museum (JN.XIII.54 and 286). In his final statement on the subject, "Civilization," (1870), he flatly counts the blacks among the races he deems incompatible with civilization and hence doomed to gradual extinction (W.VII.20).

In the case of woman, similar assumptions should logically lead to similar conclusions. It is true that Emerson did not take quite as gloomy a view of the possibility of raising woman to man's level through education; emotionally as well as mythically, he was unable to see her as a "pre-Adamite"—one of his names for the black man (JN.VII.84). But it certainly has been demonstrated that he felt that woman in important respects is a kind of "undevelop'd man" and definitely represents an evolutionary impasse as far as the expansion of man's power is concerned. Accordingly, there is reason to believe that he abstained from prophesying her obsolescence in an explicit manner in part because the cultural situation would hardly have permitted it in her case, and in part because the abolition of woman was difficult to imagine at the time, barring an apocalyptic development leading to the restoration of the original Adam.

Also—be it said without malice—Emerson had a vested interest in the continued existence of woman such as she was; he was, in fact, quite aware that a wife could administer powerfully to a man's physical well-being. This may well have contributed to his lack of interest in the less radical solution of the problem posed by woman which consisted not in abolishing her as a sex but in relieving her of some of the "femininity" that made her so tragic in his eyes. Whitman appears to have felt that one of the prime tasks of American democracy was to correct the injustice done to woman through the evolution of a handicapping femininity.[4] But Emerson, as already shown, tends to back away from the idea that the "tragedy" of woman might be a cultural rather than a natural given. One also notes his interest in the theories of a certain Dr. Vethake, who argued that "society was fast arriving at the excess of democracy, universal abolition," including "the absolute extinction of the feminine principle," but that when it did, woman would rise up and reassert the difference between her and mankind (JN. VIII.341–342).

This bent does not prevent Emerson from pursuing his monistic dream of the original Adam, however—the solution to the problem of femininity which best agrees with his metaphysical and futuristic ideas. A good illustration of the power of this dream is offered by a passage in his lecture on Milton in which the tragic phenomenon of womanhood is eliminated in a striking although merely symbolic and perhaps subconscious manner. *Paradise Lost* is here described as "a poem on the subject of Adam, the first man," and it is suggested that Milton was especially well qualified to write it because of the special insight into the nature of manhood provided by his own manliness and the affinity between him and Adam: "From a just knowledge of what man should be, he described what he was." A quotation of Milton's portrait of Adam walking in Eden follows:

> His fair large front and eye sublime declared
> Absolute rule; and hyacinthine locks
> Round from his parted forelock manly hung
> Clustering, but not beneath his shoulders broad.

The remainder of the picture, outlining the charms of Adam's wife, has been excised by Emerson, who after this vindication of Milton's "purer ideal of humanity" goes on to speak of his "philosophy of chastity" and the divorce tracts, justified by the suggestion that he was "an angelic soul" (EL.I.160–163). Eve is not mentioned anywhere in the lecture, and this just might have something to do with the fact that she is as much of an embarrassment in the context of Emerson's archangelic-Adamic ideal as the black man is.

5

OPTIMISM AND EXPERIENCE:
EMERSON'S ENCOUNTER WITH
THE IRRATIONAL

As an affirmation of final order and unity, the monistic strain in Emerson's thought undoubtedly represents a kind of optimism. But this optimism is something which he could maintain only by dint of disregarding certain things in his experience and in human life in general. This again is not easy to do without ever betraying the dualistic anxieties which make such a procedure desirable in the first place and which so often, and not least in his case, lurk beneath the cheerful surface of philosophical monism. The sex-related facts of life in particular seem to be a weak spot in his monistic armor, a threat to the cherished notion that the world is ultimately rational and everything nicely under control. In *Nature*, things like "sleep, madness, dreams, beasts, sex" are called "not only unexplained but inexplicable" (W.I.4). Apparently they are among the "disagreeable appearances" which he hoped to see eliminated in the millennial "kingdom of man over nature" which he still anticipated at the time (W.I.77).

Emerson definitely tries to dispose of these appearances in his essay on love, and here, too, what one might call his philosophical squint is very much in evidence: His announced desire to treat his subject exclusively from the idealist point of view is justified not only through statements concerning the alleged harmfulness of sexual enjoyment but also with reference to what he sees as the general painfulness of erotic experience in the sphere of generation (W.II.171). The flight into monism is hardly less obvious in a later essay, "Experience," where personal experience is declared not painful enough and irrelevant to one's essential life. On the surface, this may sound like optimism of the most radical kind, and yet the author's way of challenging life to make him suffer and realize that he exists seems somewhat overdrawn and due to an overdose of Mithridates' medicine. This is especially true of his suggestion that he would be willing to "pay the costly price of sons and lovers" for the experience of grief (W.III.48).

The personal and experiential background of essays like "Experience" and "Love" is fairly obvious, and the same thing can be said about the unfavorable view Emerson takes of "the facts of life" in *Nature*. Nevertheless, it would be a mistake to take it for granted that his personal experience (in the narrow sense) is the only, or even the main source of the squint toward dualism which complicates his sexual monism. We must remember in this context the hostile view of sex characteristic of the religious faith in which he was brought up. Even more crucial is the attitude of his Platonistic authorities, including that of Plato himself.

The fact that Plato's view of sex is also ambiguous—sometimes monistic and sometimes dualistic—needs to be taken into account by Emerson critics. Discussing his Platonism without reference to sex must necessarily result in a distortion of the philosophical background of the ambiguities besetting Emerson's own monism and hence also of any statement concerning the relation between his personal experience and his philosophical views. Before discussing the role of his life experience, I shall therefore briefly demonstrate that the ambiguity which pervades his thought from this point of view already exists in the thought of Plato and that Emerson was not entirely unaware of this.

S. G. Brown's article "Emerson's Platonism" is the ideal point of departure for such a demonstration.[1] Brown sees that the monistic and dualistic positions as such are irreconcilable (i.e., not to be "balanced") and that "it is a fair judgment against Emerson that he nowhere faces this fact directly." He also notes quite correctly that, if we do not want to dismiss Emerson as a "poet" incapable of steady intellectual focus, we must realize that the fundamental inconsistency in his thinking lies at the very heart of Platonism and perhaps "at the heart of experience itself." Nevertheless, Brown's attempt to identify the Platonistic sources in the light of which Emerson may have interpreted his own experience suffers from his failure to recognize the sexual dimension of the matter.

One problem is Brown's suggestion that Emerson's philosophical squint is due to his reading and pondering the *Timaeus*, a comparatively late work of Plato's, in the original instead of in the translation of the Neo-Platonist Thomas Taylor, on whom he otherwise relied so heavily in his study of Platonism. According to Brown, Emerson would have received a very different impression if he had seen the book through the eyes of Taylor, who in his turn read it through the eyes of Plotinus, allegedly a very consistent monist inspired by the *Republic*. This view is unsatisfactory not only because Emerson did study the *Timaeus* in Taylor's translation no later than 1842 (JN.VIII.178), but also and above all because it hardly makes any difference which text he used from this point of view: The vacillation between sexual monism and sexual dualism is not easily disposed of even in all-out attempts to do away with evil in a more general sense. In Taylor's translation, which can hardly be called an attempt of this kind, the suggestion that woman, along with the animals, represents the fallen state of man comes through with full force. In Taylor's Introduction, quotations from Proclus' Commentary on the *Timaeus* relate phrases like "the devouring jaws of nature" to the quasi-magical devouring capabilities of certain "irrational animals" and the subtly corrupting influences of menstruating women. In his ample notes, finally, Taylor—again drawing heavily on Proclus—airs questions like: "Why, therefore, are partial souls descending into generation filled with such material perturbations, and such numerous evils?"[2]

Moreover, dualistic feelings about sex, woman, and nature are not really confined to the writings of Plato's later years, witness the attempt to do away with sex and family life, and also with woman *qua* woman, which is such a crucial part of Socrates' exposition in *The Republic* and the one which seems to have fascinated Emerson more than any other part. Even the suggestion that woman is not essentially different from man, only an inferior version of him, is in the final analysis simply the reverse side of his tendency to associate the feminine principle with dark, irrational forces. Emerson gleefully juxtaposes the former part of his argument in *The Republic* with a clearly dualistic statement in Taylor's translation of *The Laws* (the very last work of Plato): "The female sex is another kind of men, more occult and fraudulent than we are through the imbecility of its nature" (JN.IX.190). But this contradiction is more than implicit in *The Republic* itself.

As for Plotinus, he cannot be said to be consistently monistic either. It is true that when he says that matter is evil, "matter" is not necessarily to be taken in the sense in which the word is used by "materialists"; to him everything is "matter" and "evil" compared with what is above it and able to inform it. Yet there clearly are passages in which Plotinus makes matter in the materialistic sense the principle of evil. More specifically, there is a tendency in the *Enneads* to regard the body, so closely associated both with nature-matter and the feminine principle, as something that ought to be shed; what in Plotinus' monistic perspective is mere "otherness" and nonexistence emerges as a formidable obstacle as soon as ethical considerations enter into the discussion. Emerson's essay on love shows the impact that the book had on him in that respect. So does *Nature,* where he not only suggests that Plotinus is as hostile to nature-matter as the Manicheans, but reminds us that Plotinus was "ashamed of his body," and that men like him "distrusted in themselves any looking back to these flesh-pots of Egypt" (W.I.58).

Thus there can hardly be any doubt that there is a close relation between the inconsistencies of Emerson's philosophical authorities and the squint which complicates his own monistic vision, including his view of sex. The question still remains as to the precise nature of his relation to these authors: To what extent can the irrational element in his own thinking be said to be the effect of his reading of the Platonists and their followers, and to what extent did he merely see in them an authoritative statement of his own experience? It would be vain to try to answer this question in any precise manner: No doubt there is a dialectic of mutual reinforcement between his own life experience and what he learned from the Platonists, but the relative strength of these forces is a matter beyond the scope of literary analysis. Yet it may not be impossible to give an idea of the absolute strength of the irrational and *hoc ipso* experiential forces which caused Emerson to see certain facts of life in two different and radically irreconcilable ways.

It should also be possible to say something about the strength of these forces at different times in Emerson's life. Indeed, this is part of the problem: Brown is not the only one who takes it for granted that the dualistic overtones of the *Timaeus* have something to do with the author's experience of old age. Ralph Inge, for instance, suggests that the later Plato was characterized by an increased ethical severity, not least with regard to sex. It is true that he traces this development to the influence of the Pythagoreans—who, he says, "preached monism on one side while making concessions to dualism on the other"—but soon afterwards he declares himself willing to "risk the epigram" that "pantheists generally become theists if they live to be seventy" (pantheism being a form of monism, theism a frequent companion of dualism).[3] In a rather similar vein, Arthur Lovejoy suggests that Schelling, a modern philosopher with whom Emerson also has a good deal in common, switched allegiance from the God of *The Republic* to the God of the *Timaeus* as he grew older, although he could not do so without betraying the idea of unity in duality.[4] Lovejoy does not explicitly state that this shift had something to do with a change in Schelling's view of sex, but such a relation is implicit in any assumption of a fundamental hostility between his two universal principles, which are thought of in virtually alchemic terms.

How, then, does Emerson perform from this point of view? The answer must be that if it is natural for a philosopher to view nature as hostile and develop dualistic feelings about sex as he grows older, this particular philosopher behaves in a somewhat perverse manner in that respect: He almost seems to have gone through the opposite development. As he himself says in the Ciceronian essay on the subject which he published in *Society and Solitude,* old age rid him of a whole "load of anxieties" that used to oppress him (W.VII.325–326).

On the whole, one must say that Emerson's attitude seems relatively "sound" in this late essay. It is true that he sounds like Schopenhauer in characterizing "the sexual instinct" as one of the "foes" we lose at every stage of life and congratulates himself on the fading of an urge that nature "reinforces" in young men "to insure the existence of the race . . . at the risk of disorder, grief, and pain." He may also seem to strike a dualistic note when he says that as a man grows older everything pertaining to procreation and "the protection of the young animal" is shed and "replaced by nobler resources." But at least sex does not pose a threat to him at this time any more than the tumor in his shoulder which "the old wife" tells him might be cancerous.

Emerson himself implies that a successfully completed career helps induce the kind of serenity described in "Old Age." He had indeed been successful not only in the sphere of spiritual creativity but in that of biological procreation as well. Since the death of his son Waldo in 1842, no more disasters had befallen his developing family. His own physical health had greatly improved compared with earlier days, and mentally he seems to have become more extroverted and sociable. It only seems natural that the cigar-smoking Emerson should take a somewhat more relaxed view of sex-related matters than the author of the *Essays*.

At the cosmic level, one glimpses a new, more consistently monistic attitude to matter and nature. Particularly noteworthy is a journal entry from 1871 which shows that Emerson himself was more or less aware of a change in his outlook. He would not feel threatened or insulted, he says, if a chemist produced "an animalcule" before his eyes; he would take this as proof that "the day had arrived when the human race might be trusted with a new degree of power, and its immense responsibility." He adds: "What at first scares the Spiritualist in the experiments of Natural Science . . . now redounds to the credit of matter, which, it appears, is impregnated with thought and heaven, and is really of God, and not of the Devil" (J.X.348).

Looking only at such passages, one might agree with Lewis Mumford's belief that Emerson's contemporaries often were neurotics suffering from warped sex lives, but that he himself was miraculously sane in this respect and thus in a position to put philosophy back on the sound basis it allegedly had in the days of Pythagoras and Plato.[5] However, apart from Mumford's characterization of Plato and the Pythagoreans, the problem is that the more indulgent attitude to sex and nature-matter was never expressed except in a sporadic and tentative manner, even in Emerson's last compositions, perhaps in part because of his continued dependence on notebooks and journals from much earlier days and in part because the sudden decline of his powers put an end to his active writing career not so long after the publication of *Society and Solitude*.

Looking at the other end of Emerson's career, one must say that not only "Old Age" but a number of other essays that he published late in life seem almost youthful when compared with some of the statements concerning sex and sex-related matters one comes across in his early lectures and essays, not to mention the journals and notebooks. In fact, considering the long-standing tendency to associate a weary or fearful attitude to sex with the onslaught of old age, it is tempting to relate this facet of his utterance to his own early feeling that he was bearing in his youth "the sad infirmities / That use to the limb and sense of age" (W.IX.381): A person doing that will naturally feel somewhat uneasy about sex. In Emerson's case, a certain lack of poise with respect to these matters is noticeable even during his in some ways quite normal courtship of Ellen Tucker, who became his first wife. Nor can one say that his early life and thought present the kind of glaring contradiction one finds in Augustine, who at the same age enjoyed sex with his mistress while philosophically embracing a personal version of Manicheism mixed with Pythagoreanism in which the feminine principle, along with matter, is treated with fear and scorn and the evil "dyadic" state of the world compared to the division of man into sexes: Ellen's groom was not equally taken with the physical side of love, although his dualistic apprehensions were sometimes overlaid with monistic ideas about angelic love.

The curious thing is that Emerson's posture did not change that much during his mature years, when his health had improved a great deal. Even during the early part of his marriage to Lidian, when he was in the process of developing a family, he could still sound like the stereotype "grey-beard." In his early lecture on love, for instance, he not only feels, or pretends to feel, that his audience might think him too old to speak of romantic and nuptial love, but suggests at one point that hardly any degree of personal beauty makes much of an impression on a person after thirty (EL.III. 54–56).

It is true that this loss of youthful excitement is supposed to be more than compensated for by a readier access to the fountain of eternal youth, i.e., upward love and aspiration. This seemingly cheerful gospel is preached not only in "Love" but also in "Circles" and other places, and many readers, including Nietzsche, have been impressed by what they are pleased to see as Emerson's refusal to "grizzle." But here again Emerson is speaking of an ideal situation rather than about the real world. Moreover, the real situation cannot be passed over entirely; even in the most optimistic section of "Circles" Emerson notes: "People wish to be settled; only in so far as they are unsettled is there any hope for them" (W.II.320). Since the reference is clearly to people's inveterate tendency to settle down and get married, the statement amounts to a concession that there is not much hope for them in the real world. Whenever Emerson chooses to speak of this world rather than of an ideal situation, thirty becomes the age after which a man, far from cheerfully loving upward and onward, "wakes up sad every morning excepting perhaps five or six until the day of his death"—to quote from a journal meditation from 1835, a few weeks before he married Lydia Jackson (JN.V.77). The philosophical rationale for such gloom is the idea that man, at least metaphorically speaking, begins to "grizzle" at that point, a phenomenon which significantly is attributed to a more "sensual" outlook: "After thirty a man begins to feel the walls of his condition"—he is not flooded by the soul any more—and he "asks himself if he has not done something that he may sit down and enjoy" (EL.III.88). The sensuality attributed to men over thirty is not explicitly described as sexual. Nor is it necessary to think that the problem of sexual indulgence is uppermost in Emerson's mind in this case. But it certainly is present, not least in the subsequent, very explicit comparison of old age to the Fall of Man—that is, man's loss of innocence.

In using the Fall as a symbol of the decline and demise of every man, Emerson no doubt felt he was drawing on the experience of the race. On the other hand, it is well known that he liked to generalize on the basis of his personal experience. His marriage to Lidian no doubt shows considerable ability to reconcile heaven and earth at the level of practical living, but it is also clear that he did not find this achievement gratifying in every respect. One reason for this is obvious: The very success of his experiment contributed not a little to the gap between the ideal and the real of which he so often complains. Unlike Augustine, who after thirty put his house in order by adopting a monistic philosophy buttressed by a monastic life-style, Emerson had most of his sexual experience after that age.

This must have been a humiliating situation from a philosophical point of view, but there is more behind Emerson's resentment than the obvious discrepancy between his theoretical and his actual position. He frequently hints that his chosen way of life, though convenient in some respects, is nevertheless potentially harmful. As an example, one may pick a journal note from 1841, the year when the essay on love was published and he had been married to Lidian for five years: "Marriage," he notes at this time, "is not ideal but empirical"; nor is "this fast union of one to one" part of "the plan or prospect of the soul." Only "a strong mind" knows how to find its advantage in it. To such a mind, "the griefs incident to every earthly marriage are the less, because it has the resource of the all-creating, all-obliterating spirit; retreating on its grand essence, the nearest persons become pictures merely. The Universe is his bride" (JN.VIII.34). The latter part of this statement may sound fairly optimistic so far as persons of Emerson's category are concerned, but one should note that the heading of the entry is "Mezentian marriage": To grasp the meaning of this phrase and of "this fast union of one to one," it is necessary to know that Mezentius, king of the Tyrrhenians at the time when Aeneas landed in Italy, was notorious for his habit of tying persons he wanted to punish face to face with corpses and leaving them to die in that situation. Apparently, Emerson found this passage in the eighth book of the *Aeneid* a good symbolic illustration of the effect marriage has on most men (the passage is obviously written from the male point of view).

Many other journal meditations on the nature of this institution are also suspicious, although the language is usually somewhat less drastic. From the early days of Emerson's second marriage one can quote an entry in which he notes: "We are imprisoned in life in the company of persons painfully unlike us or so little congenial to our highest tendencies and so congenial to our lowest that their influence is noxious" (JN.V.11). The wording is vague, but the suggested possibilities of compensation and escape point forward to a passage in "The Over-Soul" according to which the advancing soul "becomes conscious of a closer sympathy with Zeno and Arrian than with persons in the house" (W.II.275).

The same point is made in somewhat different terms in a note from 1843. Here, too, the idea of confinement appears in the association of woman with the house and the airtight indoors (man is archetypally tied to the marketplace and the open air). But the reference to a harmful and alien influence is couched in language that cannot but call to mind the conversation in the Garden of Eden during which Eve persuaded Adam to eat of the forbidden fruit: "In every woman's conversation and total influence mild or acid lurks the *conventional devil*" (JN.VIII.391).

In view of Emerson's Puritan background, it is not so strange, perhaps, that the fear of woman which contributes to his philosophical squint is commonly linked to the story of the Fall of Man. Milton, the Puritan bard whose detailed account of the Fall is even more important to Emerson than Genesis, strongly suggests that Adam would not have agreed to fall with Eve if it had not been for his excessive fondness for her, largely based on her excessive physical appeal: Too lucid to be "deceiv'd," he fell "overcome with female charms." The author of *Paradise Lost* also suggests that the Fall was inevitable in view of Eve's intellectual inferiority and heralded by the fall into sexual differentiation, belatedly deplored by his Adam.

From being a case of tragic impotence comparable to old age in a man (e.g., W.VII.320), woman thus becomes associated with the uncontrollable, irrational forces in the universe which are the *cause* of tragedy. Emerson often reminds us of woman's role in the events leading to the Fall of Man. In the early lecture where the "sensuality" and routines of life after thirty are compared to the Fall, he notes that the enemy is close like the Snake whispering in the ear of Eve (EL.III.87). Again, in "The Daemonic Love," he states that "It was ever the self-same tale, / The first experience will not fail; / Only two in the garden walked, / And with snake and seraph talked" (W.IX.109–110). This is as much as saying that the Fall is perennial. It will not avail Adam to converse with the Angel—as Milton says he does—as long as Eve will stoop to conversing with the Snake. According to a formula of Oegger's which impressed Emerson, "Man and the serpent form the right angle" (JN.V.67 and W.IV.107), but so do man and woman from this point of view. One may even say that the idea of the perennial Fall of Man amounts to another version of the vertical-horizontal diagram in which woman pulls with the full force of the devil. As Emerson puts it in a critical comment on the subject matter of the novel: *"She was beautiful and he fell in love"* (W.VII.216).

Eve's "consorting" with the Serpent has often been thought of as a kind of Fall of Woman which forever made her attractions a tool of the devil. The idea can be glimpsed in certain passages in which Emerson speculates about the possibility that woman might be naturally prone to yield to unchaste impulses and thus present a danger to man. The problem seems to have worried him a great deal. Not only does he quote Boehme as saying that temptation might "most readily" take hold of woman, "being herself a kind of temptation"—he echoes this idea on his own account: "Lightly was woman snared, herself a snare" (JN.IX.107 and 164).

Emerson's concern is genuine even when he tells himself on the basis of his own experience that the danger must not be exaggerated. Take, for instance, the note in which he vents his irritation on the Shakers for having suggested that there is something wrong about his own chosen state by "such exaggeration of the virtue of celibacy, that you might think you had come into a hospital-ward of invalids afflicted with priapism" (JN.IX.114): The passage indicates that he did not want to take the dangers of sexual incontinence in married men too seriously, but one only has to look at the immediately following page of his journal to see that the problem did have him worried at the time and that standards less strict than those of the Shakers could also upset him. He notes, apropos of Fourier's attempt to liberate man sexually: "I have observed that indulgence always effeminates. I have organs also and delight in pleasure, but I have experience also that this pleasure is the bait of a trap."

In view of the obvious relation between the trap in question and the idea that woman is easily snared because she is herself a snare, one must also say that this statement is out of line with another of Emerson's objections to the theories of Fourier and others who believe women are interested in sex: "Any body who has lived with women will know how false and prurient this is; . . . how chaste is their organization, and how lawful a class of people women are" (JN.IX.191). The whole passage reads like an exorcism.

On a much earlier occasion—at the time when he was winding up his courtship of Lidian—Emerson's need to play down the danger of woman and marriage takes the form of a sharp criticism of the author of the *Decameron* for writing as if sexual pleasure could be indulged in at will. "There is no greater lie than a voluptuous book like Boccaccio," he says, "For it represents the pleasures of appetite which only at rare intervals a few times in a lifetime are intense, and to whose acme continence is essential, as frequent, habitual, and belonging to the incontinent." This statement does not in itself suggest a dualistic squint, but Emerson adds this: "Let a young man imagine that women were made for pleasure and are quite defenceless, and act on that opinion, he will find the weakest of them garrisoned by troops of pains and sorrows which he who touches her, instantly participates. He who approaches a woman unlawfully thinks he has overcome her. It is a bitter jest of nature. He will shortly discover that he has put himself wholly in the power of that worthless slut" (JN.V.22). Here one is struck with the transformation of the conception of woman as a weak creature protected by Providence against the abuses of lecherous men into the idea of a vampire who allures them only to overpower them. Surely we are here far from Emerson's monistic view of the opposite sex.

That Emerson was subject to genuine anxiety concerning the second sex at this time can also be gathered from a journal entry that he made a few weeks earlier about a "youth" (obviously himself) who had an unusual experience while admiring a "maiden" whom he saw in a church crowd: All of a sudden, as their eyes met "in a full, front, searching, not to be mistaken glance," her face was strangely transformed. "He felt the stirring of owls, and bats, and horned hoofs, within him. The face which was really beautiful seemed to him to have been usurped by a low devil, and an innocent maiden, for so she still seemed to him, to be possessed. And that glance was the confession of the devil to his inquiry" (JN.V.8). Here the language is clearly inspired by the old New England belief in witches who have signed their souls away to consort with the devil in the wilderness.

On this occasion Emerson professes more pity than horror at

the spectacle, but in nonreligious contexts he is usually less charitable in his comments on attractive women who arouse his suspicions. In 1838, he writes apropos of an experience he had just
had: "You do not tell me, young maiden, in words that you wish
to be admired, that not to be lovely but to be courted, not to be
mistress of yourself but to be mistress of me, is your desire. But
I hear it, an ugly harlot sound in the recesses of your song, in the
niceties of your speech, in the lusciousness (forgive the horrid word)
of your manners" (JN.VII.77).

The danger apprehended here is the same as in the case of the
maiden possessed by the devil, but the image is that of the Homeric
siren, also alluded to in the *Essays* when Emerson criticizes those
who see "the mermaid's head" but not "the dragon's tail" (W.II.-
105). The sirens, as well as the witches, are among a number of
related themes that appear fairly frequently in Emerson's writings,
both during his early years and during the period that is usually
considered part of a man's maturity. The fact that they are found
almost exclusively in the journals and notebooks indicates that he
made some exceptions to the rule according to which what is most
personal is also most universal; he did not feel in these cases that
the poet should write from his experience. Nevertheless, these
themes are well worth a study, if only for what they tell us about
the odds against which he had to fight in order to reach the serenity
of "Saadi."

To the extent that they are archetypal, these themes also have
a universality of their own. One such case is the attribution of
ghoulish qualities to beautiful women. In 1837, Emerson notes with
interest that his brother Charles had once told him that a certain
married lady "had two faces, and when conversing with her, you
looked up and would suddenly find that instead of talking with the
beautiful Mrs. [name left out], you were talking with a ghoul"
(JN.V.374). This journal entry includes a cross-reference to an
earlier note concerning the experience of Pieter Camper, the anat-
omist, who after studying the Cetacea for six weeks got to feeling
that women, whether pretty or ugly, were all "marsonins or cacha-
lots" to his eyes (JN.V.299). The only obvious similarity between
a ghoul and a cachelot would seem to be that the latter, a very
large, toothed whale, also has a large appetite.

In view of the circumstance that Charles died of consumption soon after his astonishing discovery, it seems worth noting that Emerson himself records several fantasies about men being swallowed up by women during the years when his own survival was in some doubt. In 1823, for instance, he notes among a number of bizarre and cruel historical anecdotes that he had come across in the course of his reading that "a lady, of cannibal or conjugal memory, one Mrs. Artemisia, eat up the ashes of her dead husband in her meals; having heard perchance of a patriot buried in the hearts of his countrymen" (JN.II.364). The sarcastic wording—especially a phrase like "of cannibal or conjugal memory" and the mention of the lady's name, derived from that of the goddess of chastity—suggests that Emerson felt that her act was symbolic of her having already devoured her husband alive.

Soon afterwards (JN.II.405), Emerson congratulates himself on having escaped being eaten so far:

> I am not tangled in the cobweb net
> That wanton Beauty weaves for youth so knit
> To some fair maid he follows with his eye.

Here one is reminded that spiders also have teeth and devour their victims, usually, it seems, after having buried them in capsules made of secreted matter from their own bodies. The passage thus also bears some relation to the lines from 1826 in which death and inhumation are thought of as the embrace of a bride (JN.III.36):

> On me on me the day forgets to dawn
> Encountering darkness clasps me like a bride
> Tombs rise around and from each cell forlorn
> Starts with an ominous cry some ghastly child
> Of death and darkness, summoning me to mourn
> Companion of the clod brother of worms . . . .

Another symbol of the dangers of sexual attraction is rich and beautiful female hair. Such hair is archetypally attributed to witches. Plotinus, for instance, mentions the beautiful hair of Circe and Calypso as he turns them into' symbols of the sensual obstacles confronting the soul embarked for the fatherland. As for Emerson, he sometimes betrays a respect for the seductive powers of feminine hair that cannot be called entirely healthy, as when he notes in his journal: "To the youth the hair of woman is a meteor" (JN.IX.452). A somewhat later entry makes it clear that it is its bewitching character he has in mind: "A little too much in the French novel about this *superbe chevelure*. The less is said of that meteor the better. It is of quite unspeakable character, seat of illusion, and comes as near to witchcraft and humbugging, as anything in nature" (JN.X.360).

The similarity between feminine hair and snakes ties this theme to the idea of the perennial Fall. At the very beginning of his writing career, Emerson composed a ballad in the medieval style about a knight who meets a witch and jestingly asks her for a lock of her hair (JN.I.103–104). Shrieking, she plucks three hairs from her "pye-bald head" and:

> —Straight of those hairs three snakes were made,
>   That leaped on the champion good;
> And one twined round his armed neck,
>   And one twined round each hand,
> And the tails of the three in a black braid met
>   In the grisly haggis hand.

The image is clearly that of a woman who uses her powers to snare a man of the highest aims. In his final stanza, Emerson adds that the knight was not heard of again until Judgment Day.

In classical literature, Emerson early shows an interest in certain lines in Juvenal's sixth satire, in which wives are compared to Tisiphone, one of the Furies, and wifely hair to vipers: "—uxorem, Postume, ducis? / Dic qua Tisiphone, quibus exagitare colubris?" (JN.II.217). This journal note is especially significant because the Furies are not only said to twine snakes into their hair but to hold them in their hands, and everybody who comes in contact with them is supposed to go insane. Emerson's continued fascination with this theme is shown by a later journal note concerning a lady who took an egg in her hand with the result that the warmth of her body hatched it and "the little serpents came out and ran all over her hand" (JN.IV.321).

Emerson also shudders at the thought of the snakes a man might find running over his own hand if he asks for a woman's hand. He quotes "Erasmus or More" as saying that trying to find a good wife was like "putting the hand into a bag having 99 snakes and one eel" (JN.VI.154). Quoting from memory, he exaggerates a bit: In *A Prologue of Syr Thomas More* the ratio is 7:1. But the point is the same; moreover, it seems likely, at least in Emerson's case, that we are here dealing with the almost archetypal image of sexual fear that psychologists have labeled "vagina dentata." It is explicitly related to the Fall of Man in a somewhat later journal entry in which he poetically notes: "Eve softly with her womb / Bit him to death" (JN.IX.164).

Most probably, this theme also appears in a dream recorded in the journal for 1842 which, in addition to an insane person in a crib, features things like fur-muffs (female pubic hair?), empty baskets, and a saw. However, this dream is intriguing for other reasons as well, reasons that make it an appropriate final object of consideration. The dreamer reports that he was convinced that he was being exposed to witchcraft and a devilish will, and that in spite of his determination to stand up to the challenge his limbs were frozen with fear and he could not move. Nevertheless, he felt pleased as well as terrified on awakening (JN.VIII.215–216).

One analyst, Dr. L. E. Emerson, has suggested that the dream shows "how close Emerson was to the insane impulses that might lead to a mental breakdown." In his opinion, "What Emerson interpreted as a devilish Will was . . . a tendency to mental disintegration, which was overcome by his greater tendency to mental and spiritual integration, the success of which he felt as pleasing."[6] This may seem to be putting it a bit strongly, especially as Emerson appears remarkably lucid and balanced in writing this note. One also finds it hard to quarrel with his own suggestion that the dream has something to do with an extra comforter on top of three blankets, after a hearty supper. On the other hand, dreams are often retrogressive, and there are some things in Emerson's past, like, for instance, his reaction to the less than universally enthusiastic reception of his "Divinity School Address," which suggest a certain degree of nervous instability (JN.VII.126).

Thus Dr. Emerson may not be entirely wrong. But the interpreter must not ignore the fact that the threat of insanity is here projected on a woman, in accordance with the Neo-Platonistic association of the feminine with the irrational principle in the universe and Emerson's own tendency to think that all women have a streak of insanity in them. That the problem of femininity is at the core of the dream is shown not only by the fur-muffs and empty baskets and the reference to witchcraft, but also by the circumstance that the "insane person" whom Emerson says he knows well is almost certainly identical with "Nancy Barron the madwoman" mentioned somewhat earlier in the journal (JN.VII.376).

In analyzing the dream, one will find that it consists of several movements. First the dreamer finds himself in a garret (symbol of strangulating confinement) and is disturbed by the sound of a saw. Walking in the direction of the sound, he comes upon the baskets and finds that they are empty at the same time as he notices that there is no saw; he sees the baskets and the fur-muffs as "trumpery [i.e., worthless] matter" and notes that they are lying on the floor; the insane woman also seems harmless enough, lying in a crib like an infant. At this point there is a certain challenge in the fact that the trumpery matter is suddenly animated and starts flying in the direction of a dark corner—this is where he realizes that he is in the presence of "a devilish will" and feels unable to move. However, there is considerable symbolic ambiguity in this part of the dream: Wind is often synonymous with spirit in Emerson's symbolic language, and the swelling and flying fur-muffs could also be emblematic of how spirit or the male principle vivifies and impregnates matter (associated with the female principle). Thus one can understand that Emerson could feel bold and defiant as he woke, in spite of an oppressive feeling of impotence.

All of these movements need to be taken into account in discussing Emerson's comparison of the pleasing effect of the dream to the effect which the rehearsal of a tragedy might produce. It should also be noted that this comparison comes as he rehearses the events of the dream, including his own attempt at a defying stance: The pleasure is thus thought of as essentially aesthetic; it is produced by the fact that the fear that woman might be an instrument of the dark, tragedy-causing forces in the world is, as it were, counterbalanced by the suggestion that she really, in spite of appearances, is a tragic sufferer ("an insane person in a crib") and that pity rather than fear is in order, as in the case of "Nancy Barron the madwoman." Viewed in this light, the dream seems reminiscent of Aristotle's theory of catharsis, as its recorder himself seems to suggest. But it can also be said to represent in a dramatic way the use of monistic optimism as therapy for dualistic fear.

6

DIALECTIC AND MARRIAGE: EMERSON'S THEORETICAL-PRACTICAL DILEMMA

John Albee reports that Emerson once told him that it was "a great day in a young man's life" when he first read the *Symposium*.[1] Such a statement is worth pondering. Is not the *Symposium* the work in which Plato has Pausanias make the distinction between a vulgar and mundane love, the chief manifestation of which is sexual love leading to the propagation of the species, and a more exclusive, "heavenly love" whose purpose is spiritual growth? Is not the *Symposium* the book in which it is suggested that the latter kind of love is practiced by "the best men" of each generation, who as boys form romantic and lifelong friendships with other boys and then continue to seek that which is "akin" to them as adults by paying attention to handsome youths of a more recent generation? Is it not in the *Symposium* that a young man can read that those who grow up to be "the best men" marry only because it is "the custom," a duty they owe nature and the state?

The possibility that Emerson was mainly referring to the artistry displayed in the *Symposium* can be discounted because of his cavalier attitude to the formal problems of literary composition and because he is equally enthusiastic about the *Phaedrus*, Plato's other dialogue about love and dialectic (e.g., W.IV.88–89). It is certainly not a mere coincidence that the *Phaedrus* is where Socrates describes himself alternately as a midwife delivering young men not of new babies but of new thoughts and as a planter of seeds in the minds of young men which make them grow wings on which they can soar into the heaven of ideas.

Besides, the impact these ideas had on Emerson's mind can be seen in more concrete ways. There is, for instance, his literary criticism: He has a rather pronounced tendency to interpret the lives and works of his favorite authors in terms of the *Phaedrus* and the *Symposium*. In fact, even the "skeptic" among his representative men, Montaigne, becomes an orthodox Platonist when the question of his marriage comes up. One of the illustrations of his skepticism adduced by Emerson is the attitude which led him to say that he married not because he wanted to—he did not—but because it was the custom and he was not sure it was worthwhile to dodge the conventions of society (W.IV.169). In an early lecture entitled "The Heart," Emerson had already credited Montaigne with the distinction between "the natural society of marriage" and "the (celestial) society of friendship" (EL.II.288). This is of course another echo of the *Symposium*, a paraphrase of the distinction between mundane and heavenly love. At the biographical level, Emerson was fascinated by Montaigne's friendship with La Boétie. The idea of heavenly love—not to say marriage—is present in the poem which carries the latter's name (W.IX.82).

At the autobiographical level, Emerson's early journals and other works contain so many passages that are in line with Plato's views on love and friendship that it seems likely that the high opinion of the *Symposium* he communicated to Albee reflects a shock of recognition—the realization that he had always been a Platonist. As an example of early Platonic orthodoxy on his part, one may mention the scene described in the closing lines of "The Harp" (W.IX.241):

> Not long ago at eventide,
> It seemed, so listening, at my side
> A window rose, and, to say sooth,
> I looked forth into the fields of youth:
> I saw fair boys bestriding steeds,
> I knew their forms in fancy weeds,
> Long, long concealed by sundering fates,
> Mates of my youth,—yet not my mates,
> Stronger and bolder far than I,

> With grace, with genius, well attired,
> And then as now from far admired
> Followed with love
> They knew not of,
> With passion cold and shy.

That Emerson liked to think of himself as cold by nature can also be seen in his infatuation with a schoolmate, Martin Gay, in which this kind of boyish love and admiration is extended into adolescence. He appears somewhat puzzled, indeed disturbed, by the passionate character of his feelings and at one point considers burning the record of the fantasies to which it had given rise (JN.II.59 and JN.I.53–54). At this time, he could also be filled with Platonic enthusiasm at the mere sight of certain grown men, like, for instance, Professor Everett (JN.VIII.271).

Pondering these early tendencies later in life, Emerson does not fail to link them to the message delivered in his favorite Platonic dialogues. He echoes the very words of the *Symposium* in "Character": "Those relations to the best men, which, at one time, we reckoned the romances of youth, become in the progress of the character, the most solid enjoyment" (W.III.111). This statement, for some reason repeated in only slightly different terms in "Domestic Life" (W.VII.129), is significantly preceded by the suggestion that "love in the sexes" is only "the first symbol" of such friendship.

The idea that the tendency to look for that which is "akin" to one, allegedly characteristic of boys, should be extended not only into adolescence but into adulthood is expressed with particular clarity in one of Emerson's many letters to a young friend, Samuel Ward, whose acquaintance he made in the late thirties. One should note the apparent allusion to the fable of Poros and Penia (Bounty and Poverty), which may be due to the circumstance that Ward was a banker: "All men, I suppose, suffer provocations, from they know not whence, to thought and to the Celestial Bounty; but to the most it is a thing so superficial, that it blends with temperament and ends with puberty; but when those who are more godlike hear the gods, the voices remain like the sound of the sea in the seashell" (LF.44).

Accordingly, Emerson approves of "Sympathy," a poem another young friend of his, Henry Thoreau, wrote at the time and gave the subtitle "To a Gentle Boy." He immediately sent a copy of it to Ward, noting that it was "the purest strain, and the loftiest, I think that has yet pealed from this unpoetic American forest" (LF.17). Many years later—after the author's death—Emerson appears to have joined Frank Sanborn in an effort to make the public believe that the poem was really addressed to a girl whose honor Thoreau wanted to protect. But given the argument of the poem and the poet's pronounced Platonic tendencies, it seems much more likely that Emerson wanted to protect the honor of his old friend; he knew as well as Plato that the mass of people might not find such declarations as pure and innocent as he did.[2]

Emerson himself concentrated in his adult years on developing friendly relations with young men who, in the words of the *Symposium,* "had just begun to show some intelligence." His interest in Ward and Thoreau is part of this pattern. Among other instances, Charles Newcomb and Ellery Channing are interesting because his relations with them are sometimes described in terms of the symbolic marriage of males outlined in the *Phaedrus,* in which the learner is the wife of the teacher. Thus some skeptical remarks dropped by Newcomb ("San Carlo") are in the essay on Montaigne referred to as "this blow from a bride" (W.IV.174). As for Channing, there is an approving journal note stating that he had said about his own verses, which Emerson had managed to get published for him with financial assistance from Ward, that they were "proper love poems" and the "genuine fruits of a fine, light, gentle, happy intercourse with his friends" (JN.VIII.318).

It needs to be added at this point that Emerson also had some intellectual commerce with young women at this time. Caroline Sturgis is a good example of one such woman. However, he was himself aware of a personal preference for the conversation of young men. In fact, in a letter he wrote to another lady friend from England in 1847, he complains that he has not yet seen anybody "to fall in love with, neither man nor woman," adding with rare Socratic irony: "I have . . . some *youthful* correspondence,—you know my failing,—with some friendly young gentlemen in different parts of Britain" (L.III.459–460).

As for the circumstance that Emerson had long been married at that time and had two daughters and a son, he was from a philosophical point of view inclined to see it as just that—circumstance (cf. W.IV.128 and 178). Indeed, with respect to his choice of partner, he almost immediately begins telling himself that he married "impersonally" (e.g., JN.VII.336), a phrase that can only be taken to mean that any available candidate as suitable as Lidian would have done just as well. At least as much as Montaigne, he gives the impression of having married because it was "the custom."

Emerson was, however, shrewd enough to suspect that marriage might help the best men to set their aims high and steady by taking care of various practical matters and offering them a solid earthly base—a dangerous admission in that it leaves the door open for disappointments. It is easy to see that everything did not always go so smoothly in his household. Not only was he subject to strains that are common to most husbands and fathers—the Platonist in him was never entirely reconciled to having to prove that he was not "a metaphysical lover" but a man who enjoyed "the homeliest pleasures and attractions by which our good foster mother Nature draws her children together" (L.I.434). As for Lidian, she was never quite comfortable with her husband's not completely theoretical stress on "impersonal love" as the signum of genius, especially not after it began to take the form of a tendency to seek beauty and virtue everywhere and have intellectual offspring all over the place. Her need for personal attention goes a long way towards explaining why he more often focuses on the noxious rather than the beneficial aspects of marriage whenever he concedes that this institution is not merely circumstantial in the sense of leaving him exactly where he would have been anyway.

Quite logically, Emerson takes a dim view of the dialectical situation of the mass of married people, those whom Plato refers to as "the many." Their problem, as he states it in his vague-yet-clear way, is not simply the dangers of sensuality as such; there are also the children who are a common result of men's willingness to take the bait of nature. They are nice and necessary, of course, but the responsibilities they impose may easily impede the spiritual progress of the parents. Women are in particularly bad shape, so far as their ability to grow wings and soar during their fertile years is concerned. But the men are also punished; a growing family will turn most of them into breadwinners catering to the material needs of their dependents to the detriment of their own mental growth. The result in both cases is premature "grizzling" (cf. W.II.319).

Alternatively, Emerson portrays the parents themselves, the couple immersed in generation, as "children." This can be an indulgent or euphemistic way of speaking of this side of human life, as in the quoted letter to Lidian. But more often the image carries with it a note of impatience, the idea that the delights of "the nuptial chamber" easily become "a child's clinging to his toy," to quote from the passage in *Representative Men* in which Emerson denounces what he sees as Swedenborg's fanciful belief that the institution of marriage will be improved and justified in heaven (W.IV.128). In other words, this imagery also suggests that marriage may easily result in arrested development, a veritable lapse in the scale of being.

One text in which this theme is conspicuous, "Initial, Daemonic, and Celestial Love," is especially noteworthy because the "fond children" the poet addresses at the beginning of "The Celestial Love" appear to be Samuel and Anna Ward, who had just gotten married at the time it was written (W.IX.114). If Carl Strauch is not entirely wrong, the first part of "The Daemonic Love" reflects the feeling of exclusion Emerson felt as the doors of the nuptial chamber closed on these friends of his.[3] Sherman Paul, who also recognizes that Emerson was upset by this marriage, suggests that the reason was that he had been living their courtship "vicariously."[4] But this is hardly enough to explain what we know about the affair, including the words used at the beginning of "The Celestial Love." The truth is that Emerson had been courting Samuel vigorously in the Platonic manner while basking rather cautiously in the personal beauty of Anna. Without doubt Anna has something to do with the "dangerous Beauty" which in the poem does not limit itself to snapping family bonds but supplants "Friends year by year more inly known." That he worried more about the prospect of losing Ward than about what might happen to his relations with Anna can be seen in a series of letters to Margaret Fuller in which he comments on the matter. In one of them he complains about Ward's prolonged honeymooning; in another he seems reconciled to the thought of letting Anna go, but declares that he expects to keep the friendship of Ward, while commiserating with Fuller, who, he says, stands to lose both (L.II. 367–368 and L.II.327–328).

Was Emerson also the prey of more altruistic apprehensions— did he actually fear that things might not after all follow the Platonic scenario in the Wards' case and that the groom in particular might suffer a fatal setback in his cosmic career because of the excessive physical charms of the bride? It is impossible to tell with certainty. Implicitly, such a setback is the corollary of Ward's failure to act like one of "the best men" and consider his marriage a mere concession to custom, and if he lost interest in the "sympathy" Emerson had discussed with him in so many letters it would by definition mean that he had ceased to listen to the divine voices in the manner of those who are "more godlike." But Emerson understandably does not touch upon this aspect of the problem in his letters to Margaret Fuller. As for the newlyweds, he could hardly be expected to sermonize them beyond the generalities of "The Celestial Love" concerning "smoke in the flame" and the need to mount "another round" on the heavenly stair.

On the whole, Emerson had reason to be circumspect in his treatment of marriage as a poet, essayist, and lecturer to audiences that counted few dedicated Platonists. Vagueness and indirection were not his only recourse in this respect. Occasionally he abandoned the strict construction of Plato's doctrine in favor of modifications aiming at making his views more palatable to a modern public. It would be easy to demonstrate such a slanting in "The Initial, Daemonic, and Celestial Love," but "Love" offers an even better example from my present point of view.

In the essay, too, nuptial love is described as a half-baked product—the delight of children. But at least at first this is done in a more positive way than in the poem. It is actually argued that falling in love with a member of the opposite sex and getting married is a first step on the heavenly ladder, a marvelous introduction to universal and impersonal love. Such a view is hardly in line with the teaching of the *Symposium* or the *Phaedrus*. It is true that Plato uses nuptial love as a symbol of the higher love of that which is akin (male). But this does not mean that he sees it as a first step in the right direction. On the contrary, he makes it very clear that this step is the forming of romantic prepuberty relations with members of the same sex and that even at an adult age nuptial love is fundamentally irrelevant to the real business of the best men and a preoccupation with it a sign and cause of the inferiority of the masses.

Emerson's deviation from Plato's doctrine of love in this respect is all the more surprising as "Love" contains so many direct echoes of the *Symposium* and the *Phaedrus*. The essay begins with an allusion to the concept of "celestial love" (as modified by Plotinus). Its author is also close to the *Symposium* when he says that the kind of beauty which is worthy of our love does not belong to the person or body, that the feelings it inspires do not "point to any relations of friendship or love that society knows and has," but "to a quite other and unattainable sphere, to relations of transcendent delicacy and sweetness, a true faerie land; to what roses and violets hint and foreshadow" (E.I.147; cf. W.II.179). The same things hold true of his suggestions that the aspiring soul, in order to approach that sphere, must avail himself of more than one "beautiful soul"—that a whole "ladder of created souls" is needed if he is to ascend "to the highest beauty, to the love and knowledge of the Divinity." In an allusion to the *Phaedrus,* Emerson notes that the ascending movement, once begun, is irreversible (W.II.182–184).

Ralph Rusk rightly says that "the exotic homosexual elements" in the *Phaedrus* and the *Symposium* were "conveniently ignored" in Emerson's attempt to reconcile Platonic theory and marriage.[5] Yet this reconciliation does not come that easily. In trying to achieve it, Emerson must also ignore the discrepancy between some of the things he says and some of the most basic assumptions he has in common with Plato. It is one thing to ignore Plato's lack of interest in heterosexual relationships in discussing affinity-based love and friendship, as he to some extent does in the companion essay on that subject; it is another thing *partially* to ignore his own and Plato's tendency to view procreation as an evil flowing from the Fall of Man, as he does in "Love": Incongruities of this kind make "Love" look not so much like a successful reconciliation of two divergent views of marriage and sexual love as a rather contradictory statement in which the author tries to gain the confidence of and reassure his readers before telling them what he really thinks about the whole matter.

For instance, there is sometimes a wide discrepancy between

the diction Emerson uses in one part of "Love" and his usage in other parts of it, or in the majority of his essays and lectures. Thus the "initial" or "nuptial" love is at the beginning of "Love" described alternately as "a divine rage and enthusiasm" and as "a celestial rapture out of heaven," as if the distinction between the mundane and the celestial love is not going to be made soon afterwards. By the same token, certain words which often carry a sinister connotation in his works, like "witchcraft" and "private," here appear in a quite positive sense. Even the word "passion," which usually stands for something that ought to be avoided at every price, has been rehabilitated. Especially surprising is the suggestion that we "glow over these novels of passion"; Emerson's low opinion of novels and novel-readers is well known.

This element of ambiguity is reinforced by the circumstance that the positive sense of such words as often as not is undercut by added remarks in the very contexts in which they appear, as, for instance, when the "witchcraft" of young affection is said to affect circumstances which in themselves are "accidental and trivial." On the whole, the syntax Emerson uses in this essay is unusually labyrinthine, even for him, and the paragraphing also contributes to a blurring of the argument which has the double effect of neutralizing statements that are not in line with his orthodox Platonism and of sweetening the medication to the extent that it is Platonistic enough to seem harsh to readers who take an uninitiated and commonsensical view of nuptial joys.

It should be noticed that the dualistic view of sexual love which Plato shares with the authors of the New Testament is amply represented in Emerson's essay on love. In the midst of the seemingly enthusiastic account of young love, there are overt warnings concerning the inadvisability of seeking one's satisfaction "in the body." He obviously agrees with the ancient Platonists suggesting that the souls who do that will reap "nothing but sorrow" because body is "unable to fulfil the promise which beauty holds out" (W.II.181). Especially clear, although wrapped in imagery, is the following suggestion that the lovers ought to become inflamed by a love of "the true palace of beauty" and let it extinguish "the base affection, as the sun puts out the fire by shining on the hearth" (the hearth is a common symbol of domestic life).

Perhaps a Victorian with Emerson's clerical background could not be expected to say anything positive about the physical aspects of love even if he were not a committed Platonist. But what of the absence of any sustained reference to the rearing of children as a central purpose of marriage and to the children themselves as a bond uniting the parents? Ironically, he himself notes in a journal entry made a few years later that marriage and procreation are such important and "inevitable" facts of life that an author who omits them "has set a date on his fame" (JN.XI.131). Had he not been a father long enough at the time when the text of "Love" was finished to see the relevance of this topic to his subject? A more probable explanation is that the facts of life that have to do with generation generally speaking are an embarrassment from the Platonistic point of view and that giving any kind of relief to the subject, positive *or* negative, would make the main thesis of "Love" seem absurd.

What Emerson is trying to argue is that the time of sexual activity and the rearing of children is a more or less parenthetical part of the man-wife relationship to be followed by "the real marriage," planned from the beginning by Nature and the true justification of the attractions surrounding the nuptial bower with its stress on merely personal love. At this higher stage, man and wife have discovered that "all which at first drew them together" was "deciduous" and had "a prospective end, like the scaffolding by which the house was built." As a result, "They resign each other without complaint to the good offices which man and woman are severally appointed to discharge in time, and exchange the passion which once could not lose sight of its object, for a cheerful, disengaged furtherance, whether present or absent, of each other's designs" (W.II.187).

The drawing apart is said to be furthered by the very activity which is henceforth to be the main spiritual benefit of the marriage: the mutual criticism based on an ever-increasing knowledge of each other's flaws and merits. This activity represents a "purification of the intellect and the heart from year to year" in the sense that the greater understanding of human frailty which is the result of daily and intimate exposure to another person teaches one not to take occasional weak behavior personally, while at the same time making one realize that the merits which once made one deify the person in question belong to the Deity alone.

In this particular context Emerson suggests that man and wife can and should "represent the human race to each other." But it is typical of the ambiguities that pervade the essay that this suggestion of marital self-sufficiency clashes with his previous stress on the idea that one beautiful soul is not enough to make the aspiring soul ascend to the vision of heavenly and universal beauty. According to this part of his argument, the marriage must be opened up because man and wife cannot really represent the human race to each other.

The hint that it takes many rungs on a ladder of human beings to reach heaven, not to mention the suggestion that the soul is not twin-born but must reach its goal alone—such ideas make it legitimate to wonder whether Emerson really feels that there are any good reasons for preserving a marriage in the long run, apart from rather mundane and expedient considerations. A journal meditation from the year when "Love" was published suggests that he did have some doubt on that score: He notes that marriage "plainly" ought to be "a temporary relation"—adding that we do not exist in heaven, and that men in their natural state cannot be trusted with full liberty in this respect (JN.VIII.95). In "Love," he limits himself to noting that the nuptial relation per se is "a temporary state," adding somewhat apocryphally toward the end that "the objects of the affections change, as the objects of thoughts do" (albeit "slowly and with pain").

The originality of the view of marriage put forward in Emerson's essay on love is best appreciated if one compares it with the attitudes of the writers Emerson explicitly lists as his authorities along with Plato. One may begin with Plutarch, the "middle" Platonist, who owes his admittance to this august company to his dialogue on the same subject, a full-length discussion of the respective merits of boy-love and marriage.

The influence of this work on Emerson's essay is undeniable, and yet it would seem that Edmund Berry exaggerates when he argues that the Platonism in "Love" seldom comes straight from Plato but is usually derived from Plutarch, that, in fact, "only Plutarch's attitude and treatment of love seem to be adapted to Emerson's mind." It is especially hard to follow Berry when he says that one reason why Emerson preferred Plutarch to Plato is that the former remains "on the human level" and only briefly resorts to "Platonism and the higher world," his own aim being to "fortify the conscience and give hope and understanding to the ordinary American."[6] Plutarch does indeed leave Platonism and the higher world alone; he pointedly interrupts a digression on this aspect of Plato's doctrine, with its negative view of sexual pleasures, as irrelevant to the matter in hand. But Emerson stresses exactly what Plutarch omits. By contrast, he entirely ignores another significant development in Plutarch's dialogue, the author's passionate defense of woman qua woman and his characterization of sexual intercourse and procreation as a participation in "great mysteries."

Perhaps one can say that Plutarch in this case shows more common sense than Emerson. The same thing can paradoxically be said of Apuleius, author of the fantastic tale about Cupid and Psyche and the third ancient authority listed in "Love." The story of how the boy-god Cupid falls in love with a beautiful female child called Psyche and "marries" her by slipping invisible into her bed one night; how they are estranged when she contrives to catch a glimpse of his beautiful body (he does not want to be identified because he fears the reaction of his mother—here, clearly, equated with the mundane Venus); how they are finally reunited and formally wedded in heaven after the pregnant Psyche has rejoined him at his mother's house and overcome all the obstacles raised by the angry goddess: all of this can, if read allegorically and in a generous spirit, be construed as the story of the individual soul's progress toward spiritual love. But there is no particular need to read it in that manner. Apuleius' purpose is clearly as much to entertain as to instruct; his risqué story reads quite well as straight fairy tale, and with respect to allegorical interpretations—well, the burden of proof is on the reader.

As for Milton, the most modern authority adduced in "Love," Emerson to some extent appears justified in suggesting that he shares his view of sexual love and marriage: There is something of his "real marriage" about the nuptial ideal projected in the *Doctrine and Discipline of Divorce,* and Emerson can be said to allude to that text in his reference to the difficulties which great men allegedly experience in trying to find a congenial wife. Like Emerson, the author of this tract tries to upgrade marriage by downgrading sex. Among other things, he chides Paul for seeing this institution as primarily a fleshly union ("It is better to marry than to burn"), explaining that there are three levels or "ends" to marriage—namely, "Godly society, next civill, and thirdly, that of the marriage bed." To underline this point, he adds that "the cherfull help that may be in mariage toward sanctity of Life" is "out of question . . . the purest and so the noblest end of that contract" (here the phrasing directly calls to mind Emerson's "cheerful and disengaged furtherance"). The circumstance that Milton almost entirely fails to take the rearing of children into account in his discussion—another thing that he has in common with Emerson—is thus easily related to the fact that he, too, prefers to evaluate marriage in terms of man's progress as a pilgrim in an alien world.

However, the difference between Emerson and Milton from this point of view is considerable. Milton, loyal to his Christian faith, does not urge a progressive loosening of the bond between man and wife on the grounds that it hampers them in their cosmic careers. He claims the right to divorce a wife who does not meet his requirements, but these requirements pertain to an ideal which clearly implies that marriage is to be a permanent, not a "temporary" affair. In fact, the illustration of this ideal brought up in the *Doctrine and Discipline of Divorce* is the prelapsarian "marriage" of Adam and Eve.

If one looks at the way in which this marriage is described in *Paradise Lost,* one will perceive another important difference between the two authors. To some extent the portrayal of the first couple looks like a travesty of the eros-anteros relationship described in the *Phaedrus*—with Adam as the teacher and Eve as the student. But their teaching and learning is mingled with conjugal caresses in a manner that is not Platonic. On the whole, the naked bliss of our first progenitors is painted in colors which betray an appreciation of the physical side of love which one will look for in vain not only in Emerson's essay on love but in all of his works. The only thing in the Puritan epic that is in line with the argument of "Love" is the speech in Book Eight in which the Angel, alarmed at Adam's praise of Eve's not so intellectual beauty, warns him that "the sense of touch whereby mankind / Is propagated" is also the delight of the beasts, and that he must turn his back on "passion" and love only what is "human" and "rational" in his spouse if he is to climb the heavenly ladder.

The two remaining European authorities on love listed by Emerson in his essay on the subject—Michelangelo and Petrarch—are quite different from Milton in that their Platonism enters into an uneasy alliance with the courtly conception of love rather than with the heroic-biblical view of woman reflected in *Paradise Lost.* In Michelangelo's case, the conflict between orthodox Platonic aspiration and courtly love can be seen in the contradiction between sonnets like the one in which he states that woman is too "dissimil' " to inspire a man in his scaling of the transcendental heights and the group of poems whose purpose is to enthrone Vittoria Colonna as the emblem of ideal beauty and virtue. However, even his celebration of her lends very limited support to the argument presented in Emerson's essay on love. There may be something of "the real marriage" about Michelangelo's relations with this aging aristocratic widow: The "heyday of the blood" is definitely a thing of the past for both parties, and the affair might seem to illustrate the idea that "the high progressive, idealizing instinct" predominates at the later stages of life. The problem is that their love story is rather different from the evolution of nuptial love and marriage discussed in "Love" in that there is no initial stage and no marriage. Moreover, Michelangelo seems too obsessed with one particular "door" to "the society of all true and pure souls" to fit Emerson's scenario for that time of life. There are also indications of frustration; there certainly is nothing "cheerful" about the verses in which the great artist celebrates Vittoria before and after her death.

In this and other respects, Michelangelo is of course following in the footsteps of Petrarch: The author of *Rime in vita e morte della mia donna Laura* first saw his lady in church at Easter time and insistently compares his own "passion" for her to the crucifixion of Christ. Even more than the lover of Vittoria Colonna, he projects the image of a man fixed forever in the adoration of one woman. These similarities to Michelangelo also make Petrarch a dubious authority for the theories put forward in "Love." The differences between the two make him even more so: More dependent on the troubadour tradition, Petrarch sings the praises of a woman married to somebody else. Moreover, he often does so in sensuous language more suitable for a troubadour hoping for a

ᅠ

"guerdon" (reward) than for a man motivated by pure Platonic love.

Emerson himself seems to have sensed that none of his authorities had treated the subject of true love in a fashion that was entirely satisfactory to him. After listing them as teachers of the new-old doctrine he himself is outlining, he cryptically adds, "It awaits a true unfolding in opposition and rebuke to that subterranean prudence which presides at marriages with words that take hold of the upper world, whilst one eye is eternally boring down into the cellar." It also appears that he later found a truer unfolding in Dante's *Vita Nuova,* a work to which one can find no reference in "Love."

This omission is curious because Emerson had earlier been in the habit of associating Dante with Petrarch and Michelangelo as Platonic poet-lovers (EL.I.115 and EL.II.264). Apparently, there was a lull in his enthusiasm for Dante about the time when the relevant passages in the essay were first written (1838).[7] He may also have thought it a bit too peculiar to be adduced in a discussion of nuptial love and marriage.

Petrarch and Michelangelo are also peculiar from that point of view, of course; but Emerson certainly has a point when he notes—in 1843—that the *Vita Nuova* is "almost unique in the literature of sentiment" (JN.VIII.369). This little book represents a drastic break with the courtly tradition, in comparison with which Petrarch's and Michelangelo's later attempts to reconcile courtly love with Platonistic and Christian ideas look like backsliding. They do, after all, celebrate adult women with experience of marriage and sex; Petrarch's love is even technically adulterous. Their common master, on the other hand, does away with these things altogether. He explains that he first saw Beatrice when she was only a child of eight, and she conveniently dies as soon as she gets old enough to be married and have children. Thus Dante's love story is a kind of *reductio ad absurdum* of courtly love in which the *Frau* is eliminated from the *Frauendienst.* The reconciliation of Platonic love and aspiration with the love of the opposite sex is achieved in an equally paradoxical manner: Innocent girl-love is substituted for innocent boy-love as a first step on the heavenly ladder.

Emerson did not in the least mind the uniqueness of the *Vita*

Nuova as such. He liked everything about it, and not least the scarcity of "events" which along with the admittedly fictitious name of the heroine lends an almost impersonal character to Dante's love. The central event, Beatrice's death and ascension to heaven, effectively transforms her into an image of transcendent and intellectual beauty, the inspiration of a love which seeks not biological but spiritual increase. One may quote from Emerson's own translation:

> . . . the pleasure of her beauty
> Withdrawing itself from our view
> Becomes spiritual beauty and grand
> Which through the heaven expands,
> The light of Love, which greets the angels.

Thus Dante contrives to have it both ways: In a sense, Beatrice remains forever his first and only love, and yet she is a perpetual invitation to enter what Emerson calls "the society of all true and beautiful souls"; indeed, his fidelity to her also requires him to do so. Jealousy within this society is also ruled out in this context: Already during Beatrice's lifetime it was said that

> . . . her beauty is of such virtue
> That no envy proceeds from it to others
> Rather it makes them go with her clothed
> With gentleness of love and of faith.

In his journal, Emerson shows his awareness—and appreciation —of these things by associating the book with Hafiz and "Saadi apud Goethe" (an allusion to Goethe's Platonistic explanation of the boy-love discussed in Saadi's *Gulistan*). A few pages earlier, he refers to a manuscript in which Margaret Fuller had narrated some of her own experiences of suprasexual love and friendship as "Nuovissima Vita" (JN.VIII.372 and 369). Indeed, he sent the copy of the Italian edition he used for his translation as another gift to Samuel Ward, then married to Fuller's "Recamier." It is, he notes, in his journal, "the Bible of Love" (JN.VIII.430).

The question is whether Emerson's obvious tendency to iden- tify with the lover of Beatrice extended to his retrospective inter- pretation of his relations with Ellen. So far as I know, there is no statement in his writings that explicitly links the two, nor could anything of the kind be expected. But the circumstantial evidence is strong. In fact, the similarities between the life stories of the two women and the roles they played in the lives of the men who loved them are so striking that they shed light on Emerson's "dialectical" view of his own love life, whether he consciously thought of them as the reason for his enthusiasm for the *Vita Nuova* or not.

Ellen was not eight when Emerson first met her, but she was eight years younger than he was, and at least one friend refers to her as his "child-wife."[8] Moreover, she died at the same age as Beatrice, and both deaths precipitated a crisis in their lovers' lives. Dante began his "new life" by seeking consolation in the idea of friendship, and in addition to the *Vita Nuova* wrote the *Convivio*—the name is an acknowledgment of his debt to the *Symposium*—in which he further elaborates his ideal of angelic love-friendship. A rather similar interest is noticeable in Emerson's journals from the years after Ellen's death (e.g., JN.III.274). It is true that he decided to marry again (Dante married Gemma Donati), but his "new life" came with his acquisition of the "new friends" he alludes to in "Friendship."

An equation of Ellen and Beatrice on Emerson's part may seem unlikely or arbitrary since he actually married the object of his early love. But it must be remembered that he was not a pedant in matters of literary identification. Moreover, both he and his first wife were in poor physical shape during their brief marriage. In fact, there are indications that he knew that she was doomed at the time of their wedding, and not long after her death he expressed doubts concerning his own chances of survival (L.I.354). Thus it seems likely that the stress was on spiritual love and "increase" throughout their relationship. This is certainly the way he himself represents it in immediate retrospect: Not only does he suggest that she was called hence by an "impatient heaven"—exactly what Dante says about Beatrice—she is also like the heroine of the *Vita Nuova* described as an angel joining the other angels in heaven. In the verses which he kept composing at this time, he constantly refers to her as "the innocent child," "my undefiled," and "she who was fair / After another mould than flesh and blood" (JN.III.232–235).

Regardless of whether the equation of Ellen and Beatrice was consciously a part of Emerson's identification with Dante, it is clear that the image of Ellen and the idea that there is only "one first love" (JN.III.227) became very useful to him in countering the efforts of women who, as he saw it, were trying to make him reverse the dialectical ascent that was supposed to be irreversible. Lidian in particular was to find the ghost of Ellen barring any attempts on her part to make her relations with her husband more "personal." In "A Letter," a poem written after the death of Ellen, he had vowed to leave town and camp out in the country, taking his books and the "reliquaries" of his "dead saint," in order to "dwell / In the sweet odor of her memory" and aim his "telescope" at "the inviolate sun." In a sense this is exactly what he did in moving out to Concord with his second wife: The telescope aimed at the sun is a good image for the studies on which he concentrated from then on. As for the "reliquaries," one notes his reading and editing of Ellen's poems, some of which were first published in the *Dial* and then in the *Poems* of 1847 as part of a modest but unmistakable effort to celebrate Ellen as an immortal symbol of universal beauty.

This celebration was oral as well as written. Over the years, Lidian had to listen to more than one sermonette about the incomparable beauty and virtue of Ellen. To some extent she went along with this cult, or seemed to do so—her suggestion that they christen the first daughter Ellen, which Emerson greeted with such satisfaction (JN.VII.170), could also be a sly attempt to clothe Ellen with flesh and blood and in the process get more of a personal stake in her.

In a letter he wrote his wife from England in 1848, Emerson commends her for the nice things she had said about Ellen's letters to him, "the precious file," which he apparently had asked her to read.[9] They came, he says, "out of a heart which nature and destiny conspired to keep as inviolate, as are still those three children of whom you send me such happy accounts" (L.IV.54). At the same time, he almost seems to reproach Lidian for not having been there to see Ellen and thus not understanding why the sun had seemed to set in his life when she died. It looked like more than a coincidence that this letter was written only a few weeks after the one in which he tells his wife that "a photometer cannot be a stove" and that he cannot write the love letter she has been asking for, but which he really owes the whole human race (L.IV.33).

After his return to Concord—eagerly anticipated by Lidian— he notes in his journal that "a noble woman is moral, is a Beatrice" and that her lover, in his concentration on "universal aims," is really courting her. The problem, he adds, is that he dares not believe that she has not excepted herself in accepting this view: He is forced to believe that she will delight in his uniform preference for virtue over ordinary joys "with the solitary exception of preferring total union with her to the virtue of the Universe" (JN.XI.429). This sardonic remark shows that Emerson remained convinced that from the point of Platonic dialectic the only perfectly safe women are dead women.

7

DIVINE AFFILIATION AND EARTHLY PARENTS: EMERSON AND THE FALL OF MAN

In examining Emerson's view of fleshly parenthood with respect to his own parents, one immediately notices his tendency to discount the importance of fathers to the spiritual formation of their offspring: "Fathers wish to be fathers of the mind as well as of the body of their children," he once notes in his journal, "But in my experience they seem to be merely the occasion of new beings coming into the world" (JN.V.188). In view of the importance books assumed in his life and his utter failure to quote his father on any subject, one may conclude that he is also drawing on his personal experience when he on a much later occasion distinguishes between good and bad fathers in these terms: "If a man happens to have a good father, he needs less history; he quotes his father on each occasion,—his habits, manners, rules. If his father is dull and unmentionable, then his own reading becomes more important" (J.X.197).

The low opinion the mature Emerson had of his own father from this point of view is expressed quite explicitly in a letter he wrote to his brother William in February, 1850: "This is the third application within a twelve-month that has come to me to write a memoir of our father." He has no recollections, he says, that can serve such a purpose: "I have never heard any sentence or sentiment of his repeated by Mother or Aunt, and his printed or written papers, as far as I know, only show candor and taste, or I should almost say, docility, the principal merit possible to that early ignorant and transitional *Month-of-March,* in our New England culture" (L.IV.178–179).

This verdict ought to be remembered in any discussion of what Henry Nash Smith, alluding to one of Emerson's poems (W.IX.6), has called his problem of vocation."[1] His decision to resign from the ministry, the calling which he in a very real sense had inherited, was not necessarily based solely on contemptuous feelings for his own father: Not very long after he broke away from the ministry, he notes in his journal that he wants to be "a true and free man" and therefore does not want to be "a woman, or a king, or a clergyman" (JN.IV.306). The association of clergymen with kings obviously suggests a threat emanating from them; one is reminded of a passage in "Self-Reliance": "Society everywhere is a conspiracy against the manhood of every one of its members" (W.II.51). On the other hand, the simultaneous reference to women is scornful as well as a hint as to the nature of the danger he wanted to evade. Not only in "Self-Reliance," but throughout his career, he associates the clerical vocation with effeminacy. In "The American Scholar," he reports that he has "heard it said that the clergy . . . are addressed as women, that the rough, spontaneous conversation of men they do not hear, but only a mincing and diluted speech" (W.I.94). Even more biting is the reference to this professional category in *The Conduct of Life,* twenty-three years later: "The clergy have bronchitis, which does not seem a certificate of spiritual health. Macready thought it came of the *falsetto* of their voicing" (W.VI.284–285).

One is reminded both of this characterization of clergymen and the suggestion that they pose a threat to manhood and freedom when one reads the following account of the father-son relationship in another essay in *The Conduct of Life,* whose categorical nature indicates an autobiographical connection: "We stand against Fate as children stand up against the wall in their father's house and notch their height from year to year. But when the boy grows to man, and is master of the house, he pulls down that wall and builds a new and bigger" (W.VI.30). The "house," usually a symbol of feminine conventionalism, is here manifestly identical with the "house" which he earlier in the same essay says every spirit makes for itself and is then confined in. As for the scenario suggested in the second sentence, Emerson followed it very closely in deciding to worship in a larger temple than his father.

The ironic part of it is that the first sentence in this statement suggests admiration and emulation at least as much as scorn. In fact, the contempt implicit in the final rejection of everything the father stands for is really predicated on an internalization of the need to catch up with him, which in the final analysis is indistinguishable from Emerson's desire to climb the heavenly ladder and become one with his Heavenly Father. The passage evokes in an uncanny manner his stress on individual self-transcendence, conceived of as man's "continual effort to raise himself above himself, to work a pitch above his last height" (W.II.307). Significantly, the same ambivalent attitude to his father is expressed explicitly in a journal note from the time when *The Conduct of Life* was published: "We admire our fathers quite too much. . . . Rather let us shame the fathers by superior virtue in the sons" (J.IX.309).

There is of course nothing strange or unusual about the fact that Emerson in a sense holds two contradictory views of fatherhood: His more favorable view is clearly based on early impressions; a child cannot see his father in the same light as the adult will, and perhaps most adults are somewhat ambivalent in their view of their progenitors for this reason. If the discrepancy seems unusually large in Emerson's case, this is easily explained by the circumstance that he lost his father so early and therefore may not have proceeded to a reexamination of his case until he was a grown man worshiping great men. Such a situation certainly does not further the development of a balanced and integrated view.

On the other hand, one is struck by the fact that resentment of his father's power is present already in Emerson's account of an incident in his childhood which, he says in the previously mentioned letter to William, virtually sums up his recollection of the pastor of the First Church: "I was eight years old when he died, and only remember a somewhat social gentleman but severe to us children, who twice or thrice put me in mortal terror by forcing me into the salt water off some wharf or bathing house, and I still recall the fright with which, after some of this salt experience, I heard his voice one day (as Adam that of the Lord God in the garden), summoning us to a new bath, and I vainly endeavouring to hide myself."

The impact of this experience is reflected in various cryptic allusions to the paralyzing influence of fathers. Particularly noteworthy is a passage in "The American Scholar" in which Emerson says that he looks upon the discontent of the literary class as "a mere announcement of the fact that they find themselves not in the state of mind of their fathers, and regret the coming state as yet untried; as a boy dreads the water before he has learned that he can swim" (W.I.109–110). After reading the letter to William, one will see that he is here chastising "the literary class" from the vantage-point of a member of it who has left his father behind and learned to do what this potentate tried to make him afraid of doing.

The difference between "the Lord God in the garden" and his mediocre minister, which Emerson could not help noticing as he grew up, also made it difficult for him to identify with his mortal father. Even acknowledging the affiliation is in his case a sign of real dejection, a desire to humble himself of the kind recorded in a poetic fragment (W.IX.356):

> If thou go in thine own likeness,
> Be it health, or be it sickness;
> If thou go as thy father's son,
> If thou wear no mask or lie,
> Dealing purely and nakedly . . . .

Looking back on such moments in a more optimistic mood, Emerson tells himself that it is useful to "break off your association with your personality and identify yourself with the Universe" in times of trial (JN.V.391). "The victory is won as soon as any soul has learned always to take sides with Reason against himself; to transfer the *Me* from his person, his name, his interests, back upon Truth and Justice, so that when he is disgraced and defeated and disheartened . . . he bears it well . . . records all these phenomena, pierces their beauty as phenomena, and like a god, oversees himself" (in other words, when he becomes his own "Lord God in the garden").

On another occasion, Emerson reminds himself that while "the highest behavior" consists in identifying with the universe, and assuming that one is representative of the human race, one must yet at the same time "be able continually to keep sight of his biographical *ego*,—I had an ague, I had a fortune; my father had black hair, etc., as rhetoric, fun, or footman, to his grand and public *ego*, without impertinence or ever confounding them" (JN.XI.203). The somewhat whimsical reference to the color of his father's hair in this context—dropped when the passage was used in a lecture (W.XII.62)—is a striking illustration of Emerson's tendency to associate his physical father with what he saw as his own lower, mundane, and somewhat ridiculous biographical self, as distinct from the higher, ideal identity to which he aspired.

Yet neither the split in Emerson's perception of his father nor his dissatisfaction with the mortal one would seem so remarkable if it were not for the circumstance that what he says about mothers and motherhood in some respects follows a similar pattern. Commenting on his mother's death in 1853, he says in a letter to Carlyle: "It is very necessary that we should have mothers,—we that read and write, to keep us from becoming paper" (CEC.498). This might sound like a rather positive statement, coming from one so prone to consider his books as important as any mortal relationship. But the suggestion that it is good for poets to be reminded that they are born of woman is hardly representative of his usual stance. As a rule that fact of life is the object of more somber meditations. In more buoyant moods he is apt to trace his origin to a divine Mother of a kind that exists only in books.

A good illustration of the latter tendency as it pertains to poets is a journal entry which went into the portrayal of Shakespeare as the universal poet in *Representative Men*. In arguing that mortal parentage and other biographical facts are irrelevant in accounting for the works of a genius like Shakespeare, Emerson writes: "We are very clumsy writers of history. We tell the chronicle of parentage, birth, birthplace, schooling, companions, acquisition of property, marriage, publication of books, celebrity, and death, and when we have come to an end of this external history, the reader is no whit instructed, no ray of relation appears between all this lumber and the goddess-born." (JN.IX.314–315). The goddess in question is obviously identical with "the Muse" who "betrays" herself to her son, "the poor young poet," in "Nature" and the one referred to in "Woodnotes," where the poet, clearly an ideal self-projection of the author, is called "Muse-born."

In more frankly autobiographical contexts Emerson must of course abandon the image of Orpheus, son of Calliope, but that does not necessarily mean that he becomes more realistic in describing his own beginnings: "Five rosy boys with morning light / Had lept from one fair mother's arms," he chants in "Dirge," as if his mother had been a divine virgin who somehow managed five immaculate conceptions. The euphemistic reference to "arms" also suggests the misty ideas that a child might have of generation and birth. The idealization of the young woman who bore him on the basis of his childhood's perception of her—at the expense of the "Madame Emerson" of his later days—thus corresponds quite well with the rift in his view of his father.

There is a difference, of course: While the Reverend William Emerson died when his son was still a child, Ruth Emerson simply changed into an old woman. But so far as the son was concerned, the difference may not have been that great: the "one fair mother" was as gone as the impressive symbol of power he continued to associate with "the Lord God in the garden." As he could not help noticing as a grown man, his mother was not exactly "fair" from an objective standpoint. Nor had she ever been, judging by the one extant picture of her.

More importantly, Ruth Emerson was not what her son with Plato called "a beautiful soul," a person whose conversation furthers one's spiritual development and rise in the scale of being. Perhaps this shortcoming would have been less painfully noticeable if it had not been for the comparison which inevitably arose with Waldo's two other "mothers." Conway speaks very appropriately of "the three Fates" who presided over Emerson's life.[2] The latter's childhood, even more than Thoreau's, was dominated by women, and it so happens that two of them, Sarah Alden Ripley and Mary Moody Emerson, were extremely strong-willed and at the same time brilliant women. Sarah Alden Ripley was also a prodigy of learning. Her friendship with Emerson irritated Aunt Mary, who complained about her undue and harmful ascendancy over her nephew. On the other hand, it is his relationship with his aunt that he compares to Molière's relationship with his "old woman" (JN.V.250).

According to a saying of Goethe's, "the excellent woman is she, who, if the husband dies, can be a father to the children." And there can be no doubt that Aunt Mary was a more "excellent" woman than the widow in these terms: After William Emerson's premature death, she burst into the family to fill the vacuum, and Ruth herself conceded that her sister-in-law was fit for this role, and even that she possessed some traits that reminded her of her departed husband.[3]

As for Emerson himself, he clearly tends to look upon Aunt Mary rather than his father as the person carrying on the family's religious tradition (JN.VII.446). If he found too much "docility" in the minister, he constantly pays tribute to the masculine qualities of "Amita": Not only does she not, like other women, bring a "conventional devil" into the house with her, she is able to "soar" into regions entirely separate from the sphere of household matters (JN.VIII.105). "Alone among women," she had genius and a "representative life" (L.I.133 and W.X.399). The manner in which he speaks of her effect on his personal intellectual development forms a striking contrast with his denial that his father might have had any such influence.

Michaud characterizes this element in Emerson's spiritual formation by saying that Mary Moody Emerson, when she finally died in 1863—ten years after Ruth Emerson—"had born him for half a century in her womb" and that "it was she who had created him."[4] That may be putting it a bit strongly, but Michaud's image, with its implicit opposition of the mother's womb to the virgin, almost male, "womb" of the spinster aunt does bring out the contrast between a man's fleshly birth and his spiritual birth. In "The Nun's Aspiration," a poem about Aunt Mary, Emerson himself does not hesitate to extol her virginity in a manner that is far from flattering to the ordinary run of women who condescend to be wives and mothers. Nor is there any doubt that he was more satisfied with his spiritual and intellectual formation, as symbolized by the influence of "Amita," than with the physical frame conferred on him by his mother in conjunction with his father.

The depth of his dissatisfaction with his biological heritage can be measured by the fact that the matter tends to come up not only in his journals and letters but also in his published works. In "Worship" in *The Conduct of Life,* for instance, he mentions among autobiographical defeats that he would fain consider irrelevant to the final round in his life's struggle (in which he vows to prevail) that "my race may not be prospering; we are sick, ugly, obscure, unpopular. My children may be worsted" (W.VI.235). These examples of autobiographical defeats clearly reflect his own original situation, not to mention the many tragedies which befell his family: Not only did his father pass away prematurely—his little sister, not mentioned in "Dirge," died in infancy; two of his brothers died without producing any offspring; another of the "five rosy boys" turned out to be an imbecile; Ralph Waldo himself fought tuberculosis for years; his first son died at the age of five.

In judging the manner in which Emerson holds his ancestors and specifically his parents responsible for these disasters, one must, however, keep in mind that he does not usually interpret them in the light of the scientific laws of heredity, of which he quite naturally had a vague idea, but in terms of his own theory of "compensation" and the doctrine of "correspondences" between the physical world and the moral-spiritual realm. Any kind of violation of the ideal and moral order of things, he believed, would unfailingly bring retribution in the physical sphere in the form of ill health and mediocrity. Conversely, he insists throughout *The Conduct of Life* that all the good things of life—health, beauty, success—naturally gravitate to the families of those who live in accordance with moral and universal law.

As for the role of fathers and mothers, one may say that Emerson's pessimism is particularly obvious in "Fate," where, among other things, he wonders rhetorically how a man is to "draw off from his veins the black drop which he drew from his father's or mother's life" (W.VI.9). With respect to the former possibility, he alludes darkly to weak and sensual men whose very talent, if they have any, "draws off so rapidly the vital force that not enough remains for the animal function . . . so that in the next generation, if the like genius appear, the health is visibly deteriorated and the generative force impaired." There is no explicit personal reference here, but the statement certainly fits his own family history. It also fits the analysis given in "Terminus," a poem from the mid-sixties in which Emerson very specifically blames the relatively early decline he anticipates on sexual excesses on the part of his ancestors and especially, it would appear, on the part of the man who actually gave him "breath":

> Curse, if thou wilt, thy sires,
> Bad husbands of their fires,
> Who, when they gave thee breath,
> Failed to bequeath
> The needful sinew stark as once,
> The Baresark marrow to thy bones,
> But left a legacy of ebbing veins,
> Inconstant heat and nerveless reins,—
> Amid the Muses, left thee deaf and dumb,
> Amid the gladiators, halt and numb.

With respect to the possible guilt of mothers when their sons are not robust, Emerson speaks in more general terms in "Fate": "Men are what their mothers made them" (W.VI.10). But it is easy to show that there may be a personal reference in this case too. There is, for instance, the journal entry from 1859—the year before the publication of the essay—in which he asks: "Shall I blame my mother, whitest of women, because she was not a gypsy, and gave me no swarthy ferocity?" (JN.XIV.283). The answer is here supposed to be no, but the passage seems to refer back to "Romany Girl," the poem in which Emerson takes such a dim view of "pale" New England womanhood, and the very fact that he keeps asking the question is significant.

The passage obviously does not amount to an overt suggestion on Emerson's part that his frail constitution was due to "sensuality" on his mother's part; he cannot be expected to be as explicit in her case as he is about his father. However, the fact that he calls Ruth Emerson "whitest of mothers," a quality opposed not only to "swarthy ferocity" but to sensuality, suggests that he is accusing himself of doubting the purity of his mother. The poetic cross-reference here is "Saadi," the poem about his ideal poetic self, where the pessimistic attitude adumbrated in the first part of "Fate" is criticized as readiness to "smite the white breasts which thee fed."

That Emerson would be capable of harboring such doubts will seem less strange if one remembers that he—again in "Fate"—extends the concept of adultery far beyond the extension already made by Jesus according to Matthew 5:28: "Jesus, says, 'When he looketh on her, he hath committed adultery.' But he is an adulterer before he has yet looked on the woman, by the superfluity of animal and the defect of thought in his constitution. Who meets him, or who meets her, in the street, sees that they are ripe to be each other's victim." The idea that some husbands and wives are, as it were, condemned to a kind of moral "adultery" by their very constitution is not explicitly applied to his own parents, and yet intellectual mediocrity is exactly what Emerson charges his parents with as an adult.

One can go even further and say that Emerson's retrospective vision of young Ruth Emerson as a goddesslike virgin mother was threatened by the mediocre condition of human life itself. The circumstance that man reproduces in the same manner as the animals, to which he alludes so wryly in "The Poet" (W.III.37), makes it difficult to discount the signs that procreation is a sensual (and hence mortal) rather than a spiritual (and creative) act. In a journal entry which also contains his earliest quotation of Dante's "O virgin mother, daughter of thy Son," he assures himself that "in the mother's heart every sensation from the nuptial embrace through the uncertain symptoms of the quickening to the birth of her child is watched with an interest more chaste and wistful than the contemplations of the nun in her cloister" (JN.IV.257). Nevertheless, he feels compelled to add that "the low minded visitor" (who could it be but himself?) of a pregnant woman has "the ignorant impertinence to look down and feel a sort of shame."

Part of the problem is that it is not just a matter of the attitude of the mother during the act leading to conception. The Puritan code inherited by Emerson agrees with the dictum of Peter Lombard: "Omnis ardentior amator propriae uxoris adulter est" (any more than normally ardent lover of his wife is an adulterer). Moreover, excessive ardor in the husband will necessarily taint the wife who provides the carnal pleasure, whether she shares it or not. In fact, some degree of "ardor" is a necessary part of the act that leads to conception. Thus Emerson can ponder in his journal the way in which nature conspires against the "dignity and welfare" of women by making them objects of sexual desire. He does not wonder, he says, "at her occasional protest, violent protest against nature, in fleeing to nunneries, and taking black veils." Love is supposed to right "all this deep wrong," but how can it do that, except in theory: "Who ever knew in real life a genuine instance of seasonable love?" (JN.XI.31–32).

DIVINE AFFILIATION AND EARTHLY PARENTS

Melville's *Pierre,* written about the same time as Emerson's journal meditation, offers some illuminating sidelight on this issue, with special reference to the father-mother relationship. Pierre and his widowed mother exist in a paradise of their own making, until the day when the son discovers that his father was not the person he had taken him for. An old letter reveals that he had had an adulterous relationship with another woman. This relationship of his father's sensuality drags his "lovely immaculate mother" from her pedestal; she is reduced to a mere woman, a sex object. In a passage calculated to evoke the bedroom scene in *Hamlet,* Pierre quarrels and breaks with his mother.

Emerson's family situation, needless to say, was rather different. Yet this story, taken as an allegory, reminds one of how he as he came of age discovered his father's mediocrity, by definition a sign of sensuality. In fact, there is an almost literal analogy between the two discoveries in that his was also due at least in part to a perusal of old papers. Is it too much to assume that what he says about his father's achievement in his letter to William has something to do with the journal page on which his father tells himself —in vain—to "shake off sloth" and "banish lustful thoughts and foolish, childish imaginations" in order to produce works which both his enemies and his friends will see as the fruit of genius and laborious habits?[5]

The most intriguing parallel between Melville himself and Emerson is their common fascination with the bedroom scene in *Hamlet.* This unpleasant conversation is caused by the prince's discovery, at the very time he is coming of age, of his mother's sexuality—apparently it had never occurred to him that she might be an object of desire to other men, let alone that she could have passionate inclinations of her own, until the day he learned that she was going to remarry. It therefore seems significant that the only other scene in *Hamlet* that made a comparable impression on Emerson is the one in which the spirit of his godlike father revisits "the glimpses of the moon" to complain about his wife's remarriage and charge that the mediocre Claudius has not only replaced but destroyed him. It also looks like more than a coincidence that Emerson's admiration for this scene is expressed in the already mentioned discussion of Shakespeare where genealogical and other biographical data are dismissed as "lumber" bearing no relation to "the goddess-born." This statement agrees only too well with Hamlet's rejection of his mother, especially as Emerson, like Melville, sees Hamlet as a self-projection of Shakespeare's and hence an image of universal man.

With respect to Emerson's reading of the bedroom scene, one notes that he does not seem to see anything harsh or blameworthy in Hamlet's treatment of his mother. On the contrary, he suggests in one of the passages where this scene is praised (JN.VII.14) that it consistently portrays Hamlet as "an inborn gentleman." Even allowing for the possibility that he is here using the word "gentleman" more in accordance with the definition given in "Manners" than with ordinary modern usage, this judgment is remarkable since many, perhaps most, readers are likely to agree with T. S. Eliot that the prince's reaction to an in itself commonplace event like his mother's remarriage is "in excess of the facts as they appear."[6]

Other critics, including Freud himself, have not hesitated to put forward an Oedipal explanation of Hamlet's problems.[7] As a matter of fact, Melville's *Pierre* already constitutes an interpretation along these lines in the sense that the "Oedipal" overtones of the book could hardly be more obvious, although it was written before the birth of Freud. If one were to provide historical proof that a New Englander of that time could read the play in the same spirit, one might mention the case of Charles Newcomb, the friend whom Emerson enigmatically calls his "best key" to Shakespeare (JN.XI.172). Newcomb had a frankly Oedipal relationship with his widowed mother and lived with her until the age of forty-five, when she died. Having feared that she might remarry, he ponders the case of Hamlet in his journal and explains that "the largeness of the filial relationship" justifies the prince's expostulations.[8]

Emerson himself must probably be acquitted of having read *Hamlet* in a similar manner. His discussion of the play is too tantalizingly rhapsodic to permit any firm conclusions in this respect. One *is* tempted to link his fascination with the bedroom and ghost scenes with his suggestion that a schoolboy can "detect secrets of highest concernment yet unpublished" in *Hamlet* (W. III.63). This dubious generalization certainly suggests a personal connection, and it would be natural to assume that Emerson as a schoolboy feared that his mother might remarry, and therefore saw Hamlet as a kind of brother-in-arms. But this is only a guess, and even if it were correct, it would not prove an Oedipal attachment on Emerson's part: In an orphaned *schoolboy* such apprehensions may be normal.

It is perfectly clear, however, that Hamlet's reaction to his mother's marriage was of great metaphysical importance to the adult Emerson as an image of man's discovery of the role played by passion and lust in the human condition. Quite early—while he was still in college—he looked upon Hamlet as a fellow believer in angelic love-friendship of the kind that he later on (JN.IX.222) was to associate with Charles Newcomb. Among the "consideranda" jotted down in his notebook for 1822 are these lines from Hamlet's conversation with Horatio: "Give me that man / Who is not passion's slave, and I will wear him / In my heart's core, aye in my heart of heart" (JN.I.193). It is also certain that he sensed in Hamlet's soul, and in his own, something like the sex nausea which a number of modern critics have attributed to Hamlet.[9] His repeated allusions to the prince's suggestion—in the ghost scene— that we are all "fools of nature" can hardly be interpreted in any other way, at least not the one in "Nature," where the wording ("Are we tickled trout and fools of nature") reminds us not only of his tendency to see sex as the trap of nature, but also of a curiously incoherent phrase in the journal for 1841: "we tickled trout, we nose-led bullocks" (JN.VIII.88). Significantly, the passage in "Nature" is followed by a reference to Oedipus, even in pre-Freudian times a natural symbol of the mess to which sex can lead.

In "Experience," the essay where the Hamlet-studying schoolboy is mentioned, the theme is treated in a somewhat different fashion. In the area where Emerson states that he would be willing to "pay the costly price of sons and lovers" if grief could put him in touch with reality, the stress is on the isolation of bodies and souls in a world that seems to have no more substance than a dream. This kind of speculation, including the suggestion that death may be the only cure of his malady, seems reminiscent of Hamlet, and sure enough it is followed by another allusion to the "fools" of nature.

Somewhat later in the same essay, this discussion is resumed

127

and given a twist that makes one think of Hamlet's recent vogue as an existentialist: "It is very unhappy, but too late to be helped, the discovery we have made that we exist. That discovery is called the Fall of Man." While the discovery is presented as that of the age, it is clearly also that of each individual who has come of age in that age. What we are dealing with is an application of the distinction between existence and essence to the problem of sex, love, and parenthood, which in certain respects calls Sartre's *Nausea* to mind. Before the end of the paragraph, we have read again about the incurable isolation of all souls, the inequality of "each subject and each object," and our growing self, which "rooted in absolute nature, supplants all relative existence, and ruins the kingdom of mortal friendship and love."

Emerson does not again allude to Hamlet in this paragraph, but there is every reason to think that he has him in mind here, too. He habitually associates the discovery of our fallen, existential state with Hamlet, and more than once suggests that the reason this play of Shakespeare's is so popular in the nineteenth century is that this age has finally caught up with the prince in this respect. In one of the lectures in "The Philosophy of History" (1837), he notes: "We are become philosophic. The age is infected with the malady of Hamlet, 'Sicklied o'er with a pale cast of thought.' Our eyes are opened. We know that we are naked, we seek to be clothed" (EL.II.180).

Most remarkable because of the way in which it ties in with this thought complex—and indeed ties everything together—is a poem called "Philosopher" (W.IX.374–375) in which Emerson at the age of fifty analyzes his relationship with his mother, who had just died. The focus is on what he has allowed his philosophy to do to his love for her:

> Philosophers are lined with eyes within,
> And, being so, the sage unmakes the man.
> In love, he cannot therefore cease his trade;
> Scarce the first blush has overspread his cheek,
> He feels it, introverts his learned eye
> To catch the unconscious heart in the very act.
> His mother died,—the only friend he had,—
> Some tears escaped, but his philosophy
> Couched like a cat sat watching close behind

> And throttled all his passion. Is't not like
> That devil-spider that devours her mate
> Scarce freed from her embraces?

This poem is indirectly linked to Emerson's reading of the play about the philosopher-prince. In an area of "The American Scholar" where the age is also called "philosophical," the language sometimes resembles some of the phrases used in "Philosopher," and Hamlet is mentioned by name: The time, says Emerson, "is infected with Hamlet's unhappiness,—'Sicklied o'er with the pale cast of thought' "; it is the age of "Introversion," and "we are lined with eyes" (W.I.189). Significantly, these statements lead to the passage in which Emerson, alluding to his own childhood experience on the seashore, advises the "literary class" not to allow themselves to be paralyzed by their memories of fathers whom they know they have outgrown.

An important difference between the passage in "The American Scholar" and "Philosopher" is the tone in which they are written. In the former case one is struck with the cheerfulness with which Emerson implicitly dismisses his memory of "the Lord God in the garden" who once tried to push him around. The poem prompted by the death of Ruth Emerson is, by contrast, a very somber meditation. The self-accusations, coming from a man who habitually projects the image of a dutiful son, seem "in excess of the facts as they appear." They suggest, in fact, that he believed he had treated his mother as roughly as Hamlet treats his, and the comparison seems apt in the sense that Hamlet also has his moments when he fears that his suspicions are really the work of the devil.

This still does not explain the image of the devil-spider in Emerson's poem. In order to do that, it will be necessary to abandon Hamlet, although not necessarily his problems. It seems most likely that the source of this feature is Crashaw's "Satan," the only full-length poem by this author included in Emerson's *Parnassus*.[10] The devil-spider of "Philosopher" is in Crashaw's poem represented by an allegorical Satan lurking in the abyss, like a spider at the center of his net. Satan typifies reason and intellect baffled and indignant at the mystery of the Incarnation and especially the Immaculate Conception:

But these vast mysteries his senses smother,
And reason,—for what's faith to him!—devour,
How she that is a maid should prove a mother,
Yet keep inviolate her virgin flower;
How God's eternal Son should be man's brother,
Poseth his proudest intellectual power;
    How a pure spirit should incarnate be
    And life itself wear death's frail livery.

In his own poem Emerson is comparing his own intellect and philosophy (the "devil-spider") to Crashaw's Satan and accusing himself of unjustly doubting his mother's purity and his own status as a child of God. In these terms, too, the Fall of Man is the moment when intellect expels us from the garden.

8

THE IDEAL STATE OF MAN: EMERSON'S ANGELIC DREAM

After abandoning his hopes for a millennial revolution in which the poet would play a leading part, Emerson still continued his quest for the great author-messiah whose work would not leave him where it found him but introduce him to a new heaven and a new earth, if only symbolically and on a momentary basis. In spite of the biblical language he often uses in this context, he did not limit his search to Christian books and authors. In fact, a journal entry from 1845 suggests that Plato's *Republic* might be such a work (JN.IX.221).

The most striking thing about this statement is the proviso it contains: *The Republic,* says Emerson, might have the desired effect if a proper "class of two" could be established and there were someone to read it with. This remark indicates that he felt the need for a study situation à la Plato's *Phaedrus* and shows how closely associated his vision of redemption is with his yearning for friendship. Significantly, Plato's State is linked a few pages earlier to Augustine's City of God, one of his major symbols of friendship (JN.IX.214).

Such a view of *The Republic* is easier to understand if one remembers that the book is a blueprint for the restoration of man to what Plato in the companion volume *Timaeus* calls his "first and best state"—to the extent that this can be done by political means. The phrase calls to mind the old Judeo-Christian dream involving the restoration of the "original"—that is, angelic and pre-Eve—Adam. Even Plato's highest class of men, the guardians, are not angelic in the technical sense, of course, but they are at the top of a hierarchy vaguely similar to the feudal vision of heaven and are comparable to archangels in some of their functions. The comparison seems all the more apt as the carnal birth of each individual in Plato's State, regardless of class, is to be systematically obfuscated by various means, including the famous community of women. Within the guardian class, the usual sexual dichotomy is to be ignored as much as possible and friendship between androgynous individuals is to replace the bonds of family and domestic life, which are declared harmful to the State and painful to the individual.

In spite of the drastic nature of Plato's recommendations for the regeneration of man, Emerson sometimes endorses the book with polemic fervor. In the journal entry linking it to *The City of God,* he states categorically that the objections to *The Republic* are "shallow." The kind of objections he has in mind can be gathered from the essay on Plato in *Representative Men,* for which the journal meditations serve as a preparation.

One line of defense is based on the idea that Plato is first of all a poet: Most of the arguments in his writings, says Emerson, "might have been couched in sonnets: and poetry has never soared higher than in the Timaeus and the Phaedrus." Thus, "All his painting in the Republic must be esteemed mythical" and done without any thought of ever instituting his plans. The community of women, for instance, is only an "emphatic way" of expressing "a high scheme," in this case "his absolute privilege for the best," the "premium which he would set on grandeur" (W.IV.89).

Further light on Emerson's "mythical" reading of *The Republic* is shed when he seizes the offensive in order to defend the "grandeur" of the guardians and their portrayer: "Let none presume to measure the irregularities of Michael Angelo and Socrates by village scales." The mention of the archangelic artist-poet at this point shows that Emerson is no longer merely restating Plato's position but is arguing his case—or the case of grandeur—from his own total experience. The juxtaposition of Michelangelo and Socrates is somewhat cryptic, but the context, notably the suggestion that Plato's dialogues are the kind of stuff that sonnets are made of, indicates that he associates the bold proposals made by Socrates in the fifth book of *The Republic* with the intrepid expressions of Platonic love to be found in Michelangelo's sonnets, mentioned on the previous page.

There is also a journal passage combining an attack on "village" mentality with a defense of *The Republic*—including the community of women—based on the idea that the book was a poetic statement as inspiring as "the morning mountains" to wise souls (JN.XIV.168). Interestingly, this entry begins as a defense of Emerson's friend Alcott, whom he had long associated with Plato's State and its guardians, and who is here said to have "magnificent views" and habitually look "to the government of the County; of the state; of Nature. Nothing less." It thus seems natural to see this passage as a comment on the problems Alcott, never a prophet in his own village, had specifically in trying to establish an ideal community on his own terms. One problem was Mrs. Alcott, whose resistance also thwarted Emerson's charitable offer to include her family in a limited version of Plato's State in which the two households were to have their table but not their children in common.[1]

Needless to say, Emerson never believed that a full-scale political realization of Plato's State was possible. In fact, after speaking about his fascination with it, one must also speak about the misgivings he occasionally expresses with respect to this possibility. Even in the essay on Plato, he feels that he has to point out that the ideas of *The Republic* cannot be instituted "without peril of charlatanism," and there is reason to think that this problem also limited its usefulness as a symbolic focus-point in his dreams about the redemption and ideal state of man. He never rejected the book completely, but from certain points of view he clearly felt that it needed to be supplemented and corrected by other visions and images. It was not just that, as he was forced to recognize, *The Republic* seemed "Mahometan" to women (JN.IX.184): Moods change, and examining Plato's "sketch" in a more sober spirit, he was naturally himself beset by misgivings concerning the manner in which the Ideal State is supposed to be established and maintained.

Some of his doubts are vented in the essay entitled "Politics" (1844). Plato is there mentioned along with Paul as a man of truth who "forever" compels the system of society to "gyrate" around him (unlike men like Pisistratus and Cromwell, who can only achieve this feat "for a time"). But Emerson also anticipates his own suggestion in the essay on Plato that the ideas of *The Republic* would fail in real life. Legislation, he points out, cannot outpace the moral level of the individuals who make up the population: "the State must follow and not lead the character and progress of the citizen." The goal of social evolution is "the appearance of the wise man," and in a sense the State exists only to educate him: With the appearance of the wise man, the State "expires" because it is not needed. "The wise man is the State" (W.III.199–216).

With this plea for gradualism, Emerson is obviously dissociating himself ever so cautiously from the attitude of Plato. He does so even more in his portrayal of the wise man, not least when he says that the latter "has no personal friends" because "he who has the spell to draw the prayer and piety of all men unto him, need not husband and educate a few to share with him a select and poetic life." This is a more universal kind of friendship than that shared by Plato's guardians, and it is easy to see the biblical inspiration of the suggestion that the wise man's relation to other men is "angelic," that "his memory is myrrh to them; his presence, frankincense and flowers." Emerson is at one with Plato in noting that we live "in a very low state of the world," but he is implicitly including the author of *The Republic* when he critically remarks: "The power of love, as the basis of a State, has never been tried" (W.III.216–220).

However, Emerson himself does not say unequivocally that a State based "on the principle of right and love" is a real political possibility. He refers sarcastically to the representatives of the conventional wisdom who cannot "hide their contempt" if they come upon anyone who entertains such hopes, but instead of a personal confession of faith, his peroration contains the more oblique statement that he has "just been conversing with one man" (apparently Alcott), "to whom no weight of adverse experience will make it for a moment appear impossible, that thousands of human beings might exercise towards each other the grandest and simplest sentiments, as well as a knot of friends, or a pair of lovers" (W. III.221).

This is as much as conceding that the society of the wise man is also mere dream and poetry, at least for the time being. To the extent that Emerson is only looking for a symbolic and imaginative fulfillment of his millennial yearnings, this might not seem to make any difference; but it appears that he himself found the scheme a bit too vague to offer much of a foothold for the imagination, even in day-dreaming. More important, the society of the wise man is not one that can be started with a few like-minded persons. Like Plato's utopia, it is either there in its entirety or it is not there at all. For these reasons some other established images of spiritual neighborhoods had a clear advantage.

Among these images is that of the kingdom which is "not of this world" and yet, according to one reading of the words attributed to Jesus, "among you." This spiritual realm, which somehow is capable of coexisting with the mundane and political sphere, is a place one can join at any time without waiting for its completion. It keeps growing, like the mustard seed, with every new proselyte. It is the society of those who have been reborn in the spirit and who through the annulment of their fleshly birth have become brothers and sisters, the children of a Heavenly Father.

Emerson uses the idea of a spiritual brother-sisterhood of this kind fairly frequently. One finds it not only in letters to women like Margaret Tucker, the sister of his first wife, and Elizabeth Hoar, the bereaved fiancée of his brother Charles, but also in his correspondence with recently acquired women friends, like Caroline Sturgis, and with Samuel Ward. Indeed, judging by a letter he wrote from England in 1848, he even tried to hold his second wife, Lidian, to this vision (L.IV.33).

However, this scheme also has its drawbacks from Emerson's point of view. It aims at the desexualization of love, but the distinction between the two sexes is otherwise left intact, as if in recognition of the fact that this is only a kind of half-way house. For this reason he tends to fuse this image with the more radically other-worldly version of the kingdom of heaven, where, again in Christ's own words, there are no men and no women, and hence no brothers and sisters—only angels. His fascination with this scheme transpires in the speculation about the possibility of a love-friendship raised above the distinction of sex, which was one of his consolations during the months following the death of his first wife (JN.III.274). During the time when he was enlarging his acquaintance with several new friends (a few years into his second marriage), he writes raptly about how joyful it is to find that "spirits can meet in their pure upper sky without the help of organs" (JN.VII.512).

The idea that one can join this celestial neighborhood without permanently leaving the world is apparently something that Emerson largely owes to the teachings of Swedenborg. Although he disapproved of the latter's doctrine of heavenly marriage, he was greatly taken with the idea that the individual even in this life has access to a "spiritual world" in which souls associate entirely according to "affinity." Ironically, this on one occasion led to a slip which had unintended consequences. In spite of his dislike for Swedenborg's conjugal eternities, he happened to end a letter to Margaret Fuller with the suggestion that they had recently been inhabiting a "particular house in heaven" just like Swedenborg's couples (L.II.328). Fuller answered by complaining that his "light" would never understand her "fire"—another Swedenborgian allusion—and making other suggestions that made it necessary for Emerson to tell her in no uncertain terms that she was not supposed to discuss their relationship in an explicit and personal manner and that she must remember that their friendship "should be one incompatible with the vicious order of existing society, and should adjourn its fulness of communion into pure eternity" (L.II.352 and 385).

In spite of this tactical retreat, Emerson stuck to the image of an "amphibious" existence, which suited him better than any other (cf. W.III.229). In a journal entry from 1842, he speaks of a "class" of persons "born into a new heaven and earth with organs for the new element and who from that Better behold this bad world in which the million gropes and suffers. By their life and happiness in the new," he adds, "I am assured of the doom of the Old, and these therefore I love and worship" (JN.VIII.185). This way of looking at his new friends—the ones he had been alluding to in "Friendship" (1841)—is obviously inspired by John's vision of a New Jerusalem, a much safer image than Swedenborg's heaven in discussing nonsexual friendship.

On the other hand, the New Jerusalem described in Revelation also presents a problem in that it, strictly speaking, is not a place

THE IDEAL STATE OF MAN

to which the aspiring soul has immediate access: One does not transport oneself into that heavenly air and back to this world in the way in which Swedenborg claims to pass from one sphere to the other. The ideal Christian image of the possibility of an amphibious life is another city—Augustine's City of God. Seemingly more removed from the earthly sphere than the kingdom which is "among you," it is like this version of heaven thought of as open-ended, if not universal: It envisions the building of a perfect society as a historical process uniting more and more souls in a blessed fellowship existing independently of the residual mundane sphere and yet effecting the transformation of this sphere into itself.

Emerson has more than one way of showing that he sees the City of God as a symbol of the heavenly society of friendship. The link is implicit in his association of Augustine's City with the beauty of sunsets, a phenomenon which he frequently sees as the symbol and promise of friendship (W.I.17, LF.44–46, JN.VII.461–462). Explicitly, this symbolism is present in "Culture," where he quotes from a German Romantic to illustrate his thought: " 'We four,' wrote Neander to his sacred friends, 'will enjoy at Halle the inward blessedness of a *civitas Dei,* whose foundations are forever friendship' " (W.VI.156–157).

The kind of friendship Emerson has in mind in "Culture" is clearly angelic and based on the concept of amphibiousness. In the same context he underlines that what he associates with the City of God and views as the most heavenly flower of civilization is the union of friends who "live in different streets." Long before the publication of *The Conduct of Life,* he had used the same phrase in "New England Reformers" to make the point that the Brook Farmers and other people trying to institutionalize an ideal society were not approaching the problem in the right spirit: "The world is awaking to the idea of union," he says, but any worthwhile union must be "inward" and represent "the union of friends who live in different streets and towns" (W.III.265).

The conception of friendship as the driving force in history is frequently met with in Emerson's works (e.g., JN.X.327). Sometimes the idea is developed in a way that conjures up the image of a heavenly free-masonry reminiscent of the City of God. The outstanding example of this phenomenon is probably the last part of

"The Celestial Love," where he describes a breed of men who "have heartily designed / The benefit of broad mankind" and whose "cords of love so public are / They intertwine the farthest star."

A more static and also more pagan note is struck when Emerson resorts to what must be considered his favorite amphibious scheme, that of the "heaven of letters" (JN.VII.68). No doubt it contains Stoic elements, but the idea of authors and readers united across the gulfs of time and space is also perfectly in line with the Plotinian conception of the union of great and related souls regardless of the age and country in which they live. In fact, Plotinus first uses the term "amphibious" to describe such men. To Emerson, the proof, as it were, of the possibility of such relations is the "friendship" of Montaigne and Plutarch, which he does not see as a one-way thing: "Montaigne, whilst he grasps Etienne de la Boéce with one hand, reaches back the other to Plutarch" (W. X.300). Emerson himself seems to have found a source of inspiration in Plutarch's way of "living" with the heroes and authors he wrote about. He also has a tendency to single out pagan authors in arguing the possibility of this brand of amphibious life and love: As a young man, he fired off a "letter to Plato," presumably in answer to those which Plato had written him (JN.II.246–249). In the essay on "History" he describes the kind of relationship he can have with a man like Plato (or Pindar) in these terms: "When I feel that we two meet in a perception, that our two souls are tinged with the same hue, and do as it were run into one, why should I measure degrees of latitude, why should I count Egyptian years" (W.II.26–27).

On the other hand, the rhetoric used by Emerson often has a Christian ring even when he is discussing "the heaven of letters": "What new heavens and new earths," he exclaims apropos of Landor's *Imaginary Conversations,* associating the book with Montaigne's *Essais* as evidence and guarantee of the existence of a "literary world" (JN.VIII.38). Carlyle, to whom he was first introduced through a letter Landor wrote for him in Rome, avers in a chapter of *Sartor Resartus* called "Organic Filaments" that "there is a living, literal *Communion of Saints,* wide as the World itself, and as the History of the World." Quite fittingly, then, Emerson once states that he does not even need to read Carlyle's works, since at any time he can sit with him under a tree in paradise and hear much better tales from his own lips (JN.V.454–455). After Carlyle had advised him that John Sterling had "fallen overhead in love with a certain Waldo Emerson," he began corresponding with this writer, whom he had never met, and soon assured him that their relations were both "holy" and "eternal" (CSE.28). This relationship is integrated into the fellowship of all great souls—the dead as well as the living—on the basis of their common love for Montaigne (JN.VIII.376 and W.IV.163).

In a sense we are here dealing with a Romantic cliché; Emerson could also find the idea in Coleridge—in *Biographia Literaria,* as well as in *The Friend.* Yet Emerson is distinguished by the extent to which he placed his hopes in this heaven and actually lived in it. No doubt the dream of a "heaven of letters," like his other dreams of amphibious life, satisfied a profound need in his case, enabling him to see himself as a not entirely mortal man sharing in a divine existence. As for the mundane obligations that could not be escaped, he had the satisfaction of knowing that even Plotinus' Rational Soul had its higher and lower spheres of activity.

In looking for specific references to the things from which Emerson's "heaven of letters" was to serve as a refuge, one cannot help noticing the stress placed on the evils of domestic life. In "The Over-Soul," for instance, he says that as a mind grows and begins to "converse" with "Truths that have always been spoken in the world," it "becomes conscious of a closer sympathy with Zeno and Arrian than with persons in the house" (W.II.275). Since these two gentlemen are Stoics, the passage shows the combined influence of this school and Platonism, whose hostility to family life has already been mentioned. First of all, however, Emerson seems to have been impressed by the example of Jesus, whom he sees not only as a champion of angelic love and friendship but as a man who actually left his earthly family behind to follow his own divine calling. The first series of *Essays* alone furnishes a number of echoes of gospel passages suggesting as much: "I shun father and mother and wife and brother when my genius calls me" (W.II.51). "With every influx of light comes new danger. Has he light? . . . He must hate father and mother, wife and child" (W.II.99). "Jesus says, Leave father, mother, house and lands and follow me" (W.II.343).

How much this matter still weighed on Emerson's mind toward the end of his career is perhaps best shown by "Domestic Life" (1870). This essay represents an attempt to open up marriage and family life by turning the house into a "university," as Lord Falkland did according to Clarendon's portrayal of him. The house of a truly great man, says Emerson, is one to which the great repair for conversation. Significantly, he explains that love between the sexes is very much inferior to friendship, a relationship described as "the happiness which where it is truly known postpones all other satisfactions" (W.VII.129). In a sense, he is here trying to eliminate the need for amphibious excursions into the spiritual world as much as circumstances might allow. On the other hand, the persistence of the angelic theme suggests that the idea of a universal intellectual community available in this life is yet another version of his Protean dream of heavenly love and friendship: Sexual differentiation is eliminated almost as radically as in the heaven of Christ. As all known angels have male names, so do a great number of great souls listed in this essay. Besides the wife, referred to as a potential obstacle to the realization of the "university," the "Gorgon of Convention" (W.VII.133) is virtually the only feminine creature mentioned. Children are said to have "angels' flesh"; a boy is "the little Adam," as if he were not born of woman; "blushing boys," not girls, are said to perform the household chores.

Not entirely by coincidence, Clarendon is the source on which Emerson draws in the area of *English Traits* where he describes the aristocratic gentlemen who once ruled England. As he portrays them, their way of life also represents a subordination of family life to loftier considerations. The gentlemen in question are described as androgynous—terrible to their enemies and affectionate in a "domestic" way as soon as they are not engaged in war. But this domesticity is obviously supposed to be a qualification for the administration of the State and the Empire as much as an asset in the narrower task of rearing children and producing the next generation of gentlemen. Moreover, what really interests Emerson here is the situation of great seamen, like Rodney, Collingwood, and Nelson, who by their duty to the larger family of the nation are kept away from their homes for years at a time. Judging by the chapter entitled "Race," such men in the meantime get their emotional satisfaction from a comradely love inextricably bound up with their love of the homeland (W.V.67–68).

The fact that these gentlemen, as Emerson sees them, have traits reminiscent of Plato's guardians as well as of the angels obviously goes well with the subordination of domesticity to higher aims which he attributes to them: The incompatibility of family life with the kind of totalitarian society in which they belong is as obvious in the New Testament as in *The Republic.* Moreover— and this makes it possible and necessary to examine Emerson's dream about man's ideal state from a different and yet not unrelated point of view—this totalitarian society is based on the maintenance, and in Plato's case on the systematic breeding, of a certain type of superior man. In spite of his continued interest in eugenics at this time (e.g., JN.XIII.107 and 438), Emerson does not propose anything similar to Plato's schemes, but he does advocate the superiority of the English nation and the English "race" even more strongly than Plato urges that of the Hellenes in *The Republic.* What is more, *English Traits* contains explicit and implicit cross-references between England and Plato's State and between the English and the angels.

For instance, in his account of an interview with Wordsworth during which he brought up the *Republic,* Emerson quotes the poet as saying that "we [i.e., the English] have embodied it all" (W.V.295). He does not exactly endorse the idea in this particular context, but in the next chapter he states that England, while not "the ideal framework," is nevertheless "the best of actual nations."

As for the link between the angelic kingdom and England, it is established in the very area of "Race" in which the androgynous nature of English lords is dwelled on. It is implicit already in the rapt description of the alleged physical characteristics of the English, blue eyes and blond hair, which were traditionally attributed to angels and children. The explicit connection between the attractions of this natural aristocracy and angelic beauty is the allusion to Pope Gregory's comment on some young English captives: "Non Angli, sed angeli." This is the very historical quotation that Melville adduces in his portrayal of Billy Budd, the handsome English sailor, as an androgynous, angelic, and heaven-born man who is everybody's friend.

Possibly, views of this kind were quite common among New

England intellectuals at the time. Nevertheless it seems noteworthy that Emerson shares them with his friend Alcott, the man whom he once calls "the Plato of New England" and, as mentioned, associates with the guardians of *The Republic*: Alcott also betrays a tendency to link people's moral level to their physical appearance, in the process distinguishing between an angelic type of man with blue eyes and blond hair and a diabolical type characterized by the opposite traits. Thoreau seems to have passed the test—he is called "a descendant of the Scandinavian Thor" in Alcott's journals—but Hawthorne did not: "There runs a drop of dingy Roman life in his veins," says his fellow Concordian.[2]

Emerson is less personal, of course. But the moral implications are not absent from his own division of humanity into different categories according to physical characteristics. In "Race," he sees the "dark complexion" of the Roman as a more or less alien admixture in the English blend of bloods; indeed, even the Normans are seen as examples of moral and physical deterioration in this context compared with the more purely "Scandinavian" component. By the time he wrote *English Traits,* he had clearly come to share Alcott's—and Wordsworth's—conviction that his English ancestors represented "earth's first blood" (cf. JN.X.509).

In the journals which Emerson kept in the fifties, one notes a passage in which he suggests that "the beauty of the blond race" betokens great reserves of "mental and moral power" and is to be hailed as "a new morning that dawns on men" (JN.XIII.325). As we saw, the ideas expressed in *The Republic* are associated with the morning in another journal passage from this period which also involves Alcott. Even without this connection, it would be difficult not to relate this statement concerning fair hair and blue eyes to yet another journal entry from this time, in which the future of the American Republic, as it were, is made a hostage to the prevalence of these physical traits: In suggesting that an elite, the "America-loving" part of mankind, gravitates to this part of the world, he specifies that "it is the light complexion, the blue eyes of Europe that come: the black eyes, the black drop, the Europe of Europe is left" (JN.XI.398).

In factual terms this statement seems so unrealistic, even for the times, that one is tempted to interpret it as wishful thinking based on color symbolism of a rather abstract kind. Yet one can understand that some readers, no doubt also familiar with what he says about the Scandivanian "race" in *English Traits,* have applied the passage in a rather concrete manner. Thus C. G. Shaw suggests that Emerson anticipated Nietzsche both in his stress on blond beasts and Aryan blue-eyedness and in his "hard and cold" view of the family. At first, Shaw's association of blue eyes and intellectuality seems symbolic: "Where do we find bluer eyes, where is a deeper, brighter blue-eyedness?" he asks apropos of Emerson himself. But he suddenly becomes very literal when he goes on to warn the American Republic against the dangers of immigration from southern Europe: "Shall we let the immigrant destroy our intellectualism?"[3]

Emerson's own position on race is actually hard to pin down, especially in modern terms.[4] He is capable of saying in his journal that his aesthetic sensibilities were offended by some bearded Polish Jews whom he saw in the Allston Gallery, and also of implying that their looks proved their moral inferiority (JN.VII.221–222). But he can also ridicule those who explain the sorry state of the world with reference to alleged conspiratorial activities of "men of dark complexions" (W.XI.418). Ultimately he escapes the charge of placing "racist" limitations on his gospel of universal, angelic, and intellectual love, not so much because he sometimes says things on the other side, nor because of the dreamy and symbolic nature of many of his statements, but because he also anticipates Nietzsche in viewing *all* of mankind as "human-all-too-human" and hence, strictly speaking, unworthy objects of an upward and aspiring love.

In the final analysis, Emerson's universal love is only another name for universal hate. Such a position follows with necessity from his refusal to be quite satisfied with anything short of the ideal state of man. It is this logic which causes him to repeat again and again (e.g., JN.IX.377) the sentence "I like man, not men." It is also what makes him say, after noting that "Nature is loved by what is best in us": "It is loved as the city of God, although, or rather because there is no citizen" (W.III.178). Perhaps the application of this view to the theory of angelic love and friendship is particularly clear in certain letters to Caroline Sturgis written in 1840–1841. In one, he speaks about a "hating love," based on the assumption that you do not love anybody for what he is, only for what he, like you yourself, represents—that is, God (L.II.338). In another, the question "Who is fit for friendship?" is answered by "Not one," and the paradox of universal-angelic love is expressed in the following way: "Multitude in our philosophy is a sort of name and title for the devil, yet one would dream away his soul in extasy at the faintest prophecy of dwelling in a universe of angels" (L.II.386).

Another facet of the same paradoxical view of friendship and love is Emerson's tendency to seek the fulfillment of his ideal in other regions than those of real life, where by definition it is unrealizable. In this context, the image of the heaven of letters serves him very well: "The best souls in the world love books the best," he says in an early lecture (EL.III.44). But most of the books in question apparently were written long ago. In "The American Scholar," we are told that the aspiring scholar, if he is to make proper progress and not lose heart, must often "forego the living for the dead" (W.I.101). So must the poet; "Saadi," the poem in which his ideal self-projection is described as the angelic lover of all and sundry, also contains those startling and not quite integrated lines: "Seek the living among the dead,— / Man in man is imprisoned."

On the whole, Emerson's favorite images of amphibious life are still useful when he looks at things from this point of view, but they are often complemented or modified by various other themes. For one thing, the stress is on solitude even more than on union when the safeguarding of the ideal is uppermost in his mind. In "New England Reformers," he says sternly, apropos of certain attempts to build an ideal community, that "no society can ever be so large as that of one man" (W.III.264–265). In "Character," he quotes two lines from his own poem "The Celestial Love" ("When each the other shall avoid / Shall each by each be most enjoyed") and adds that when people travel to meet "all the greatness of each is kept back"; it is "as if the Olympians should meet to exchange snuff-boxes" (W.III.112–113).

What Emerson is seeking is of course not a merely physical solitude. It is equally important to preserve it when the friend is present: "Now I will identify you with the Ideal Friend, and live with you on imperial terms," he tells Caroline Sturgis; "Present, you shall be present only as an angel might be, and absent you shall not be absent from me" (L.II.334). Indeed, sometimes—as in May, 1842, when he was dreaming of establishing a neighborhood of beautiful souls in Concord—he seems to have felt that physical propinquity, by removing the disgust and depression of visitation," might actually make each member "more completely isolated and sacred than before" (JN.VIII.173).

The idea that we do not have to and must not "descend to meet" (W.II.199 and 278) is further underlined by suggestions that we should take our cue from the cold intellectuality of Plotinus' highest hypostasis, the Rational Soul. The coldness with which divine individual souls meet each other is stressed in "The Celestial Love," and in "Poetry and Imagination" Emerson triumphantly points out that "even Swedenborg, whose theory of the universe is based on affection," concedes that the best souls in his heaven live alone (W.VII.6). One should also note his marked preference for the cherubs, the angels who know most, over the seraphs, the angels who love most (e.g., L.IV.33). The rarefied air of Mount Olympus —if not the actual habits of the Homeric gods—is of course the best image of this coldness: "Let us sit apart as the gods, talking from peak to peak all around Olympus" is the advice given in "Manners," characteristically followed by this assurance, or warning: "No degree of affection need invade this religion" (W.III.137).

Emerson also makes the Greek gods, as well as the angels, the models of another virtue, silence, which he often sees as essential to a pure and Platonic love: "They love, but name not love," he says with reference to them in a poem called "Eros." By the same token, he himself does not mention by name any of the "new friends" he alludes to in "Friendship"—"for an old shame before the holy ideal," one learns in "The Poet" (W.III.42). The only way of declaring one's love is thus that of poetic symbolism, or some other mode of indirect expression which at the same time is a kind of reticence or silence: "In good society,—say among the angels in heaven," he notes in his journal, everything is "spoken by indirection" (JN.VIII.99–100).

From this point of view, Emerson's position can probably be said to be summed up in his early suggestion that genius is essentially "finer love, a love impersonal" (W.I.217–218). He was keenly aware that this was not the popular view. Nor was he fatuous enough to think that he had permanently risen to the level of genius in this respect: His writings are full of denunciations of his own tendency to idealize and idolize persons. Sometimes, as in "Circles," self-criticisms of this kind appear in the midst of an eloquent vindication of the primacy of the ideal: "I thought as I walked in the woods and mused on my friends, why should I play with them this game of idolatry? . . . O blessed Spirit, whom I forsake for these, they are not thou! Every personal consideration that we allow costs us heavenly state. We sell the thrones of angels for a short and turbulent pleasure" (W.II.307).

The many references to angels in Emerson's discussions of universal and impersonal love cannot conceal the fact that he is placed in stark opposition to Christian doctrine with its stress on charity, especially as he explicitly rejects this sentiment along with sexual love. His attitude is understandable in that Christian charity, while defined against erotic love, is nevertheless just as "personal" and "downward" and hence not in every respect easily distinguishable from it or less reprehensible from a strictly Platonistic point of view. On the other hand, it is a moot question whether Emerson does not sometimes go further than Plato himself in theorizing about these matters. The relationships which Plato's Socrates has with young men are supposed to be nonsexual, but they can hardly be called impersonal or angelic, and he certainly takes a charitable view of their lack of true knowledge.[5] Emerson's theoretical intransigence seems to separate him from Plutarch, the "middle Platonist," who is known not only for his appreciation of nuptial love but also for his φιλανδρωπία, a term which definitely translates as "love of men" rather than "love of man."[6] His main philosophical support would seem to be Neo-Platonism: He chuckles in his diary over the neo–Neo-Platonist Thomas Taylor's characterization of Christianity as "a certain most irrational and gigantic impiety" (JN.IX.49 and JN.X.485). He himself echoes the Neo-Platonist view when he criticizes what he calls "popular" Christianity for failing to see that persons cannot be invested "with the rights of ideas" (JN.VII.512–513).

The idea that Christianity is a two-story house is important to Emerson whenever he feels embarrassed by the painful discrepancy between his Platonism and the religion in which he was brought up. In his journal, he once makes the distinction between an "esoteric" and an "exoteric" (popular) brand of Christianity, the former being virtually indistinguishable from Platonism (JN.V.31).

In an early lecture, he even suggests that Paul says that "God is no respecter of persons," taking a statement in Acts 10:34 in what he is pleased to call "the philosophical sense of the text" (EL.II.278). The factual basis for such a dichotomy of the Christian message is obviously brittle. Paul clearly puts charity at the top in I Corinthians and even in that context suggests that speaking with the tongue of angels is not enough if one does not possess that attribute. The closest Christian parallel to Emerson's view would seem to be Augustine, who under the influence of Neo-Platonist thought modifies the idea that Christian charity is modeled on the downward élan of a personal God by arguing that it is not the imperfect human being who is the object of neighborly love but the neighbor as he will be "when God is all in all."

Emerson's problem with what he saw as "popular" Christianity is understandable in terms of his philosophical commitment. It is not just that charity addresses the person and the body; he respects both as symbols of "something far greater," and this, as he kept telling Margaret Fuller and Caroline Sturgis, is the only sound basis for friendship between human beings. The problem is that charity cannot really be fitted into this symbolistic framework. Indeed, it is, as Pascal points out, the only thing that is not symbolic. What is more, not only does charity address the body; judging by the Greek word used to describe the sentiment in the first chapter of Mark ($\sigma\pi\lambda\alpha\gamma\chi\nu\iota\sigma\theta\epsilon\iota\varsigma$), it also has its origin in the body, more precisely in the bowels, the part of the body which Plato in the *Timaeus* disparagingly compares to the women's quarter in a house. It is, in short, in every way irrelevant to the idea of "intellectual" love which dominates Emerson's vision of the ideal state of man.

Logical as it is from his own philosophical point of view, Emerson's hostility to Christian charity nevertheless surprises by the very violence of its expression. One is tempted to look for some nonphilosophical reason contributing to his determination to stress this aspect of his thought in the face of the "prejudices" of the world and, one should add, in spite of his own posture as a private citizen, which was often quite different. One clue is the passage in "Intellect" in which he says that intellect is "void of affection" and "eviscerated of care" (W.II.326–327). The point is that intellect is capable of separating the person who has it from his own sufferings as well as from those of others; and to a man who has suffered a good deal in his own body during the earlier part of his life and seen a lot of suffering in others, such a belief in the therapeutic, not to say redemptory, virtues of "intellect" may not be without a special significance. It is sometimes suggested that Emerson's philosophical optimism, his reliance on the exalted sphere of intellect, and his corresponding dismissal of the mundane sphere of mere personal worries and sorrows—his own as well as those of others—contributed to his ultimate recovery.[7]

By no coincidence, this recovery followed rather quickly after his resignation from the ministry. He had never felt comfortable in this role, and one reason for his uneasiness seems to have been exactly his pastoral duty to attend the sick and the dying at a time when he needed a more uplifting spectacle. An early journal meditation prompted by complaints from some parishioners that he did not seem to commiserate sufficiently with the suffering clearly shows—in spite of the Christian language which he was still using at the time—that he thought them guilty of weak self-indulgence and that his real duty was not to be sick and dying with them but to show them the Truth that alone could help them and himself regardless of whether they lived or died (JN.III.312). After his resignation from the Second Church, he felt increasingly free to say so openly and in public, as he did in the "Divinity School Address" (W.I.148). Even more explicit is the essay "Self-Reliance," where the section on prayers, in addition to some words in praise of "the self-helping man," features a denunciation of the "base" kind of sympathy which makes us "come to them who weep foolishly and sit down and cry for company, instead of imparting to them truth and health in rough electric shocks, putting them once more in communication with the soul" (W.II.78). His lasting need to justify the posture which had characterized him as a minister is reflected in "Considerations by the Way" (1860), where, along with the condemnations of the masses which discredit Adamhood, one finds an anecdote about "a clergyman" who spent his time with the sick and the dying: Emerson says he told him that he seemed to him to need "quite different company" and quotes Dr. Johnson's dictum, "Every man is a rascal as soon as he is sick" (W.VI.263–264).

After he had resigned from the ministry and begun his real lifework, Emerson's critique of charity focuses to a considerable extent on the ability of friends and relatives to prevent one from doing one's own thing. Even in the "Divinity School Address," he tells his listeners to "study the grand strokes of rectitude: a bold benevolence, an independence of friends, so that not the unjust wishes of those who love us shall impair our freedom, but we shall resist for truth's sake the freest flow of kindness and appeal to sympathies far in advance"; it is suggested that in this way we will show "the angel" (W.I.149). In "Self-Reliance," a striking passage falling within this category combines an allusion to Jesus' dismissal of his earthly family with a reference to a private kingdom which is not of this world: "Friend, client, child, sickness, fear, want, charity, all knock at once at thy closet door and say, 'Come out unto us.'—Do not spill thy soul; do not descend; keep thy state. . . ."

Here, too, we are listening to a man who is trying to bolster his own self-confidence. Emerson was by no means an insensitive person; he was, on the contrary, often bothered by a guilty conscience with respect to close ones who had died. More especially, he could not overcome a gnawing feeling that he had not sufficiently demonstrated his love for Charles and Ellen, in spite—or perhaps because—of his admiration and respect for their supposedly angelic nature. This uneasiness even found expression in "Love" and in part explains his dismissal of experience in favor of the ideal in that essay: "I know not why, but infinite compunctions embitter in mature life all the remembrances of budding sentiment, and cover every beloved name. Every thing is beautiful seen from the point of the intellect, or as truth. But all is sour if seen as experience" (W.II.71).

We shall come full circle if we consider the fact that the sufferings of loved ones, as well as his own, are also among the things that push him into taking refuge in some imaginative version of man's amphibious state. The idea of a "heaven of letters" seems to have been particularly helpful in this context. In a letter to Aunt Mary, he notes, after mentioning the past suffering of Ellen and his own uncertain health: "I am entering into acquaintance with Goethe, who has just died" (L.I.354). To the end of his writing days, he continued to seek this kind of redemption in literature: "It is relief," he says in a late journal note, "to read some true books, wherein all are equally dead, equally alive" (J.X.15).

9

MUTABILITY: EMERSON'S
TRANSFORMATION OF AN
OLD HUMAN GRIEVANCE

Emerson often indulges the dream of an amphibious life making heaven accessible to the aspiring soul seemingly imprisoned in clay. But this is not the only way in which his imagination deals with the possibility of angelic love and friendship in this life. It would have been strange if it had been: After all, such visits to heaven are by definition temporary, and even the brightest of human souls must spend most of its time in this world. In his search for some additional imaginative scheme which might be helpful in coping with the problems flowing from that dilemma, Emerson could find inspiration in the works of the originators of the idea of an amphibious life, Plato and Plotinus: They hold that even the brief visits in the higher world, often of an ecstatic character, would not be possible without the slow and sometimes painful climbing of the dialectical ladder which is eventually to lead to a permanent abode in that sphere. In this perspective, the static idea of an ideal human state yields to that of a need for improvement of one's state of being—that is, for change. At the same time, the stress on universality of communion, while not invalidated, is replaced by a stress on the need for change of partners.

One facet of Emerson's adaptation of this theme is the way in which he relates it to the problem of mutability, the phenomenon which has saddened so many generations of poets. In the process, mutability becomes as potent a source of consolation for the loss of loved ones as the idea of amphibious life (which implies that commerce with them is by no means entirely interrupted). As early as *Nature,* Emerson ends the section called "Discipline" on the note that while the human form in principle is a wonderful symbol, particular persons are by definition imperfect, and it will take quite a few of them to give us anything like a complete idea of "the resources of God." Therefore, the individuals we love are usually in one way or another "withdrawn from our sight" as soon as we have taken what we could from them, turning that into "solid and sweet wisdom" in our minds and themselves into objects of thought which will follow us everywhere (W.I.46). At the end of "Compensation," he says more explicitly: "The death of a dear friend, wife, brother, lover, which seemed nothing but privation, somewhat later assumes the aspect of a guide or genius; for it commonly operates revolutions in our way of life, terminates an epoch of infancy or of youth which was waiting to be closed, breaks up a wonted occupation or a household, or style of living, and allows the formation of new ones more friendly to the growth of character" (W.II.126). Nor is the reader allowed to think that this is a somewhat egocentric way of looking at it: Thanks to such compensations, we are told, "the man or woman who would have remained a sunny garden-flower, with no room for its roots and too much sunshine for its head, by the falling of the walls and the neglect of the gardener is made the banian of the forest, yielding shade and fruit to wide neighborhoods of men."

Even without such universal benefits, it is from this point of view irrational, perhaps insane, to grieve too deeply over the deaths of individuals, no matter how much we loved them. We are supposed to learn and progress as long as we live, says Emerson in "Love," and consequently "the objects of the affections" must change just like "the objects of thought." They do so "slowly and with pain," but "the moments" when we believe that our happiness is dependent on a particular person are a kind of disease. When we are in better mental health, we do not fear that we will lose anything by the spiritual progress we make: "That which is so beautiful and attractive as these relations, must be succeeded and supplanted only by what is more beautiful, and so on forever"

(W.II.188). The importance of this theme to Emerson personally is hard to exaggerate. In "Experience," he again says, with specific regard to our alleged inability to like anything for very long and its effect on personal relations: "Our love of the real draws us to permanance, but health of body consists in circulation, and sanity of mind in variety or facility of association. We need change of objects" (W.III.55). This passage is especially remarkable because it comes only a few pages after his seeming complaint that the loss of his first wife and his first son did not leave any permanent pain.

Nevertheless, the most striking coincidence in Emerson's handling of these two themes—amphibious access to the ideal state of man and the benefits of change—is the somewhat negative philosophical view of the home and the family, already singled out by Plato as the seat and origin of emotional suffering. In both cases he tends to measure the elevation of the individual soul by the distance it puts between itself and its original attachment to the home. Especially noteworthy in this context is the recurrence of the word "custom" as the common denominator of everything that the aspiring soul wants to leave behind: In the *Symposium*, Plato suggests that the best men marry only because it is the custom to do so. Emerson develops the theme in his own way when he compares his ideal poet to a Kalmuck who loves to "quit his home" and travel about in his wagon "to read new landscapes and old skies." It is specified that while "spirit" moves him to "roam," "custom" brings him "home again" (W.IX.311). Implicitly at least, the same symbolism is tied to his philosophical preference for friendship over marriage at the beginning of "Nature," where he— obviously referring to certain nightly excursions with Thoreau— describes how "the knapsack of custom" falls from a man's back as he leaves his "close and crowded" house and issues forth into nature: "How easily we might walk onward into the opening landscape, absorbed by new pictures and by thoughts fast succeeding each other, until by degrees the recollection of home was crowded out of the mind. . . ." (W. III.170).

However, the walking, as in Thoreau's essay on the subject, does not have to be literal. In the early lecture entitled "Home," Emerson describes a man's progress as a successive weaning from his emotional dependence on particular persons—father, mother, wife, children, friends—until he develops the readier kind of "domestication" which makes him feel at home with anybody who betrays enough of an affinity with him to yield the spiritual nourishment he may need at a given moment: At that point, says Emerson, his old familiar haunts assume an altered look—"he finds himself a stranger under his own roof" (EL.III.31).

This passage cannot but remind one that Emerson a few years later—during the months before he left for England to become "the lonely, wayfaring man" described by Scudder—actually was a boarder in his own house.[1] But the reference obviously is to Plotinus' elaboration of Plato's characterization of the aspiring soul as a wanderer and pilgrim in nature seeking his way back to his true home. One also recognizes an echo of Novalis' Platonizing definition of philosophy as properly speaking "Heimweh—Trieb ueberall zu Hause zu sein," or, as Emerson puts it, "the homesickness of the soul."

Such allusions to "the flight of the alone to the Alone" may not sound very social, but they do not in any way contradict Emerson's repeated description of angelic and universal friendship as a kind of solitude unaffected by whether the friend is absent or present (e.g., W.II.216). Moreover, even in "Home" he sees things in a somewhat social perspective when he notes that "the constant progress of Culture is to a more interior life, to a deeper Home." Nor should one ignore the reference to Augustine's City of God, one of Emerson's major images of the possibility of an amphibious life and a large affinity-based acquaintance, but also of historical progress toward a universal home. In a sense we are not so far here from his disciple Whitman's vision of a humanity, or the better part of humanity, on the road propelled by comradely love.

Certain cross-references between "Home" and "History" are particularly significant in this respect: Some of the phrasings used in the essay to argue that history is really universal autobiography—that in reading about the great characters of the past we are actually getting acquainted with our own true origin and destiny—are lifted from "Home" (W.II.11 and EL.III.30). By the same token, the central idea of "Home" is quite close to what Emerson in "History" calls "intellectual nomadism," in the original edition of the *Essays* defined as "the faculty of objectiveness or of eyes which everywhere feed themselves" (E.I.19). The following sentences, also quoted from the undiluted first version, are noteworthy for the

way in which the concept of universal love is subordinated to erotic
—or, rather, "intellectual"—versatility: "Who hath such eyes,
everywhere falls into easy relations with his fellow-men. Every man,
every thing is a prize, a study, a property to him, and his love
smooths his brow, joins him to men, and makes him beautiful and
beloved in their sight. His house is a wagon; he roams through all
latitudes as easily as a Calmuc" (W.II.22).

The love described here is clearly of the angelic type: Emerson
often refers to what he on one occasion calls the "ocular" and "all-
feeding" air of heaven (W.III.12). Since the kingdom of heaven
is one of the images he uses in discussing his excursions into the
world of free love and friendship, we probably should not be surprised that Jesus, who denies that there are marriages in heaven,
is also fitted into the "Calmuc" pattern. Not only does Emerson
follow Milton in looking upon him as a champion of free love and
friendship—he suggests that Christ "was in love with his thought
and quitted all for it" (JN.V.482). The thought in question obviously is the thought of the heavenly home which the advanced
soul carries with him wherever he goes, according to "Home." In
another journal, Emerson says that Jesus "builds his house on the
road" (JN.XI.177).

Conversely, Emerson's objection to Swedenborg's doctrine of
heavenly marriage is due to the circumstance that it is heretic from
the Platonistic no less than from the Christian point of view. To
him, Swedenborg, like Milton, distorts the idea that the earth
mirrors heaven to the point of reversing it when he argues that
"the departing soul finds such a world as it left" (JN.XIII.335–
336; cf. J.X.191). In Milton's case, he must be thinking of the
passages in *Paradise Lost* describing the inhabitants of heaven
eating and making love. Swedenborg is guilty of stating that there
are men and women in heaven and that they marry, each couple
moving into its own house. Their situation is not unlike that of
Milton's Adam and Eve at the moment when Satan comes upon
them "imparadis'd in each other's arms," as he enviously puts it.
Emerson is less envious: To him Swedenborg's idea of heavenly
bliss represents "a child's clinging to his toy; an attempt to eternize
the fireside and nuptial chamber; to keep the picture-alphabet
through which our first lessons are prettily conveyed" (W.IV.128).

Clearly, Emerson feels that Swedenborg is not doing justice

to himself in *Conjugal Love*. The argument of this book, he says in "Swedenborg, or, the Mystic," is stated in such a manner that it does not provide "that scope for ascension of state which the nature of things requires" (W.IV.127). However, in another area of the same essay, where the reference is to *The Economy of the Animal Kingdom* (as elucidated by J. G. Wilkinson), Swedenborg is seen as a prophet of evolution promising the "ascent" of things "into daemonic and celestial natures."[2] Significantly, Emerson is especially impressed with the idea that the brain may eventually be able to shed the trunk and exist independently in a state of androgynous fertility. Such a development, he says, is not only in agreement with a certain passage in the *Timaeus*—the grand rhymes and echoes it involves are the mark of "a daring poetic synthesis" showing that the author sees better than anybody else the Protean "flowing" of nature (W.IV.108–112). What a pity, then, that he should end up pinning his doctrine of heavenly love "on a temporary form," as if he could not see that marriage is simply the first symbol of angelic friendship.

Curiously, Emerson's own account of the doctrine set forth in *Conjugal Love* and *Heaven and Hell* suggests that there is plenty of scope for progress in Swedenborg's spiritual world: "In heaven," Emerson quotes, "the angels are advancing continually to the spring-time of their youth, so that the oldest angel appears the youngest" (W.IV.126). We are not far here from Emerson's own suggestion in "Circles" that "whilst we converse with what is above us, we do not grow old, but grow young," a phrasing demonstrably derived from a passage in *Heaven and Hell*. By the same token, we are reminded of Emerson's own Platonic stress on beauty of soul when we find him noting that, while the virgins Swedenborg saw in heaven were beautiful, the wives were incomparably more beautiful and went on increasing in beauty forever. Why, then, does he take such a dim view of the dialectic potential of heavenly marriage?

The answer is: for the same reason that he doubts the usefulness of earthly marriage in this respect, especially from the man's point of view. He was entirely convinced by Swedenborg's idea (already to be found in Milton and St. Paul) that woman is essentially the learner in her relation to the husband; in fact, the Preface to *Representative Men* contains a reference to his belief that the wife through daily association arrives "at the intellectual and moral elevations of her husband" (W.IV.26). However, if this is the case, marriage offers slim opportunities for the husband to rise in the scale of being, and in the end there is bound to be stagnation for both. As he puts it in the same Preface, "It is observed in old couples, or persons who have been house-mates for a course of years, that they grow like, and if they should live long enough we should not be able to know them apart. Nature abhors these complaisances which threaten to melt the world into a lump, and hastens to break up such maudlin agglutinations." Obviously there is no reason to perpetuate such a situation in the next world.

Perhaps one can say that Emerson unconsciously corrects Swedenborg when he attributes to him the idea that "the marriages of the world are broken up"—*Conjugal Love* only states that false marriages are discontinued in heaven (W.IV.125). But he is revising the book very deliberately when he suggests that "the true subject" of *Conjugal Love* might be conversation. At that point he has already corrected Swedenborg by stating that the loves and friendships of "progressive souls" are invariably momentary: "*Do you love me?* means, Do you love the same truth? If you do, we are happy with the same happiness: but presently one of us passes into the perception of new truth;—we are divorced, and no tension in nature can hold us to each other." He goes on to suggest, "Heaven is not the pairing of two, but the communion of all souls," and finally gets to the most remarkable part of his argument—the idea that we "change sexes" every moment in the spiritual world: "You love the worth in me; then I am your husband: but it is not me, but the worth, that fixes the love; and that worth is a drop of the ocean of worth that is beyond me. Meantime I adore the greater worth in another, and so become his wife. He aspires to a higher worth in another spirit, and is wife or receiver of that influence" (W.IV.128–129).

In this startling and, needless to say, quite free-wheeling interpretation of Swedenborg's doctrine of marriage, the beloved person obviously does not stand for ideal perfection, but only for a truth which the lover has not yet perceived and which to him appears higher than the truth he previously possessed and thus capable of raising him in the scale of being. This Platonic way of linking the love of persons to the love of truth is not in itself new in Emerson's works: In "Circles," for instance, he links the suggestion that "No love can be bound by oath or covenant to secure it against a higher love" to the search for new truth that makes the thought we knew before look trivial rather than sublime (W. II.319–320). In the essay on Swedenborg, however, we have a much more radical and also more elaborate statement of this doctrine. It is linked very firmly to the idea of the evanescent and "fluctional" character of the symbolic phenomena of this world.

Emerson's theory of conversation is also quite unequivocal on another score. No doubt its origin has something to do with certain journal meditations concerning the possibility of finding a way to "correct" marriage by looking at "how the facts stand in heaven." But the very journal passage from which these words are quoted (JN.VIII.95) indicates that he is not interested in sexual licentiousness. So do his discussions of his relations with his new female friends, which are behind these meditations. He may sign himself "Your facile Waldo Emerson" in a letter to Margaret Fuller (L. III.147), but that is just meant as a pleasant reminder of the universality of angelic love. Another letter to her, ending with the words "Instantaneously yours" (L.II.400), is clearly a joking and yet serious allusion to the momentary character of the embraces in Swedenborg's heaven and in his own theory of conversation as "the practice and consummation of friendship" (W.II.206–207).

In view of the friendships Emerson formed at the time when he first developed his theory of conversation, there can be no doubt that it, originally at least, was intended to apply to conversation between men and women as well as to conversation between men of the kind his "author" Montaigne discusses in his essay "De la conference." Indeed, there is every reason to think that Emerson felt his theory represented a refinement not only on Swedenborg's doctrine but on that of Plato himself. He has made room for women in Plato's dialectic scheme, while at the same time doing away with the last vestige of ambiguous attachment to mortal beauty still adhering to the teachings of the *Phaedrus* and the *Symposium*. However, even apart from the fact that the symbolic dichotomy on which his own scheme is based implies that women are not likely to play the "husband's" role in conversation with men, there is something inherently strained and awkward about a symbolic pattern inviting a man to see himself as the "wife" of somebody who is perhaps in a quite literal sense somebody else's wife. One is not surprised to find Emerson balking at the idea of admitting women to the Town and Country Club a few years later, when the novelty of his venture into symbolic extramarital romance had worn off.[3]

A certain lack of respect for the conversational ability of women is also reflected in the variation of the theme in which conversation becomes "intellectual nomadism." The state of woman in a nomadic society, whether Asian, African, or American Indian, was usually one of subjection. In the case of the Moslem Nomads who interested Emerson most in this context, those of the mid-eastern and north-African deserts, the inferior status of woman is well documented. The nomad of the desert is also the epitome of the outdoor way of life Emerson associates with the masculine principle. Nor is that all: The sterility of the desert and the unearthly emptiness of its landscape remove it from any association with the feminine principle; leaving a man alone with the horizon and the sky, the desert is the transcendental landscape par excellence.

The close connection between Emerson's concept of "intellectual nomadism" and his theory of conversation can be glimpsed in the very context in which he corrects Swedenborg with obvious reference to what he sees as the possessiveness of wives: "The Eden of God," he says, "is bare and grand"; it is "like the outdoor landscape remembered from the evening fireside; it seems cold and desolate whilst you cower over the coals, but once abroad again, we pity those who can forego the magnificence of nature for candlelight and cards." He is here referring to a snow-covered landscape, the nearest New England equivalent of the desert.

Certain medieval Persian poets play a prominent role in Emerson's imaginative celebrations of "intellectual nomadism" as the right angelic kind of friendship. The Persians were hardly as nomadic as the Arabs—the Shiraz of Saadi and Hafiz in particular seems far from a desert—but in "Saadi" Emerson nevertheless places his alter ego in a cottage "on the desert's yellow floor" (W.IX.135). In the same poem, Saadi is portrayed as a representative of universal love. It is true that Emerson in this case stresses that Saadi does not have to leave his cottage door and seek all over for a friend— the friend is right there, provided he has nomadic eyes. But this is only stating the idea in a paradoxical manner: Since the intellectual nomad finds friends everywhere, he does not have to go anywhere. Besides, one notes that in the ode by Saadi ("Von Hammer, p. 208") which Emerson is adapting in this area of "Saadi," the idea of moving from one friendship to another is stressed as much as the idea that there are friends everywhere (J.IX.538–539). In another poem involving "Saadi," Emerson slyly introduces the idea of nomadism by bestowing the title of "cameldriver" on the lowly man whose demeanor makes him scorn the fame of Timour and who in real·life seems to have been none other than his neighbor Edmund Hosmer, "the Napoleon, the Alexander of the soil" (W.IX.323 and JN.VIII.238).

Intellectual nomadism of the pure and simple "forever onward" type is more often tied to the image of the Arab Bedouin living in a tent. In the last paragraph of "Love," for instance, where he is arguing that the true lover seeks virtue and wisdom everywhere, Emerson says that "we are often made to feel that our affections are but tents of a night." The same theme is used in "Compensation": "We linger in the old tent," but "The voice of the Almighty saith, 'up and onward forevermore!'" In the same paragraph, the suggestion that we ought to let our "angels" go so that "archangels" may come in points up the interchangeable character of angelic love and "intellectual nomadism" as literary themes: There seems to be cross-reference here to "Give All to Love," the poem in which the reader is told to keep himself forever "free as an Arab" of his beloved, remembering that "When half-gods go / The gods arrive."

The circle of the horizon, the most obvious feature in the landscape of the desert, is another important image Emerson uses in his discussions of endless individual progress: "The Arabs measure distance by horizons," he once observes in his journal, adding that the scholar ought to do likewise (J.IX.523). At the beginning of "Circles," he points out that the horizon is "the second circle after the eye," and although he does not explicitly say so, it would seem that if "our life is an apprenticeship to the truth that around every circle another can be drawn; that there is no end in nature, but every end is a beginning"—then the Arab desert is the most fitting symbol of our situation. The theme also proves an efficient one in tying the love of persons to the love of truth(s): "There is no outside, no inclosing wall, no circumference to us. The man finishes his story,—how good! how final! how it puts a new face on all things! He fills the sky. Lo, on the other side rises also a man and draws a circle around the circle we had just pronounced the outline of the sphere." In these terms, a man's growth is indeed seen "in the successive choirs of his friends" (W.II.307).

Another nomadic note is struck in "Circles" when Emerson writes: "I unsettle all things. No facts are to me sacred; none are profane; I simply experiment, an endless seeker with no Past at my back." At the moment, he is obviously speaking of his own method of intellectual seeking. But the theme is tied to the love of persons in the next paragraph, which ends with the words "People wish to be settled: only as far as they are unsettled is there any hope for them." This part of the essay urges the idea that "the coming only is sacred" and that old truths and loves lose their claim as soon as new and higher ones enter our field of vision (W.II.318–320).

The hostility of this doctrine to timbered houses, the indoors, and the home and hearth needs no further demonstration. But it is worth pointing out that Emerson explicitly thinks of himself as an Arab in these terms. When he notes "Only so much of Arabian history can I read, as I am an Arabian within" (JN.V.286), the cross-reference is to "History," where the argument for "intellectual nomadism" is accompanied by a stress on "creative" or "active" reading—that is, identification with the author. In another journal entry, Emerson gets quite personal: "Yes, I resent this intrusion of a few persons on my airy fields of existence. Shall our conversation when we meet O wife, or sister E[lizabeth], still return like a chime of seven bells to six or seven names, nor we freemen of nature be able long to travel out of this narrow orbit? Rather I would never name these names again. . . . Beware of walls; let me keep the open field" (JN.VII.515). As if fearing that Lidian might be leaning over his shoulder and reading what he had just written, Emerson adds as an afterthought: "Yet though I start like a wild Arab at the first suspicion of confinement, I have drank [sic] with great joy the contents of this golden cup hitherto."

Nobody knew better than Emerson himself how much he needed his home and the people in it: While chafing in theory against the bonds and responsibilities of marriage, he carefully refrained from any acts that might jeopardize his own domestic base. However, it would hardly be fair to accuse him of hypocrisy in this respect: Even apart from his great personal need for tranquillity, his philosophy is ultimately so radical that he simply had to be one of those speculators who, in the words of Hawthorne, "conform with the utmost quietude to the external regulations of society" because "The thought suffices them, without interesting itself in the flesh and blood of action." At the same time, his philosophical hostility to marriage and what it stands for is at the very core and center of his world-view; so far as the "thinker" is concerned, the theory of conversation and the doctrine of "intellectual nomadism" lead us straight to the essential, not to say the quintessential, Emerson. The theme has great integrative potential.

Take, for instance, the idea that all symbols are "transitive" (W.III.34), and that we therefore must "give ourselves the lie" if we want to remain true: Obviously it has a bearing on Emerson's method of composition as well as on his way of thinking. As already mentioned, Emerson insists that the poet must "see the Proteus," and significantly he does so not only in the essay on Swedenborg and the essay "The Poet" but also in one of his discussions of Saadi (W.VIII.64). The prose-writer must operate in like fashion, although in his case a renunciation of excessive coherence and consistency is what is required. In the Preface to the *Gulistan*, Emerson characterizes Saadi's prose style by saying that he "saharized" the mind (G.xi); the phrase admirably fits his own aphoristic style, which tends to confer considerable autonomy on the paragraph and even on the sentence. Apparently this stylistic trait, to some extent at least, was achieved through a deliberate cutting out of transitions, paradoxically justified by the idea that nothing is true but in transition.

The methods of the lover, the thinker, and the poet are thus fundamentally one and the same, so far as Emerson is concerned. What is more, he also suggests that the behavior of his great individual is really only a reflection of the method of nature: As the lover-thinker-poet stays young and continues to draw new and ever-larger circles by changing his loves, thoughts, and symbols, so nature shows its abhorrence of everything that is old by changing and at the same time slowly improving the creatures it pours forth. "Horsed on the Proteus, / Thou ridest to power" (W.IX.288), says

Emerson in one of his poetic discussions of the importance of love and poetry as a vehicle of historic-evolutionary progress. "The Method of Nature" ends with the words "through universal love to universal power" (W.I.224). Allusions to the nomadic way of life also appear in this context: "We dwellers in tents, we outlines in chalk, we jokes and buffooneries," he once exclaims in his journal (JN.IX.378).

The integration of Emerson's philosophy in terms of flux and change actually goes even further. In a complete unification of the field, God is also brought into the picture, and his method turns out to be remarkably like that of the nature which he animates, not to mention that of the poet-thinker-lover: "All forms are fluent and as the bird alights on the bough and pauses for rest, then plunges into the air again on its way, so the thoughts of God pause but for a moment in any form, but pass into a new form, as if by touching the earth again in burial, to acquire new energy" (JN. IX.301).

Speaking of this "law" of metamorphosis, Emerson does not hesitate to invoke Pan, whose priest the poet is supposed to be. This of course has to do with the circumstance that some Neo-Platonists liked to interpret the name of this god with reference to τὸ πᾶν, or "the All." But in Emerson's poetry, Pan usually becomes a symbol of the life force, as, for instance, in "Woodnotes" (W.IX.58):

> Onward and on the eternal Pan,
> Who layeth the world's incessant plan,
> Halteth never in one shape,
> But forever doth escape,
> Like wave or flame, into new forms
> Of gem, and air, of plants, and worms.

A specifically nomadic note, as distinct from the purely Protean theme, appears a page later in the same poem, where the god assumes a curious similarity to the roving lover-thinker-poet imaged in "The Humble-Bee":

> As the bee through the garden ranges,
> From world to world the godhead changes;
> As the sheep go feeding in the waste,
> From form to form He maketh haste;

> This vault which glows immense with light
> Is the inn where he lodges for a night.

Emerson has been accused of a failure to perceive that his conception of a universe in which everything, including the godhead, is in a state of flux and transition does not jibe with his subscription to the Platonic vision of a divine world of unchangeable archetypes raised above the sphere of mundane flux.[4] From the point of view of logical consistency, one must agree that it would have been better if he had consistently stuck to his own brand of pantheism, according to which man and the whole universe are permeated and kept going by a steady influx of divine energy. From a purely literary point of view, there usually is not much of a problem: There is no clash between the reference to Plato's archetypes in "The Celestial Love" and the universal flux described in "Pan," unless the two texts are wantonly juxtaposed.

Emerson has good reasons for abandoning his pantheistic standpoint in certain contexts, as, for instance, in "The Celestial Love." This doctrine goes quite well with his idea of the "flowing" hero who "conspires" with the divine will which informs him and whose willing instrument he is in its carrying out its plan for his race or nation, as part of the grand evolution of humanity leading to universal power (cf. W.VI.23–24). But it does not really fit the situation of the Platonic truth-seeker trying to rise above the unstable world of appearances and catch a glimpse of the realm of unity and permanence. In Plato's dialectic, the idea of flux, far from having anything to do with a divine inspiration with which one is supposed to "conspire," is associated with the state of forgetfulness characteristic of profane souls. It is the wash of events and circumstance which carries us away from our higher duties. The best Emerson can do to bridge the gap between the two schemes is to see the moments of mundane oblivion as the result of a temporary withdrawal of the influx of divine energy—"a vast ebb of a vast flow" during which purposeful "flowing" is replaced by aimless drifting. Significantly, this point is made in an area of "Circles" where he has been dwelling on the idea that there are "no fixtures" in nature or the universe at large, and that the same fluidity is characteristic of men in their slow climbing of the "mysterious ladder" leading to greater power as well as to larger "choirs" of friends (W.II.305–307).

This is not the only ambiguity affecting Emerson's positive view of flux and transition as the process through which God's work is carried forward. According to the Platonic scenario, the change of thoughts and loves is not an end in itself; often painful and laborious, it serves the very definite purpose of raising the aspiring soul to the level where it can behold the realm of final and absolute beauty. Emerson, on the other hand, has a tendency to cheerfully stress the endlessness of the quest he is referring to. Not least his image of "intellectual nomadism" leads to a tension between the assumption that it represents a movement toward an all-important goal and the attitude expressed in the formula: "Not in his goals but in his transition man is great" (EL.II.158).

In "Circles," Emerson not only characterizes himself as an "endless" seeker, but also as a man without "a Past" at his back, a phrasing which denies that there is any accumulation of wisdom along with the existence of a definite goal. Clearly, we are here close to the intellectual "Don Juanism" that Rougemont attributes to Emerson's reader Nietzsche, in which new and youthful ideas are so attractive that frequent marriages and infidelities are indispensable to the thinker's happiness.[5] The phrase perfectly fits the heavenly "conversation" with which Emerson replaces Swedenborg's doctrine of heavenly marriage.

The idea that heaven is not so much the state toward which the aspiring soul moves as the movement itself, or each stage of the movement, is often stated quite frankly by Emerson. In "The Poet," he says that "every heaven is also a prison" (W.III.33). In "The Sphinx," he suggests that there are many heavens along the road and that they successively destroy each other: "The heavens that now draw him / With sweetness untold, / Once found,—for new heavens / He spurneth the old." One of his favorite Moslem poets is adduced to make a similar point: "It was no Oxonian," he notes in *English Traits*, "but Hafiz, who said, 'Let us be crowned with roses, let us drink wine and break up the tiresome old roof of heaven into new forms'" (W.V.258). Is it a coincidence that he uses the same verb in suggesting that the marriages of this world are "broken up" in Swedenborg's heaven?

Emerson's journal translation of the cupbearer poem he paraphrases in *English Traits* shows that Hafiz is proposing a liberating God-drinking of a pantheistic kind (JN.IX.398). Apparently, Emerson felt quite close to him in this respect. The Bacchus in his poem of that name, which is partly inspired by another poem by Hafiz, is not so different from his conception of Pan in, say, "Woodnotes." At this level, too, it is often difficult to see any ultimate goal or meaning in the undulation of the universe. "Woodnotes" is again an example in point: Pan's laying of "the world's incessant plan" seems as endless as his pouring of his wine "To every age, to every race" (W.IX.58).

One is struck by the somewhat nihilistic-sounding ring of some of Emerson's descriptions of the evolution of the universe from this point of view. In "The Over-Soul," where "drinking" the soul of God is a theme frequently referred to, he also dwells on the fluidity of time, space, and everything in nature: "The landscape, the figures, Boston, London, are facts as fugitive as any institution past, or any whiff of mist or smoke, and so is society, and so is the world. The soul looketh steadily forwards, creating a world before her, leading worlds behind her. She has no dates, nor rites, nor persons, nor specialties, nor men. The soul knows only the soul . . ." (W.II.274). This attitude of the soul is brought out even clearer in "Woodnotes":

> What recks such Traveller if the bowers
> Which bloom and fade like meadow flowers
> A bunch of fragrant lilies be,
> Or the stars of eternity?
> Alike to him the better, the worse,—
> The glowing angel, the outcast corse.

In "Pan," one image ("Ebbs the tide, they lie / White hollow shells upon the desert shore") calls to mind certain lines by Omar Khayyám, another Persian poet whom Emerson "translates" on occasion and according to whom human life is "One moment in Annihilation's Waste" and a caravan starting "for the Dawn of Nothing."

This Eden is indeed bare and grand, and yet even when he strikes this note Emerson does not intend to dishearten his reader. In "Woodnotes," we are definitely invited to become as "free and libertine" as Pan by identifying with the god and adopting his grand perspective. In "Pan," the final words stress renewal and eternal youth; the music of Pan is compared not to the gift of

Liber-Bacchus but to the spermatic foam out of which Aphrodite was born:

> But not the less the eternal wave rolls on
> To animate new millions, and exhale
> Races and planets, its enchanted foam.

One must conclude that to Emerson the idea that the individual and the universe exist only in transition is exhilarating.

10

HEAVENLY INFLUENCE: THE *INFLUXUS MYSTICUS* IN EMERSON'S THEORY OF FRIENDSHIP

It is easy to exaggerate the cold intellectuality of Emerson's conception of "universal" love and friendship. This element is definitely present in his chief images of this relationship—the society of cherubic souls dwelling in rarefied ether, and the nomadic souls roaming the desert in search of a momentary embrace under a starlit heaven—but these images hardly sum up his utterance on the subject. Just as the stress on change characterizing his theory of "intellectual nomadism" modifies the impression given by his various conceptions of a heavenly state, so both these ideas of "impersonal" love are balanced, or contradicted, by a strongly emotional strain. Occasionally, he denounces his own "personal" and emotional approach as a series of unfortunate lapses, but one only has to read his essay "Friendship" to see that he does not always see the two attitudes as mutually exclusive.

Paradoxically, marriage and intercourse are even more important figures in this context than in Emerson's discussions of impersonal-universal love. He is haunted by a vague fear that even "the language of love" will seem "suspicious and common" compared with the "select and sacred relation" that he is analyzing in "Friendship," but apparently there is no real alternative (W.II.201). It is easy to say that like attracts like and verbally erase the differ-

169

ence between "friendship" and sexual love, as he does in this essay, but in the end the human mind finds it difficult to conceive of spiritual love or friendship except in terms of some kind of polarity, usually sexual. Moreover, the use of the lower and "common" kind of love as a symbol of the higher and "select" brand is legitimized, as it were, by the fact that a symbol by definition is inferior to that which it symbolizes. As for the risk of being misinterpreted in using sexual love and intercourse as an image of the intimate commerce of friends, Emerson seems to have felt that he could reduce and perhaps eliminate it by using such imagery only or mainly in discussions of male friendship (the possibility that such selectiveness might result in another undesirable ambiguity either did not occur to him or seemed the lesser risk in his Platonistic and Victorian perspective).

To some extent Emerson's way of resorting to nuptial language in his discussions of friendship reminds one of the predicament of the many mystics who have felt compelled to use the language of mortal love in their attempts to express how it feels to become one with God: In spite of the apparent contrast between religious and erotic feelings, they quite often use imagery suggesting that the individual soul is feminine in its relations with the Deity. Rather similarly, Emerson's nuptial metaphors tend to be predicated on the idea that his exemplary individual (usually himself) is basically feminine compared with the friend. In fact, he shows a rather pronounced tendency to use the image of the *influxus mysticus* in this context. In that respect, he goes beyond the nuptial mystique with which Shakespeare surrounds friendship in the *Sonnets* that so early fired the imagination of Emerson and his brother Charles. The closest analogy is the lover planting seeds in the soul of the beloved described by Plato in the *Phaedrus,* but the most important source of inspiration may well have been Swedenborg's doctrine of heavenly marriage, according to which the husband floods the wife with his insight and light.

Whether the analogy between mystical religious love and Emerson's version of love-friendship can entirely solve the contradiction between the emotional-exclusive and intellectual-universal facets of his theory is another matter. It would be nice to be able to say categorically that he sees friendship as a holy state comparable to marriage only in a purely metaphorical sense and that the frankly erotic language he often uses does not imply that the emotions and sensations he refers to are erotic any more than the rapt nuptial imagery of the mystic implies that he actually feels like a wife at the moment of ecstasy. But the parallels Emerson draws sometimes sound literal enough. One example is the passage in "Friendship" where he, apparently alluding to his correspondence with John Sterling (cf. JN.V.449), states that he feels "as warmly" when his friend is praised "as the lover when he hears applause of his engaged maiden" (W.II.195).

One thing in "Friendship" that definitely is not meant metaphorically is the stress on the importance of intimacy and twoness. Modifying the view of Plutarch ("a poet"), Emerson says that this pastime "cannot exist in its perfection . . . betwixt more than two" (W.II.206). Obviously his attitude is here very different from what it is in the essay on Swedenborg, where he sternly remarks: "Heaven is not the pairing of two but the communion of all souls" (W.IV.-128–129). The stress on the idea that spiritual embraces are "momentary" is also missing in "Friendship." What we do find is an analogy between the penetrating conversation of which two men are capable when they are left alone and the intimacies of husband and wife.

Emerson is also less reluctant to use suggestive language in speaking of free and suprasexual friendship and love—especially when female partners are not specifically envisaged—than he is in his discussions of sexual love and marriage. A comparison of "Friendship" and "Love" is very instructive in this respect. In the latter essay, he says that love is best when not consummated (W.II.180). There is no positive mention of either the spiritual or the physical union of man and wife. By contrast, we are told in "Friendship" that we are animated by "the hope of union with our mates" (W.II.198). Conversation is defined as "the practice and consummation of friendship," and "the high freedom of great conversation" is said to be something that "requires an absolute running of two souls into one" (W.II.206–207). Nor is that all. Perhaps the relative lack of inhibition with which Emerson here describes the intimacy of this union is best shown by the following description of the friend for whom he yearns: "Before him I may think aloud. I am arrived at last in the presence of a man so real and equal that I may drop even those undermost garments of dissimulation, courtesy, and second thought, which men never put off, and may deal with him with the simplicity and wholeness with which one chemical atom meets another" (W.II.202).

The same freedom of expression often characterizes Emerson's discussion of friendship in many other essays. One of the older meanings of the word "conversation" is sexual intercourse, and he frequently makes the point that it is accompanied by pleasure in terms alluding to this meaning: "In higher activity of mind," he says in "Clubs," "every new perception is attended with a thrill of pleasure, and the imparting of it to others is also attended with pleasure" (W.VII.227). On the other hand, pleasure is not everything: If intercourse of the lower and natural sort, to the extent that it is legitimate, has offspring as its main purpose, so does conversation. In the same essay, Emerson notes that "intercourse we must have . . . we lose our days and are barren of thought for want of some person to talk with"; thought is "the child of the intellect" and is "conceived with joy and born with joy." In another essay, he suggests—before going on to state that natural marriage is only a symbol of the higher kind of intercourse—that "The perceptions of a soul, its wondrous progeny, are born by the conversation, the marriage of souls," and that a life rightly lived therefore is "incessant parturition" (W.XII.18).

Thus Emerson has every reason to approve of Ellery Channing for saying about his own verses that they were "proper love poems" in that "they were really genuine fruits of a fine, light, gentle, happy intercourse with his friends" (JN.VIII.318). By the same token, one can understand that he writes bitterly about persons whose conversation does not lead to fruit and offspring. Alcott's is a case in point; occasionally at least, it left Emerson with a kind of post-coital depression—the unhappy feeling that "when the conversation is ended, all is over" (JN.VIII.212).

Perhaps the most important and most fruitful "conversations" Emerson had were with his favorite authors. For that reason, and because the obviously spiritual nature of this kind of intercourse allows it, Emerson uses especially strong language in speaking of the pleasures of reading. Looking back on this aspect of his career, he notes in "Books" (1870) that these influences rank not only with parents but with "lovers and passionate experiences" (W.-VII.190). Thirty-five years earlier, less than a month before his marriage to Lydia Jackson, he had already stated, "Life has few pleasures so pure and deep as that with which we sit down to read a new book of a favorite and venerated author." In the same place, he says that it is also a great pleasure to help others to have this kind of experience. All in all, "It must be our main object to consummate this marriage between the mind of the scholar and the mind of the author" (EL.I.211).

Although "the law of one to one" obviously applies in this kind of conversation as well, there is in principle no limit to the number of partners a scholar can have in a lifetime. Nor does Emerson think that there is anything wrong with versatility in this respect. In a journal entry from the following year, he discusses the benefits of his own scholarly polygamy, contrasting it with the prim inflexibility of Alcott: "I go to Shakspear, Goethe, Swift, even to Tennyson, submit myself to them, become merely an organ of hearing, and yield to the law of their being. I am paid for thus being nothing by an entire new mind and thus a Proteus I enjoy the Universe through the powers and organs of a hundred different men" (JN.V.178).

The analogy between penmanship and generation also appears in Emerson's works. His early lecture on Bacon contains the following quotation: "The images of men's wits and knowledges remain in books exempted from the wrong of time and capable of perpetual renovation. Neither are they fitly to be called images because they generate still and cast their seed in the minds of others provoking and causing infinite actions and opinions in succeeding ages" (EL.I.330). It seems probable that this statement inspired the striking passage in which Emerson defines genius as "the activity which repairs the decay of things," and then compares the transmission of poems to the spreading of agaric spores in terms that also call spermatozoa to mind (EL.III.74–75 and W.III.23).

Emerson does not always shun the direct word in discussing these influences. In "Books," for instance, he notes that Montaigne thinks books are "a languid pleasure," but that he himself finds some of them "vital and spermatic, not leaving the reader what he was" (W.VII.197). In his journal, he expresses the idea that all books are not worth reading through exclamations like "Away with your prismatics, I want a spermatic book" (JN.VII.547) and "Give me initiative, spermatic, prophesying man-making words"

(JN.VIII.148). Another entry is remarkable for the way in which it defines the difference between the two kinds of books, and suggests that there is a category of authors whom not even the spermatic words of the great writers can fertilize and enable to do something creative on their own: "Now and then, rarely comes a stout man like Luther, Montaigne, Pascal, Herbert, who utters a thought or feeling in a virile manner, and it is unforgettable. Then follow any number of spiritual eunuchs and women, who talk about that thought, imply it, in pages and volumes. . . . Great bands of female souls who only receive the spermatic aura, and brood on the same but add nothing" (JN.XIV.277).

This view of the creative powers of woman may surprise in a symbolic context in which Emerson seems more than willing to see himself in the receiving or "feminine" role. But the explanation lies in part in the ambiguous, dual effect attributed to the "spermatic" book in Emerson's use of this kind of imagery. When things are right, such books impregnate the person at the receiving end, but they make him pregnant with a male thought which when uttered is capable of impregnating others. In other words, a "spermatic" word or book is "man-making" in the sense that the reader, by momentarily submitting and "being nothing" to it, is himself transformed into a more masculine agent. It is a matter of finding oneself by losing oneself. Significantly—and this is the most obvious reason why the process is not seen as humiliating—the great author is viewed as a mere channel through which divine Soul flows. In this sense even the master assumes a passive and "feminine" role.

The idea is elaborated in "The Problem" with immediate reference to Michelangelo (W.IX.8). With respect to authors and readers, the same thought is expressed in "Literary Ethics," where Emerson says that an able man is "nothing else than a good, free, vascular organization, whereinto the universal spirit freely flows," and that "the student . . . is great only by being passive to the superincumbent spirit" (W.I.165 and 182). The latter phrasing, by no means unusual in Emerson's works (cf. W.XII.303), reveals his debt to Plotinus, who sees Intellect as "incumbent" on the world-soul, or *anima mundi* (the third hypostasis). Plotinus also teaches that thoughts are creative powers and speaks of "spermatic words."

Perhaps because of the old tendency to view femininity as a lack of masculinity, the mystical opposition of divine masculinity and individual femininity sometimes yields to that of greater and lesser masculinity. This variation of the theme also occurs in some of Emerson's uses of the great men of the past, and notably in a free-wheeling application of the names Swift gives to two warring factions in "A Voyage to Lilliput," based upon the end at which they break their eggs (JN.XI.173):

Bigendians	Littleendians
Plato	Alcott
Swedenborg	Very
Shakespere	Newcomb
Montaigne	Channing
Goethe	RWE
Napoleon	Thoreau

The key pair here is obviously Goethe-Emerson. In spite of certain reservations, Emerson had long admired Goethe and grate-fully noted down any resemblances between his own thoughts and habits and those of this great man. Whether all of the other "Littleendians" felt a special affinity for the authors they are paired with is uncertain. On the other hand, one does note that the other "Bigendians" together with Goethe make up the full list of authors discussed in *Representative Men*. In a sense they are all Emerson's "Bigendians," as well as those of his friends. Perhaps these juxta-positions serve the purpose of fortifying him in his own determina-tion to see each of these friends as another self by associating them with a great author representing a larger cut of the "Aboriginal Soul" in which all men share and through whom they can all identify with one another in love and aspiration.

More surprisingly, Emerson is also capable of accepting the less virile end in relation to some of his live friends. This would seem to take a much greater amount of humility, but apparently he felt that the idea that "a great man is always willing to be little" (W.II.117) applies in this case, too. He was willing to go quite far in this respect. At the beginning of their acquaintance, he paradoxically describes Alcott as if he saw himself as the "Little-endian" of the man he was later to identify as the "Littleendian" of Plato. In spite of a bad cold, he says, he could see plainly that he was conversing with "the most extraordinary man and the highest genius of the time. . . . The steadiness and scope of his eye at once rebukes all before it, and we little men creep about ashamed" (JN.V.328).

Emerson's willingness to be little is linked to his theory of "conversation" in an even more striking manner in a somewhat later journal entry (JN.VII.6), in which incidentally the friend referred to is Alcott:

> I told my friend last night I could think of nothing more deeply satisfying than to be shut up in a little schooner bound on a voyage of three or four weeks with a man—an entire stranger—of a great and regular mind, of vast resources in his nature. I would not speak to him; I would not look at him . . . I would roll in my berth; so sure should I be of him, so luxuriously should I husband my joys that I should steadily hold back all the time, make no advances, leaving altogether to Fortune for hours, for days, for weeks even, the manner and degrees of intercourse. Yet what a proud peace would soothe the soul to know that . . . here close by me, was grandeur of mind, grandeur of character; that here was element wherein all I am, and more than I am yet, could bathe and dilate, that here by me was my greater self; he is me, and I am him.

This outpouring is inspired by what happened during Emerson's voyage from St. Augustine to Charleston in the company of Achille Murat, the naturalized nephew of Napoleon and son of the king of Naples, whom he met and conceived a vehement admiration for during his convalescence trip to Florida in 1827. According to the family tradition, the weather was bad, and the two actually spent a good deal of time in their berths (Murat in the upper, Emerson in the lower).[1] The impact that this experience had on Emerson is also reflected in a number of allusions to it in his works, including the last book he personally saw through the press (W.VII.12 and 219).

One might say that Emerson does not see Murat as merely the "Littleendian" of Napoleon here: At the time, meeting someone like "Prince Murat" was to him almost like meeting the emperor himself. Fairly soon, however, he was to become more particular—so particular that he was on the whole limited to living with the great in the vicarious manner described by Plutarch in "Timoleon." On one occasion, he notes somewhat condescendingly in his journal that "Women read a book to find a hero whom they can love" (JN.XIII.16), but his own browsing in Plutarch and other like-minded authors is not really that different: Strikingly often, the heroes in literature are discussed from a feminine point of view in his writings. In "The Doctrine of the Soul," for instance, he devotes a page to the personal appearances of various Greek heroes as portrayed by Helen sitting on the wall of Troy (EL.III.12). In "Character," the image of the divine man whose mere appearance "alters the face of affairs" is conveyed through the reaction of Iole on the occasion when she first saw Hercules (W.III.90).

The role played by the eye in such contexts is remarkable. Its importance is in line with the idea that the lover, like the inhabitant of heaven, is all eyes (W.II.175 and W.VI.289), but beyond that we are here dealing with the archetypal analogy between eating and love-making. Emerson speaks of the lover's way of looking at the beloved object as a kind of feeding, whether he is discussing what he calls "intellectual nomadism" or the air of heaven (W.II.23 and W.III.12). Hero worship is no different from this point of view, judging by "The Uses of Great Men." On the first page (W.IV.3), he says that those who lived with the great "found life glad and nutritious," before going on to suggest that "Life is sweet and tolerable only in our belief in such society" and that "actually or ideally, we manage to live with superiors." A few pages later, one finds the following quotation from John Sterling's "Daedalus":

> Ever their phantoms arise before us,
> Our loftier brothers, but one in blood;
> At bed and table they lord it o'er us
> With looks of beauty and words of good.

Sometimes, the incorporation of the hero's virtue by his worshiper is seen as a kind of liberation, or redemption. In "Fate," for instance, Emerson says on one hand that the eye of a hero has "the force of sunbeams," on the other that "A personal influence towers up in memory only worthy, and we gladly forget numbers, money, climate, gravitation, and the rest of Fate" (W.VI.30). Possibly he is actually thinking of some personal experience in this case, but the passage is most easily related to what he says about the influence of great men in "The Transcendentalist," based upon his reading of Landor's *Pericles and Aspasia*: "Everything admonishes us how needlessly long life is. Every moment of a hero so raises and cheers us that a twelvemonth is an age. All that the brave Xanthus brings home from his wars is the recollection that at the storming of Samos, 'in the heat of battle, Pericles smiled on me, and then passed on to another detachment'" (W.I.350).

Pictures of heroes can also be helpful. There is a journal entry —curiously evocative of the quoted lines from Sterling's "Daedalus" —in which Emerson describes how he feeds his eyes on a portrait of Washington, at the same time indulging in a veritable orgy of symbolic sexual polarization: "The head of Washington hangs in my dining-room for a few days past, and I cannot keep my eyes off of it. It has a certain Appalachian strength, as if it were truly the first-fruits of America, and expressed the Country. The heavy, leaden eyes turn on you, as the eye of an ox in a pasture. And the mouth has a gravity and depth of quiet, as if this MAN had absorbed all the serenity of America, and left none for his restless, rickety, hysterical countrymen" (JN.XIII.63).

An important variation on this theme is the comparison of a man's eyes to the effect of a waterfall, one of Emerson's favorite symbols of the Over-Soul (e.g., W.IX.369). To some extent, this image is tied to the appearance of a man whom Emerson had seen in the flesh, although they were not otherwise acquainted: Daniel Webster. At least until he came out in favor of the Fugitive Slave Bill, this statesman was a symbol of virility as well as a hero to Emerson. On one occasion, he refers to him as the only "notable" American who does not have a feminine mind (JN.IX.452). Moreover, he is especially fascinated by Webster's "great cinderous eyes" (JN.VIII.323) and speaks of the "terror" they produce in the beholder (JN.VIII.326). The terror factor is also present in a statement by Elizabeth Hoar on the subject, Emerson's approving quotation of which further underlines the essentially feminine quality of his response to Webster's eyes: "E[lizabeth] H[oar] says that she talked with him as one likes to go behind the Niagara Falls, so she tried to look into these famed caverns of eyes, and see how deep they were" (JN.VIII.361).

This journal passage should be compared with a somewhat earlier entry, which the editors of the *Journals* suggest might represent "some vision." It does seem reminiscent of the vision of Hermes described in *The Divine Pymander*. On the other hand, visionary or not, it may just as easily have been inspired by Webster, especially as rivers and cataracts are brought into the picture: "I beheld him and he turned his eyes on me, his great serious eyes. Then a current of spiritual power ran through me and I looked farther and wider than I was wont, and the visages of all men were altered and the semblances of things. And when I came out of his sight, it seemed to me as if his eyes were a great river like the Ohio or the Danube which was always pouring a torrent of strong, sad light on some men, wherever he went, and tinging [*sic*] them with the quality of his soul" (JN.VII.439; cf. J.V.537).

Emerson's abiding fascination with this theme is reflected in his use of this passage in "Character," where he says of the influence of a true master, "A river of command seemed to run down from his eyes into all those who beheld him, a torrent of strong, sad light, like an Ohio or Danube" (W.III.94). Here it is particularly easy to see the analogy with the descending river of divine power which, according to another essay, makes Emerson put himself in "the attitude of reception" (W.II.268).

Quite early Emerson defined friendship as an "idolatry" (JN. III.274). To him, as to some of his Transcendentalist friends, it became a kind of substitute religion, in terms of which the friend stood not only for the Over-Soul but for the Messiah. He is describing his own attitude when he says in "The Transcendentalist" that the friend must be an "influence" so great that "though absent he should never be out of my mind, his name never far from my lips; but if the earth should open at my side, or my last hour were coming, his name should be the prayer I should utter to the Universe" (W.I.346).

Pursuing the sexual analogy, one can say that the idea of friendship as redemption in Emerson's thought replaces the more conventional Romantic idea according to which marriage is the salvation of man through the quasi-divine intervention of a savior-wife. Not surprisingly, it was during the loneliness he experienced after the death of Ellen and his resignation from the ministry that Emerson turned in earnest to the dream of the messiah-friend, in many respects indistinguishable from his dream of the hero-friend. Judging by "Written at Rome," so different in tone from "Written at Naples," the monuments of the Eternal City gave him new hope that "the hour of heaven" would come and "the man appear." So did the letter to Carlyle which Landor presented him with in Rome.

Craigenputtock may have shown Emerson his "potential heaven" (cf. JN.V.54). On the other hand, his long and often troubled friendship with Carlyle is a good illustration of what was bound to happen whenever his acquaintance with a friend went much beyond the kind of brief commerce he had with Murat. Very soon he began to discover traits in his friend which made him wonder whether the moment of heaven had really arrived. Nor does he always seem too shaken by these frustrations. On the contrary, he is quite capable of making room for them in his theory of spiritual progress through conversation with many souls, as in a journal note echoed at the beginning of "Love": "Every promise of the soul has twenty or twenty thousand fulfilments. . . . The first friend the youth finds, he cries: 'Lo! the hour is come and the man; the promise is fulfilled.' But in a few days he finds that it was only a quasi-fulfilment, that the total inexhaustible longing is there at his heart still; and is aspiring to grander satisfactions" (JN.VII.523).

It is hard to escape the impression that Emerson is content to keep on waiting for the messiah, even if it means that a Carlyle must be reduced to another "harbinger of a greater friend" (W. II.214). But his conviction that "every hero becomes a bore at last" (W.IV.27) does not only serve to keep the fabulous dream alive: It is also a way of offsetting his own idolatrous tendencies and thus regaining his philosophical balance. It would certainly be a mistake to think that he is always content to be a "Littleendian": His willingness to be little is matched by an equally conspicuous willingness to belittle his great men. Thus, after several journal entries extolling Alcott as the most "majestic" converser (e.g., JN.VII.177), Emerson one day sits down and writes: "I shed all influences—Alcott is a tedious archangel" (JN.VII.539).

It is probably fair to say that as Emerson advanced in years and fame he increasingly enjoyed the groom's part in "the practice and consummation of friendship"; his reference to Newcomb as a rebellious "bride" in the essay on Montaigne is one example. However, he always remained ambiguous on this score, for the simple reason that while his nineteenth-century Romantic individualism required him to "insist on himself," his nineteenth-century hero-worship, fusing with his Platonism, made him seek "elevating" influences.

This ambiguity affects Emerson's "conversation" with his favorite authorities of the past as well as his relations with the contemporaries whom he chose to admire. Especially interesting are certain cases in which the language of love mingles with expressions of warlike rebelliousness and hostility. One such case can be found in "Compensation," where he says: "If I feel over-shadowed and outdone by great neighbors, I can still love; I can still receive; and he that loveth maketh his own the grandeur he loves." This sounds very much like the familiar idea of ascension through love and identification with the great. But the way in which Emerson develops the theme in this essay is rather original: "It is the eternal nature of the soul to appropriate and make all things its own. Jesus and Shakspeare are fragments of the soul, and by love I conquer and incorporate them in my own conscious domain" (W.II.124). This statement seems to point forward to the mention of the cannibalistic rites of the Sandwich Islanders a few pages later; they, too, love the virtue of the enemies they "incorporate" and illustrate the analogy between eating and loving.

Another age-old analogy worth noting in this context is the one between wrestling and love-making. In "Intellect," Emerson uses the biblical image of Jacob wrestling with God to make the point that we do not have to capitulate and abdicate the self when confronted with the influence of great authors, but that it is rather a matter of forcing them to give us what we want: "Exhaust them, wrestle with them, let them not go until their blessing be won, and after a short season the dismay will be over-past, the excess of influence withdrawn, and they will be no longer an alarming meteor, but one more bright star shining in your heaven and blending its light with all your day" (W.II.343–344).

Obviously, Emerson is here trying to achieve a kind of balance between the need for "influence" and the need for personal integrity. His most concerted effort of this kind is the theory of beautiful enemies outlined in "Friendship" with reference to conversational as well as heroic friendship. In this essay there is seemingly great stress on the need for superiority in the other party: "That great defying eye, that scornful beauty of his mien and action, do not pique yourself on reducing, but rather fortify and enhance. Worship his superiorities . . . . Guard him as thy great counterpart . . . . Let him be to thee forever a sort of beautiful enemy, untamable, devoutly revered, and not a trivial conveniency to be soon outgrown and cast aside" (E.I.175). On the other hand, this statement is manifestly addressed to both parties; Emerson demonstrates his growing awareness of the need for equality by changing "thy great counterpart" to "thy counterpart" in later editions of the *Essays* (W.II.210). A few pages earlier, there is another passage stressing reciprocity, a polarity of equals: "I am equally baulked by antagonism and by compliance . . . . I hate, where I looked for a manly furtherance or at least a manly resistance, to find a mush of concession. Better be a nettle in the side of your friend than his echo . . . . There must be very two, before there can be very one. Let it be an alliance of two large, formidable natures, mutually beheld, mutually feared, before. they recognize the deep identity which, beneath these disparities, unites them" (W.II.208–209).

The rationale for this emphasis on a polarity of equals is given at the beginning of the same paragraph: "Friendship requires that rare mean betwixt likeness and unlikeness that piques each with the presence of power and consent in the other party." Freedom, in other words, is as important as polarity and equality; in fact, the importance of the two latter ingredients of friendship is that it cannot be free without them. Significantly, the idea of a polarity of equals is not stressed in Emerson's discussions of marriage, an institution which he affects to see as a kind of bondage.

In a sense even this version of friendship, so different from the theory of conversation put forward in the essay on Swedenborg, represents a pattern transferred from the domain of sexual love. Dante uses the phrase "battaglia d'amore" (battle of love) in the *Vita Nuova,* the book translated by Emerson in the early forties; Petrarch, mentioned as an authority on true love in his essay on the subject, addresses Laura as "dolce mia guerrera" (my sweet combatant); more recently, Goethe had referred to a young woman as the "schoene Feindin" (beautiful enemy) of her lover in *Elective Affinities,* a book alluded to in "Friendship" (W.II.210) and the probable immediate source of Emerson's term.

However, it is again questionable whether he is really transferring the theme from the sphere of natural sex to that of a love raised above such considerations, or simply to the sphere of male friendship. It is certainly ironic that Margaret Fuller, who rivaled Carlyle as a promoter of Goethe in Concord, should bitterly complain in a letter that he will never agree to see her as "a large formidable nature" and a "beautiful foe."[2] This may not in itself warrant the conclusion that he was unwilling to see any woman in that role. But apart from the circumstance that the "resistance" he requires in his friend is explicitly defined as "manly," the awkwardness which dogs all attempts to use sexual love as a symbol of spiritual friendship between a man and a woman is more than usually pronounced in this case.

Significantly, the lavish use of military and agonistic imagery, which should also be noticed in this context, is largely inspired by certain essays by Montaigne ("my author"), like "De l'art de conferer" and "Consideration sur Ciceron." The difficulties Emerson must have had in finding a woman whom he could see as a beautiful enemy also becomes easier to grasp if one looks at "Etienne de la Boéce," the poem in which Montaigne's relationship with La Boétie is described in terms of a marriage consummated at the altar and yet predicated on what in "Friendship" is referred to as "manly resistance." "Shadowlike" or feminine following is specifically condemned. If he could lead the way to the altar at which we can unite with each other and the Soul of All, says the speaker in this dramatic monologue, "That were a man's and lover's part" (W.IX.82).

In "Friendship," too, Emerson can be quite lyrical in his account of the union of two friends. An exclamation like "Delicious is a just and firm encounter of two in a thought, in a feeling" is followed by this effusion: "The moment we indulge our affections, the earth is metamorphosed . . . nothing fills the proceeding eternity but the forms all radiant of beloved persons. Let the soul be assured that somewhere in the universe it should rejoin its friend, and it would be content and cheerful alone for a thousand years." But the main point, even in this essay, is that the affections must not be indulged too freely; there is a point beyond which manly love must not go. In fact, when we examine what Emerson calls "the metaphysical foundations of this Elysium," we shall soon find that this view of friendship is balanced by a stress on its paradoxical nature and the idea that, strictly speaking, even friendship is an impossibility because it absurdly implies that there can be two subjects (W.II.196–197). The reasoning is essentially the same as in "Experience," where marriage is said to be impossible even "in the spiritual world" because of "the inequality between every subject and every object" (W.III.77). The argument is based on the Plotinian idea that every individual soul sees itself not as "twin-born" but as "the only-begotten";[3] in "Friendship," he twice uses the word "first-born" in a similar sense (W.II.202 and 213). The spiritual fusion of two beautiful enemies is still possible in this perspective, but only symbolically and, as it were, in a kind of fine fantasy, in which the loneliness of the only-begotten yields to the idea of the oneness of the Soul.

At this metaphysical level, the idea of equality assumes a special importance. Each of the two beautiful enemies must be able to defend his own primogeniture, and yet the battle must paradoxically end in a draw—otherwise the outcome would only demonstrate "the inequality of each subject and each object," and no bipolaric union would be possible. Perhaps the nicest illustration of this part of Emerson's theory is one of the notes he took for the composition of "Friendship," in which he quotes a few lines from Book Seven of Pope's translation of the *Iliad* as proof both of the general principle that "extremes meet" and of the specific proposition that "the sublime of War in the Iliad meets the doctrine of *one mind*" (JN.VII.162). The lines in question are the ones in which Hector tells Ajax, at the end of the single combat that ended in a draw, that they should:

> Exchange some gift that Greece and Troy may say
> Not hate but glory made these Chiefs contend
> And each brave foe was in his heart a friend.

Such passages also help us see why Emerson, unlike the less metaphysical Montaigne, feels that he must prove equal to *every* conversational challenge. He senses that his birthright is always at stake and that he might be shaken in his conviction that he is the only-begotten, if proved "unequal" even in one combat (W.II.200). He himself suggests as much by quoting sonnet no. 25 by Shakespeare (rather out of context):

> The valiant warrior famoused for fight,

> After a hundred victories, once foiled,
> Is from the book of honor razed quite
> And all the rest forgot for which he toiled.

Perhaps it is for this reason that Emerson found the theory of beautiful enemyship so difficult to apply in practice: A clear victory is obviously easier to determine and more reassuring than a tie from this point of view. Significantly, it did not help if the other party was as "military" and willing to defend his birthright as Emerson felt Thoreau was (JN.XIII.183). The more determined his younger friend was to be a "nettle" in Emerson's side, the more determined the latter became to consider him his "echo." The result, as Emerson himself sometimes suggests with some bitterness in his journal, was altercation for altercation's sake, tension without fusion.

Such experiences could only confirm Emerson's feeling that there was a deplorable gap between theory and practice. As early as "Friendship," he had noted that "Friends such as we desire are dreams and fables" (W.II.213). On the other hand, he saw no reason why he should not enjoy the dream of a beautiful enemy, just as he enjoyed the dream of the messiah-friend. Apparently it never faded. In 1859, for instance, he seems to have indulged it while taking a hot bath, thus making it a kind of "influence": "The bath, the cutaneous sublime, the extremes meet, the bittersweet, the pail of pleasure and of pain," he exclaims in his journal: "O, if an enemy had done this!" (JN.XIV.338).

Another entry from 1859, which occurs a few pages earlier (JN.XIV.331), involves John Brown, who was tried and hanged that year. This entry went into an essay called "Courage," published in 1870 (W.VII.271), which may serve as final proof that Emerson never gave up on the dream of beautiful enemyship and enjoyed this sentiment vicariously until the end of his writing career:

> The true temper has genial influences. It makes a bond of union between enemies. . . . If Governor Wise is a superior man, or inasmuch as he is a superior man, he distinguishes John Brown. As they confer, they understand each other swiftly; each respects the other. If opportunity allowed, they would prefer each other's society and desert their former companions. Enemies would become affec-

tionate. Hector and Achilles, Richard and Saladin, Wellington and Soult, General Daumas and Abdel-Kader, become aware that they are nearer and more alike than any other two, and, if their nation and circumstance did not keep them apart, would run into each other's arms.

11

ANDROGYNOUS COMPLETENESS: THE MENTAL CONSTITUTION OF EMERSON'S GREAT MAN

In the spring of 1843 Emerson participated in a conversation during which it was argued that Hermaphroditus is "the symbol of the finished soul" and that "The finest people marry the two sexes in their own person" (JN.VIII.380). There is reason to believe that this was not the only discussion of its kind in Concord in the early forties. The interest in androgyny had been flourishing there for some time, and it had certainly been stimulated by Alcott's return from England in 1842 with many books in his luggage, including a pamphlet on "internal marriage" mentioned by Emerson in "English Reformers" (UW.85). Alcott says in his journal that he does not like men who do not remind him "of the graces proper to women" and explains that "the best of Emerson's intellect" is due to the presence in him of the feminine element.[1] Another Middlesex philosopher, young Henry Thoreau, also reveals his fascination with this subject in the journal he was keeping at the time.[2] Last but not least, there was Margaret Fuller, Emerson's collaborator on the *Dial* at this very time; she has much to say about androgyny in an article in that magazine which later went into *Woman in the Nineteenth Century*.[3]

The New England discussion of androgyny was of course predicated on a similar debate that had been going on in Europe for some time and which Margaret Fuller was probably instrumental in bringing to Emerson's attention. It was she who persuaded him to read Balzac's Swedenborgian novels, *Louis Lambert* and *Séraphita,* which have androgynous heroes (L.II.246 and JN.-VII.336). Since her book includes a reference to the Saint-Simonians, who tended to see Swedenborg's hemaphroditic angel as the model of human perfection, she may also have refreshed his memory of this Utopian group; there is a note about Saint-Simon in the journal for 1843 (JN.VIII.329–330), and his ideas are alluded to in "New England Reformers" (1844). Above all, Fuller reinforced the impulse to read Goethe and the other German Romantics which Emerson had already received through his intellectual commerce with Carlyle. This is significant because to many of them—besides Goethe one may mention Baader, whom Emerson knew through Schelling (JN.IX.360)—the association of human completeness with androgyny is almost axiomatic.

It also appears that Emerson at this time was developing a new familiarity with some of the main figures in the long syncretic tradition on which the German Romantics in their turn drew in their speculation concerning the redemption of mankind through the reintegration of the sexes. His acquisition and subsequent study of the copy of *Hermes Trismegistus: The Divine Pymander* that Alcott brought home from England is worth noting from this point of view.[4] Among modern authorities, he seems to have rediscovered Boehme, whom he read in the translation by William Law, himself the acme of the alchemic-hermetic tradition in England. Swedenborg, who to some extent drew on Boehme, is also much more interesting to him during this period than he had been in the previous decade.

Emerson's reading of such texts at this time must have reinforced his awareness of the tradition according to which the first stage of the Fall of Man was the fall from divine androgyny. Since Hermes is the lengendary father of alchemy, this reading also brought a reminder of the fact that to the more metaphysically inclined alchemists the search for the Philosophers' Stone, the hermaphroditic *rebis,* was not predicated on a thirst for gold but on a longing for a redeemer capable of restoring the golden age of man—that is, his original, angelic state. This idea, both in Emerson's mind and in intellectual history, came to be closely related to the myth of the original angelic Adam, the "Adam Kadmon" of the cabalists, who in the writings of Paul becomes "the new Adam."

In order fully to appreciate how massive Emerson's indoctrination on this score actually was, one should remember that Plato himself tends to see man's sexual differentiation as a sign of decadence in the *Timaeus* and in a sense provides for his restoration to his "first and best state" in *The Republic*. The members of the highest class in this society, the guardians, are described as androgynous persons uniting the tenderness of women with male toughness.

Plato's *Republic* also illustrates a certain ambiguity in most of the related doctrines that associate androgyny and human perfection, including Emerson's. Theoretically, some women are supposed to qualify as guardians of the Ideal State, but they will obviously be relatively few, since Socrates and his friends agree that their abilities, while not essentially different so far as the administration of the State is concerned, are nevertheless not equal to those of men. Plato's vindication of women in this work is clearly a matter of logic rather than a genuine commitment to an idea of female androgyny of the kind that some Romantic updaters of his theory try to attribute to him. The heavenly equivalents of his guardians—the angels—are definitely androgynous on a male basis; they all have male names. So, of course, does Adam Kadmon, and we consequently should not be too surprised to find Augustine, who was influenced by Platonism as well as by the Judeo-Christian tradition, underlining in *The City of God* that hermaphrodites are always thought of as male and that it would be absurd to think differently.

Biological hermaphroditism does not otherwise have much to do with the angelic ideal, or with the human completeness of creative genius; it is usually looked upon as a symbol of decadence and sterility. Sometimes, however, the two conceptions of androgyny are confused. One example is the late Romantic period, which Mario Praz discusses from this point of view in *The Romantic Agony*.[5] A certain apprehensiveness on this account is noticeable in some of the early Romantics. Coleridge, for instance, pointedly says in a "table-talk" alluded to by Emerson (EL.III.80) that "something feminine—not effeminate, mind—is discernible in all men of genius."

Thus we should keep this distinction in mind in dealing with the fact that Emerson not only shares the conviction of many of his contemporaries that the androgyny of genius is reserved for men but believes that it is reflected in the physical features of great men. Femininity is a good thing when he states that Raphael "confronts us with the visage of a girl" as well as with "the easy audacity of a creator" (JN.IX.395), or says that he sees the face of Leonardo in his Medora (JN.IX.578). It is a good thing when he says of Horatio Greenough, an artist whom he personally knew, that he was so handsome that he ought to be pardoned if, as alleged, the face of *his* Medora and that of his Achilles were "idealizations of his own" (W.V.5).

All the men of genius whom Emerson characterizes in these terms are not artists; public speakers and preachers are judged in the same light: In Edward Taylor, for instance, he was fascinated by what he saw as an almost godlike power, which made everybody "willing to be nothing in his presence," but even more by the fact that he nevertheless "becomes whilst he talks a gentle, a lovely creature" (JN.VII.359–360). By contrast, he says about Garrison, a philanthropist whom he rather disliked, that he is a "virile speaker; he lacks the feminine element which we find in men of genius" (JN.IX.267).

On other occasions, Emerson is more specific with respect to the nature of the feminine element which he thinks is indispensable to genius. In another comment on the power of the great public speaker, he compares this potentate to "an Emperor," who "in his robes is dressed almost in feminine attire, because the supreme power represents woman as well as man, the moral as well as the intellectual principle" (JN.IX.21). Here we already glimpse the Romantic-Victorian conception of the wife as the ruler and moral supervisor of her husband later elaborated by Ruskin. This high estimate of woman's influence is even more striking in Emerson's description of the poet, to him the moral teacher of mankind par excellence: "When a man writes poetry," he says in one instance, "he appears to assume the high feminine part of his nature," and we consequently clothe him "in robes and garlands, which are proper to woman" (JN.VIII.356).

Emerson himself probably related this part of the poet's nature to the allegedly sibylline and oracular quality in woman which, he suggests, was appreciated even in societies in which she was otherwise held in relatively little esteem (W.XI.414). The poet, like the sibyl, is supposed to utter words which he does not understand under the influence of a higher intelligence. The difference, of course, is that a sibyl like, say, Pythia, is not usually considered a genius; she is a mere instrument of divine communication. Significantly, Emerson prefers the image of "the passive Master" (W.IX.8) as soon as the creativity of genius is stressed rather than its moral authority: This image is much less flattering to the feminine principle, since it so clearly puts the "spermatic" effect of the Over-Soul and heaven above feminine and earthly receptivity. Moreover, this role dichotomy in itself makes it awkward to apply the image to women of genius even if one believes in their existence.

Emerson's tendency to see genius as a masculine attribute also transpires in some of the alchemic variations on this theme. For instance, he says with reference to the conceit according to which the Over-Soul is equated with light (the sun): "The truth is in the air, and the most impressionable brain will announce it first, but all will announce it a few minutes later. So women, as most susceptible, are the best index of the coming hour. So the great man, that is, the man most imbued with the spirit of the time, is the impressionable man;—of a fibre irritable and delicate, like iodine to light" (W.VI.44). It is easy to see that it is great men, not great men and women, who are compared to women.

A very similar pattern is discernible when Emerson bases his discussion on the idea that the eye is the main organ of the man of genius in his capacity as "the photometer" (cf. W.II.166). Such a man, a man like himself, has "more womanly eyes" than other men (W.VIII.289). In his journal the theme is elaborated in this way: "Women see better than men. Men see lazily if they do not expect to act. Women see quite without any wish to act. Men of genius are said to partake of the masculine and feminine traits. They have this feminine eye, a function so rich that it contents itself without asking any aid of the hand" (JN.VII.310). Here it is stated fairly clearly that women, in spite, or rather because of the rich function of their eye, do not wish to act, i.e., are not creative geniuses; on the other hand, it is obviously not implied that men of genius do not ask the aid of their hand because they have this eye: Passivity of that kind is attributed to men who do not have feminine eyes—that is, to uninspired men.

What we have in Emerson's conception of the androgyny of genius, when the Romantic-Victorian idea of woman's moral superiority is not intruded, is thus plainly an upgrading of qualities which are often referred to in a derogatory manner when attributed to women and men devoid of genius. This is true not only of feminine receptivity but also of the affections which he so often associates with the feminine principle. In fact, a certain contempt for the emotions and woman shines through when he says of Goethe—a genius of whom he was somewhat distrustful—that his affections help him "like women employed by Cicero to worm out the secrets of conspirators" (W.IV.285).

Both receptivity and an affectionate disposition are also prominent features in another conception of male androgyny which is important to Emerson—that of the hero-gentleman. The greatness of this type of man expresses itself largely through action, but the difference between Emerson's hero-gentleman and his poet must not be exaggerated. He felt very strongly that "words are also actions" (W.III.8) in the case of the poet as well as that of the public speaker. Conversely, the hero is also a "passive master," a channel through which "heaven flows to earth" (W.I.210). Indeed, he is often seen as a man of genius: Emerson is hardly interested in any other kind.

Among moderns, Napoleon stands out among a number of men whom Emerson admired because they were men of genius as well as men of action. The fact that the emperor of the French was also an author of sorts further enhanced his status in Emerson's eyes. In spite of certain reservations concerning Napoleon's character, he voraciously read the *Mémorial de Sainte-Hélène,* along with any biographical materials he could lay hands on. Among the many sayings of this representative man, he quotes the following one in "Inspiration": "I am like a woman with child" (W. VIII.279).

The books about Napoleon which Emerson read can be seen as a kind of supplement to the *Lives* of Plutarch, where he could find so many men uniting heroism and genius. Not a few of these are also portrayed as men-women; Emerson was particularly impressed with Phocion and Epaminondas (e.g., W.II.260 and 257). One also notes that Plutarch himself is sometimes implicitly or explicitly seen as a man-woman in Emerson's works: His affinity for genius earns him the title of poet, and as for personal heroism, Emerson describes him in the Preface to the *Morals* as a stern Stoic "in his fight with Fortune, with vices, with effeminacy and indolence," and yet "gentle as a woman when other strings are touched" (W.X.315).

Emerson stops just short of describing Plutarch as a "gentleman" in the sense in which this word is used in "Manners": "manhood first, and then gentleness" (W.III.123). On the other hand, several Plutarchan heroes figure in "Manners" as examples of this combination, also referred to as "personal force and love"; Pericles, Epaminondas, Alexander, and Julius Caesar are mentioned along with Sir Philip Sidney, the poet-soldier who himself seems so interested in the theory of a "womanly man."[6]

The stress on androgyny is even more insistent in the portrayal of the English aristocracy delivered in *English Traits*. To some extent, this trait is there said to characterize the whole race. Emerson notes in one instance that it is reflected even in their composite language, in which "the male principle is the Saxon; the female, the Latin" (W.V.234–235). In another he suggests that "England is tender-hearted. Rome was not" (W.V.299): He finds gentle ruffians as far back as Robin Hood, "mitissimus praedonum" (W.V.68). But his main interest attaches to the military heroes of the days when the empire was won and defended. In "Race," where we are also told that "the two sexes are co-present in the English mind" (that is, in the male English mind), men like Lord Nelson, Admiral Rodney, and the Duke of Buckingham are described as "women in kindness" in their dealings with their friends and families and yet marked by "the most terrible determination" when confronted with enemies at home or abroad. The "Greek legend of *Hermaphrodite*" is explicitly invoked in this context (W.V. 67–68).

Among fictional hero-gentlemen who appealed to Emerson's imagination, one notes Hamlet. That he saw the prince of Denmark as a worthy representative of his race from this point of view can be gathered from the journal comment on his discourse in his mother's bedroom: It is "terrible," says Emerson, and yet that of an "inborn gentleman" (JN.VII.141). Emerson's perception of the gentler side of the prince transpires in his suggestion that Sidney "probably sat for the portrait of Hamlet in Ophelia's lament for his madness" (EL.I.306). In this context Ophelia dwells on the sweetness which she feels normally characterizes her betrothed, on the fact that he is a scholar and courtier as well as a soldier.

Not least in view of Emerson's strong tendency to identify with Hamlet and his creator ("gentle Will"), one may wonder to what extent he attributed this kind of spiritual completeness to himself. Sherman Paul says on this score that "he knew he was only the feminine half—the passive, receptive observer," and links this alleged one-sidedness to Emerson's need for friendship.[7] Undoubtedly, some evidence can be adduced in support of this view, which makes androgyny a matter of aspiration rather than a reality in his case. For instance, he once complains that although he is able to take in a scene through the eye and enjoy it as much as he would enjoy a picture, he does not have the hand that would enable him to paint it (JN.VII.440–441). He is slightly less humble with respect to his own poetic ability (L.I.435).

As for the other part of Paul's remark, one is again inclined to say that he is right, up to a point. Not only does Emerson form ties of friendship with men more frequently than with women (a trait not so remarkable in itself, especially in the Victorian age); he himself sometimes seems to relate his befriending of other men to his own insufficient strength and virility. During his second visit to England, he sent Elizabeth Hoar a letter in which he speaks of his "muscular neighbors" and wishes he had been "born in England, with but one chip of English oak in *my* willowy constitution," before going on to speak about his relations with "some friendly young gentlemen in different parts of Britain" (L.III.459–460). There is also the poem in which "Saadi"—that is, his poetic alter ego—grovels before the superior masculinity of "Hassan," in real life his sturdy neighbor Edmund Hosmer (W.IX.323 and JN.VIII. 238). On the other hand, Emerson was definitely also capable of finding pleasure in the company of female friends—Elizabeth Hoar is one example—and in some of his friendships with men he clearly cast himself in the male role, as, for instance, when he once refers to Charles Newcomb as his conversational "bride" (W.IV.174).

Emerson's most explicit statement of the idea that he felt the attraction of persons of both sexes because his own makeup was complex and androgynous—and thus by no means predominantly and onesidedly "feminine"—is the "Ode to Beauty," a dramatic monologue of the kind that very appropriately has been called "the poetry of experience."[8] Using an archetypal opposition of natural phenomena as an image of the sexual dichotomy, he here suggests that he is attracted by both men and women if they are in any way representative of true beauty:

> The sun and sea
> Informed by thee,
> Before me run
> And draw me on . . . .

In asking himself why he feels that way, Emerson varies one of the symbols, but the meaning is unmistakable:

> Is it that my opulent soul
> Was mingled from the generous whole;
> Sea-valleys and the deep of skies
> Furnished several supplies;
> And the sands whereof I'm made
> Draw me to them, self-betrayed?

Personal as this theory is, it also fits the image of Apollo, the androgynous god who is one of the chief symbols of Emerson's ideal world. Apollo is "ambidextrous," to borrow a word from Plutarch's dialogue on love; he is as easily attracted by male beauty as by female. This coincidence allows us to wonder to what extent Emerson's practice actually followed his theory, and to what extent he is only painting an ideal self-portrait in "Ode to Beauty."

The problem is complicated by the fact that man or woman is a false alternative in terms of another image of the ideal (and of ideal love) that is dear to Emerson: the angel. Milton may say that angels can change sex at will—something that would make them practically ambidextrous—but usually they are considered androgynous in a simpler fashion, and Emerson in particular associates them with a pure affinity-based love in which one androgynous individual knows another. In his discussions of these matters, the question of androgyny does not necessarily come up in an explicit manner; in fact, angelic love is more likely to be depicted as suprasexual. Nevertheless, the idea of androgyny is part of his doctrine of angelic love, and the theme surfaces in various ways in his writings. Thus Charles Newcomb is in one journal entry recognized as an angelic lover, in another portrayed as a person who combines the face of a girl with the aplomb of a general (JN.IX.222 and JN.XI.265). The military reference ties the suggestion to Emerson's ideas about heroic androgyny, but he also thought of Newcomb as something of a genius. Another interesting example is his view of Henry James (the elder). Emerson could feel oppressed by "the excessive virility" of people with whom he had to rub shoulders in the hotels where he had to stay during his lecturing trips, and on at least one occasion the womanly qualities which he perceived in James, along with his "heroic manners," meant "true comfort" to him (JN.XI.248).

Exactly what kind of "lover" Emerson actually was is a question which fortunately does not have to be settled here. Be it noted, however, that James does not judge him as favorably as Alcott does from this point of view and on the whole seems less gratified by the companionship than his visitor. In some comments published in *The Literary Remains,* he calls Emerson an "unsexed woman" and a "Boston belle," and recalls the frustration he experienced in trying to establish a fruitful intellectual relationship with him: Once he even pursued Emerson into his bedroom to have conversation with him concerning man's regeneration—all in vain.[9] A letter to Cabot expresses similar misgivings concerning Emerson's intellectual ability, linking them to his personal appearance: "On the whole, I may say that at first I was greatly disappointed in him, because his intellect never kept the promise which his lovely face and manners held out to me." Nor does James' opinion seem to have changed much over the years; a later letter to Cabot sounds equally bitter as he characterizes the friendship Emerson had to offer as somewhat "prim and bloodless": "I remember well what maidenly letters I used to receive from him, with so many tentative charms of expression in them that if he had been a woman one would have delighted in complimenting him; but, as it was, you could say nothing about them, but only pocket the disappointment they brought."[10]

Possibly this view of Emerson is to some extent based on a misunderstanding: James may not have been fully aware of the tendency to "tender" himself least to the person to whom he was most devoted, to which Emerson confesses in "Friendship" (W.II.-204–205), and which he there sees as a manly trait in himself. On the other hand, Emerson may not have had an entirely correct idea of the impression that this tendency might make on at least some of the persons to whom he showed his devotion in this way. In a journal entry in which he also speaks of the strongly emotional side of himself which makes this precaution necessary in the first place, he says that "Rob" (one of his personal pseudonyms) "was tender and timid as a fawn in his affections" and "assumed coldness only to hide his *woman's heart*"—succeeding so well that he "passed for a man of calculation and cold heart" (JN.VII.321).

This aspect of Emerson's theory and practice is important because it reconciles the apparent contradiction between the emotional intensity that sometimes characterizes his discussions of friendship and the rejection of the gestures of affection that goes with his vindications of the universal and impersonal nature of angelic love. In the latter phase of his theory, the mark of human completeness is not so much the ability to enjoy the company of individuals of either sex as a knack of being on friendly terms with everybody in a detached and self-sufficient way. The complete, androgynous man is only close to himself.

It is in this vein that Emerson in the Preface to the *Gulistan* calls Saadi the poet of "serenity" and "self-devotion" as well as of friendship and love (G.vii). In "Saadi," where the idea of universal love and friendship is stressed, along with emotional ambidexterity, the essential solitude of the great and creative soul is associated with bachelorhood: "Two touch the string, / The harp is dumb." This obviously has to do with the fact that Emerson, while favoring friendly "angelic" relations with individuals of both sexes, was suspicious of the "passions" which may lead two individuals to mutual dependence and to a literal form of marriage opposed to the spiritual fertility of the androgynous mind. While still at college, he had copied into his notebook as food for thought the lines in which Hamlet, after rebuking two passionate women (his mother and Ophelia), declares his love for Horatio in these terms: "Give me that man / Who is not passion's slave, and I will wear him / In my heart, aye in my heart of heart" (JN.I.193). This sums up the paradox of Emerson's own position quite well, and one is not surprised to find that Hamlet, like Saadi, always remained one of his representatives of angelic and self-sufficient love.[11]

The circumstance that Emerson considered women particularly subject to "passion" could not but affect his view of their eligibility for angelic friendship of the kind that inspires his poet. At the same time, however, it is clear that he found it convenient to stress the angelic character of his relations with women like Elizabeth Hoar and Margaret Fuller. The complications which such friendships as well as his marriage to Lidian caused him in the early forties are reflected in a journal note from that time: "A highly endowed man with good intellect and good conscience is a Man-woman and does not so much need the complement of Woman to his being, as another. Hence his relations to the sex are somewhat dislocated and unsatisfactory. He asks in Woman, sometimes the Woman, sometimes the Man" (JN.VIII.175).

Perhaps this statement does not in itself warrant the conclusion that Emerson did not believe in the existence of "highly endowed" women-men who do not need husbands to complement their being. However, other passages suggest that he saw women as essentially dependent on men for personal fulfillment. There is no indication that he is castigating the society of his time rather than referring to a natural state of things when he notes in his journal that his "paths" are not open to women and tells himself that he must not insist on "this self sufficiency of man" in conversation with ladies since it is inflicting "an unnecessary wound"— after all, there is something tragic even about the finest and most cultivated women "who have not been wives" (JN.V.410). The implication clearly is that few if any women have enough genius and androgynous completeness to make them sufficient to themselves and at the same time sufficiently creative in the spiritual sphere to forgo the biological offspring which comes with marriage.

It is not that Emerson never saw "un uomo in una donna" (a man in a woman). But unlike Michelangelo, he never did so in a positive sense, apart from a rather late discussion of "sex of mind" suggesting that some women can be creative and have masculine minds, just as uncreative men have feminine minds (W.VI.58). Even in this one case, it is implied that creativeness is a rare thing in women, and there is no suggestion that a woman's mind could be manly enough to render her as self-sufficient as a man of genius, let alone that a manly mind would make her a more attractive candidate for the celestial society of friendship. On the whole, any hint of manliness in a woman is likely to turn Emerson off rather than on. A good example is the journal report on the conversation during which it was said that "The finest people marry the two sexes in their own person": It reflects a dislike of women who presume to add a "masculine" element to their basic femininity. Far from praising them for aspiring to androgyny, he tends to view them as a kind of transvestite: "Much poor talk concerning woman which at least had the effect of revealing the true sex of several of the party who usually go disguised in the form of the other sex. Thus Mrs. B. is a man." Neither men nor viragos of this type—Emerson specifically mentions Harriet Martineau, "a masculine woman"—have a right to tell woman what her duties are; they will simply end up "describing a man in female attire." As for men, they should remember that "Women only can tell the heights of feminine nature," and that the only thing they can do for her, "whenever she speaks from herself and catches him in inspired moments up to a heaven of honor and religion," is "to hold her to that point by reverential recognition of the divinity that speaks through her" (JN.VIII.380–381).

There is something touching about the passages in which Emerson adheres to the Romantic-Victorian notions about the sibylline and morally inspiring nature of woman in this context, in spite of the condescending tone he is not quite able to suppress. Possibly he felt that, while a feminine element can be added to a basically masculine constitution with beneficial effects, the masculine element is too strong and dominant to be integrated into a feminine system in anything like a balanced manner and without dire damage to "true womanhood." If he saw the notion of feminine androgyny and the feminism he associates with it as a threat to man's role in the world as well as to femininity, he certainly conceals it well. The condescension and mild boredom which characterizes his journal note concerning his first meeting with Harriet Martineau seems entirely unfeigned: In conversing with her, he was impressed with "her speedy limits," and, he says, "What pleased me most of her communications was that W. J. Fox though of no nerve, timid as a woman, yet had the greatest moral courage, as

Charles said at my commentary, 'Go and be hanged but blush if spoken to on the tumbril' " (JN.V.86–87).

However, the best way to show Emerson's position on this issue is probably to examine his view of Margaret Fuller: If his relations with her were indeed "somewhat dislocated and unsatisfactory," this definitely has something to do with her ideal of feminine androgyny and her desire to incarnate it. Emerson was familiar with both even before she expressed them in the *Dial* article and in *Woman in the Nineteenth Century*. He clearly disapproves of her theory and takes a dim view of her personal claim to man-womanhood. In fact, it is easy to see that this yearning for a share of manhood is what he in retrospect likes least about his dead friend.

This attitude does not necessarily reflect a lack of generosity on Emerson's part. No doubt he was honestly convinced that Fuller's actual achievement was not on a par with her ambition, and it is hard to fault him on that score. Nor is there any reason to doubt that he was genuinely disappointed, in going over her papers in preparation for the memoir he had agreed to write, to find that she had hardly been more self-sufficient than most women he knew and had been hankering for a husband and a marriage all along (JN.XI.500). But one is struck by the insistence with which he links her failure to do the work of genius to her failure to achieve androgynous self-sufficiency, while at the same time implicitly criticizing her for trying to be more than a woman. On the one hand, he deplores her failure to establish a truly angelic personality; on the other hand, he seems to deplore her gestures in that direction as an attack on nature and true womanhood.

In his memoir, Emerson's double disappointment with Fuller is expressed in such a manner as to suggest that he consciously or unconsciously is trying to justify his own treatment of her to himself and the world by arguing that while she reached out for the androgyny of genius she only achieved mediocrity and—abnormality. At one level he does this by speaking about her interest in the love of the angels ("Sie fragen nicht nach Mann und Weib") in one place, while showing her essentially womanly and passionate nature in other places. To illustrate the latter aspect of Fuller, he quotes from a letter addressed to himself in which she complains that at a certain point in her life he appeared to her like an oasis, a fresh spring and a palm in the desert, but that as she approached she realized only too well that it was just a mirage (M.I.289–291). Such language is not only incompatible with Emerson's ideas of angelic love but also with his alternate theory of "intellectual nomadism." Even more significant are his suggestions that Fuller could also be passionate in her relations with women. Not only does he bring up her tendency to compare her own feelings for Anna Barker to Madame de Staël's love for Madame de Récamier (M.I. 283–284); he compares her to Sappho (M.I.228). In reporting that she kept a school for young women in Boston, he adds that her relations with her students were not "unmingled with passion" (M.I.281).

In this context Emerson also notes that any one of the sixteen-year-olds in her class would have been happy to marry Fuller had she been a man, and this statement—extraordinary in its implications if one thinks about it—suggests a very real problem that Emerson felt Fuller had and which he also found rather morbid: her wishing that she had been born a man, or, failing that, that she could play the role of a man as well as that of a woman. So far as he could see, her passionate nature and lack of proper restraint prevented her from achieving more than an inferior kind of hermaphroditism. Although he apparently approves of Milton's idea of angelic sex changes, he says that she found "something of true portraiture in a disagreeable novel of Balzac's, *Le Livre Mystique* [Louis Lambert and/or Séraphita], in which an equivocal figure exerts alternately a masculine and a feminine influence on the characters of the plot" (M.I.229). He also suggests that Fuller worried a great deal about her sexual status and that she in this context was not exempt from a touch of dark Thessalian superstition. Noting that carbuncles are male and female, she is supposed to have observed with a certain satisfaction, "Mine is the male" (M.I.219). Emerson even quotes the following lines from a poem by Fuller "To the Moon" (M.I.229):

> But if I steadfast gaze upon thy face,
> A human secret, like my own, I trace;
> For through the woman's smile looks the male eye.

At one point Emerson quotes a friend who held that "Margaret was, of all she had beheld, the largest woman, and not a woman who wished to be a man" (M.I.300). But this comes as a rather weak *démenti* at the end of a longish account of her obsessive fears concerning the value of her own achievements. At an earlier point, she is said to have despised herself and other women as lacking true genius: "She had a feeling that she ought to have been a man, and said of herself, 'A man's ambition with a woman's heart, is an evil lot' " (M.I.229). Emerson suggests that she looked upon George Sand as another would-be man who tragically failed. The Frenchwoman "has genius, and a manly grasp of the mind, but not a manly heart." Hence she is only capable of shallow remarks *"à la mode du genre féminin"* (M.I.250).

Such statements do indicate that Fuller was sometimes shaken in her conviction that "man and woman share an angelic ministry," which in terms of Swedenborg's doctrine of heavenly love means that the "heart" contributed by woman is as important as the "head" of man.[12] On the other hand, Emerson may be guilty of unconsciously editing her sayings with respect to Sand. Fuller does express disappointment with Sand in certain notes on her to which he apparently had access, but her reaction to this feminist writer— one of the first European women to smoke and wear men's pants— is rather complex and by no means always negative. She also quotes approvingly the words with which Elizabeth Barrett (later Mrs. Browning) hails the author of *Consuelo:* "Thou large-brained woman and large-hearted man / Self-called George Sand."[13] This certainly vindicates both woman's heart and the androgynous genius of Sand.

Among other statements by Fuller that Emerson fails to quote in his memoir is a passage in *Woman in the Nineteenth Century* in which she says that it is humiliating and self-defeating for members of her sex to try to be like men, and that women, if they were "free," would develop the "strength and beauty of Woman" and "never wish to be men, or manlike."[14] This statement does not necessarily contradict Fuller's ideas about feminine androgyny; rather, it suggests that true womanhood is a type of androgyny that is different from male androgyny. Significantly, she dwells on how impressed she was with Sand's womanhood in a later account of their meeting in Paris.[15] The more developed feminine personality that she hoped to see realized in the future is also suggested by her fascination with the women portrayed by Goethe in *Wilhelm*

Meister and specifically with the fact that Mignon and Theresa "wear male attire when they want."[16]

The "advanced" attitudes and mores of the women in *Wilhelm Meister* have been noticed by many: Ronald D. Gray sees them as the fruit of Goethe's alchemic speculation.[17] It is therefore worth noting that Emerson expresses such a negative view of this book in a *Dial* article of his own (W.XII.330–333) and is especially critical with respect to the men and women with whom it is filled. They are definitely not at all reminiscent of the angelic society that he dreamed about, and from this point of view, too, one can understand that he felt that Goethe had failed to become "the Redeemer of the human mind."

Emerson also draws on alchemic thought in a portrait of an admirable woman worked in at the end of the essay called "Spiritual Laws." But it is rather different from the Goethean updating of the old alchemic blueprint for man's redemption adopted by Fuller. Nor does Emerson's adaptation of a theme he found in Herbert's "The Elixir" (cf. EL.I.352) seem to admit the possibility that woman might not be free to develop her own human personality: "Let the great soul incarnated in some woman's form, poor and sad and single, in some Dolly or Joan, go out to service and sweep chambers and scour floors, and its effulgent day-beams cannot be muffled or hid, but to sweep and scour will instantly appear supreme and beautiful actions, the top and radiance of human life, and all people will get mops and brooms" (W.II.165–166).

12

METAPHYSICAL NARCISSISM: EMERSON ON MAN'S DIVINE SOLITUDE

Emerson never felt that he had been completely and lastingly successful in the search for a literary "redeemer of the human mind" to which he proceeded after abandoning his more literal expectation of a new heaven and a new earth. What he was looking for was apparently not furnished by the most impressive statements of philosophical idealism, modern or ancient: "Where is the New Metaphysics?" he asks in a late journal entry, noting that "the Kant or the Plato of the Inner World, which is Heaven, has not come" (JN.XI.438–439). On the other hand, his own writing over the years can in a large measure be seen as an effort to fill this gap; although his hostility to systematic exposition tends to obscure it, his thinking follows a definite pattern when examined from this point of view.

One of the directions of Emerson's long quest for a purely subjective mode of redemption is suggested by a fairly early journal note paraphrasing Thomas Brown's *Lectures on the Philosophy of the Human Mind:* "In every metaphysical enquiry the mind itself is the subject of analysis, the instrument of analysis, and the operator of the analysis" (JN.VI.185–186). The idea of the mind's knowledge and possession of itself is here put in as neutral terms as possible, but the sexual connotations are very clear in Horatio Greenough's characterization of Emerson's contemplative activities as "the masturbation of the brain," which the latter found piquant enough to repeatedly quote in his journals and notebooks (JN. XIII.84 and JN.XIV.204).

A more fruitful approach, perhaps, in discussing this particular aspect of Emerson's thought is to view it as metaphysical narcissism, as he himself sometimes does. The story of Narcissus, as told by Ovid, is closely related to the Hermaphroditus theme which plays such a large role in Emerson's "heaven of intellect" (JN.XIV.114). The young man absorbed in the contemplation of his own beautiful image does not know whether he is the lover or the beloved; he unites subject and object, active and passive, the roles of male and female. Like Emerson's androgynous man of genius, he is therefore essentially self-sufficient and solitary; he takes a dim view of passionate, erotic involvement with others, men or women. However, his rejection of otherness is obviously more consistent, more radical. Moreover—and this is the main difference between the two images—Narcissus is not a symbol of the "heaven of invention." He is made for contemplation alone.

Although familiar with Ovid's story, Emerson is of course also inspired by more philosophical discussions of the problems upon which it touches. Plotinus in particular seems to have been able to provide some useful hints: He specifically uses the word "otherness" to designate everything that is to be "shed"—that is, everything that has to do with the earth, the body, the person. Love, in the Plotinian view, is only the internal power by means of which the aspiring soul turns inward upon itself. In the ecstasy, it does reach its "very self," and the seer becomes indistinguishable from the seen: It is purely a matter of contemplation, of the eye, and having attained to that state even once, the soul must necessarily despise all other loves, no matter how fair it had previously thought them; they have served their dialectical purpose.

It is this kind of doctrine which explains the emphasis on self in Emerson's essay "Love" with its ultimately Plotinian message, including the seemingly commonsensical statement that the greatest benefit which love confers upon the lover is that it "gives him to himself" (W.II.177). In the companion essay "Friendship," we are told that friends must be seen as other selves, and that this is the reason why some persons are known to have exchanged names with their friends—to signify "that in their friend each loved his own

soul" (W.II.212). As for the tension between love of self and love
of others, which subsists even when others are loved as symbols of
one's ideal self, it is faithfully echoed not only in "Love" and
"Friendship" but in a number of other essays as well. Toward the
end of "The Over-Soul," for instance, the insufficiency of personal
loves and friendships is urged upon the reader in the very context
in which the author alludes to Plotinus' praise of the beauty of
the soul as "immense" and says, "The soul gives itself, alone, original and pure, to the Lonely, Original and Pure . . ." (W.II.296).

The idea that the friend is another self is clearly important
to Emerson from a purely emotional point of view, but he is usually
careful to tie it to the Plotinian concept of a "sympathy" based
on pure affinity, which again is predicated on the idea that there
is only "One Mind." Particularly noteworthy is the suggestion in
"Behavior" that the glance is "the bodily symbol of identity of
nature" and that "we look into the eyes to know if this other form
is another self." There seems to be an allusion to the fate of Narcissus in the subsequent assertion that while some eyes "give no
more admission into the man than blueberries," others are "liquid
and deep,—wells that a man might fall into" (W.VI.179–180).

The warning is not too seriously meant, but the interesting
thing is that there is a warning at all; it is slightly incongruous in
this context. Its presence is best explained by the circumstance
that Emerson apparently had feminine eyes in mind when he wrote
this, and the pleasant tone is due to the fact that the eyes in question are Ellen's. It must be said that the statement is not in every
respect typical of his opinion of feminine eyes. Michaud is right
from a psychological point of view when he says that Emerson
needed in those he loved—in Lidian as well as in Ellen—"a calm
mirror of himself . . . as serene as the sapphire of Walden," but
philosophically speaking he is somewhat wary of the glance of
woman, and the narcissistic pattern does not really apply with
respect to her.[1] In fact, a text like "Eva," whose place next to
Ellen's verses in the *Poems* of 1847 suggests that it has something
to do with her, betrays a certain fear that her traits may *not* be
"at heart my own" (W.IX.95). In Platonistic terms, women are
"dissimil' troppo," to use Michelangelo's phrase; they are subject
to suspicion from this point of view not only because they belong
to the "opposite" sex but also and above all because they are seen

as more closely immersed in nature and everything covered by the word "otherness." In this perspective they are "the nymphs" of Valéry's so Plotinian "Cantate du Narcisse."

On the other hand, the idea of feminine otherness is often present in the imagery Emerson uses in discussing the limitations of the aspiring soul's ability to identify with his friends, and this imagery is clearly related to the Narcissus theme since the subject-object dialectic between Narcissus and his image has such clear sexual overtones. We are willing to project our inner vision of ideal man on the persons we love, he says in "Friendship," but "In strict science all persons underlie the same condition of an infinite remoteness . . . . I cannot make your consciousness tantamount to mine. Only the star dazzles; the planet has a faint and moon-like glow" (W.II.196–197). The language here calls to mind the archetypal (and hermetic-alchemic) opposition of sun and moon as symbols of male and female, as well as the Plotinian dance of the universe around its Creator. The equally venerable notion that woman is man's "shadow" is paralleled in the same paragraph: "I cannot deny it, O friend, that the vast shadow of the Phenomenal includes thee also in its pied and painted immensity . . . . Thou are not Being, as Truth is, as Justice is,—thou are not my soul, but a picture and effigy of that."

This passage in "Friendship" also contains the suggestion that "the soul environs itself with friends that it may enter into a grander self-acquaintance or solitude." Here, too, one glimpses a symbolic male-female opposition: The statement is obviously based in part on the idea that "love is only the reflection of a man's worthiness from other men" (W.II.212), which again is closely related to Emerson's theory of conversation and Swedenborg's way of seeing the wife as essentially the lover and admirer of the husband's wisdom. But in a context equating self-acquaintance and solitude this conception of the friend clearly serves the same purpose as the notion that the friend is as remote and untouchable as Narcissus' image in the water. Friendship is a useful aid to self-possession, but only to the extent that it furthers the solitude which Plotinus calls "the flight of the alone to the Alone," at the end of which is the ineffable union of man and God also referred to as "self-union."

It would seem that friends are ultimately expendable in this perspective, and Emerson actually makes that point in the highly Plotinian lecture "Home." Here the progress of the individual is measured not so much by "the successive choirs of his friends" (W.II.307) as by the extent to which he has transcended his original attachment to a few persons—those of the immediate family, with whom he happened to spend his first years—and is able to "find a higher home than before . . . in souls that give back a true image of his own," regardless of where they are encountered. Eventually, at the highest level, all individual loves and friendships fade away and the aspiring pilgrim's progress toward "a more interior life" and "a deeper home" is accompanied by an interiorization and sublimation of the whole idea of friendship into a general benevolence and a feeling of being at home everywhere (EL.III.26–31).

The idea that the friend is ultimately expendable is expressed in different ways in different contexts, but usually in such a manner as to call the story of Narcissus to mind. In introducing himself to Sterling, a protégé of Carlyle's whom he was never to meet, Emerson explains that he is "a worshipper of Friendship, and cannot find any other good equal to it" (CSE.28). Perhaps it is natural, even necessary, to fall back on the worship of an abstraction in a relationship which has no basis in concrete experience. On the other hand, Emerson apparently finds this approach natural in a much more general sense: The lover described in "Love" seeks the solitude of the forest in order to savor and enjoy his love.

Toward the end of "Friendship," Emerson suggests that he has recently discovered that it is more possible than he used to think to "carry a friendship greatly on one side, without due correspondence on the other." This statement, which owes something to a coolness in his relations with Carlyle, may seem to violate Aristotle's definition of friendship as a sentiment which unlike love is necessarily reciprocated. But Emerson, who does not acknowledge the difference between friendship and love in this essay, offers the following explanation of his own position: "It is thought a disgrace to love unrequited. But the great will see that true love cannot be unrequited. True love transcends instantly the unworthy object and dwells and broods on the eternal, and when the poor interposed mask crumbles, it is not sad, but feels rid of so much earth and feels its independency the surer" (W.II.216).

The full meaning of this statement emerges in the final sentence where he, as it were, tries to answer his own interposed objection: "These things may hardly be said without a sort of treachery to the relation: The essence of friendship is entireness, a total magnanimity and trust. It must not surmise or provide for infirmity. It treats its object as a god, that it may deify both." This clearly implies that what the friend really is counts less than what he stands for in the eyes of his friend—that is, the latter's ideal self. In such a situation, confrontation with the reality can obviously be an embarrassment, as Emerson himself so often suggests. In fact, the only way of not being a traitor to one's friend may be to withdraw from his company. More than once he hints that he actually resorts to this strategem: "Cold and silent he shall be in the circle of those friends who when absent his heart walks and talks with evermore . . . . There is no deeper dissembler than the sincerest man . . . . You shall find him noble at last, noble in his chamber" (JN.VII.423–424).

This chamber is not necessarily a closet space in a house. It can be the place which Emerson, borrowing a phrase from *Childe Harold's Pilgrimage,* calls a "populous solitude." The soul whose angle of vision is right, he suggests, will see such a solitude—also referred to as "its unfathomable heaven"—"mirrored back" to it no matter where it looks in the world (W.VI.269). Here we are close to the idea that while the great man is necessarily lonely, his isolation is not one of place but of spirit. It is essentially the Plotinian idea that the divine man is capable of dwelling simultaneously in the spiritual world and in this, which Emerson sometimes develops with a remarkable stress on mirroring. In "The Over-Soul," for instance, he notes that "men descend to meet," but he nevertheless has a feeling even in trivial conversation with his neighbors "that somewhat higher in each of us overlooks this byplay, and Jove nods to Jove from behind each of us" (W.II.278).

In a passage in *Society and Solitude,* on the other hand, Emerson speaks of a "populous, all-loving solitude" which definitely is removed from the physical presence of other people, or at least from "the tattle of towns" (W.VII.175). Indeed, there are places in his works where the solitude of the countryside seems to replace even the thought of people with the thought of the indwelling Deity who in "The Over-Soul" is said to "people the lonely place." In a journal entry dating from the same time as this essay, he plays with the idea of a "New Narcissus" who from sheer naïveté would cut through the veils of illusion that hide truth from falsely educated men and perceive that the beauty of nature is an intoxicating reflection of himself no less than of God and heaven (JN.XI.39; cf. 108).

In this case, Emerson's immediate inspiration seems to be Coleridge, who in a section of *The Friend* entitled "Essays on the Principles of Method" gives a similar picture of what he calls a "Narcissus-like" adoration of nature, carefully pointing out that the young man is led back by nature not to his own personal self but to the common source of all selves. The Plotinian background of the theme is also obvious, however, just as it is in the famous passage in *Nature* where Emerson describes an ecstacy in which he loses his "mean" personal ego in the grander identity of God: "The name of the nearest friend sounds then foreign and accidental. . . . I am the lover of uncontained and immortal beauty. In the wilderness, I find something more dear and connate than in streets or villages. In the tranquil landscape, and especially in the distant line of the horizon, man beholds somewhat as beautiful as his own nature" (W.I.10).

In "Language," another section in *Nature,* Emerson adduces the Plotinian idea that the whole of nature is a mirror of the human mind as a truth which the naturalists must learn from the poets if they are to fully understand the scope and significance of their own achievement. This suggestion is followed up in "The American Scholar," where he says he is looking forward to the day when the scientist will see not only that "nature is the opposite of the soul, answering to it part for part," but that "its beauty is the beauty of his own soul." In asserting that "so much of nature as he is ignorant of, so much of his own mind he does not yet possess," Emerson even manages to give a "narcissistic" twist to the motto Socrates picked up at Delphi: "And, in fine, the ancient precept 'Know thyself,' and the modern precept, 'Study nature,' become at last one maxim" (W.I.87). In a much later journal note, nature is from this point of view compared to "a chamber lined with mirrors" (JN.IX.352).

Speaking about the poet himself, Emerson mentions Narcissus in a passage where he characterizes symbolism as "the looking glass raised to the highest power" (J.VIII.99). As seen by his poet, the world is definitely a "palace" or "chamber" of mirrors (JN.VIII.16 and JN.IX.352). In some ways, one can even say that it is reminiscent of Swedenborg's heaven, where love is based on pure affinity and "what we call poetic justice takes effect on the spot" because "everything is as I am" (W.IV.125). Thus one may apply to him, or to his ideal self-projection, the poet, what Sartre says about Baudelaire, a reader of Emerson who was also fascinated by Swedenborg's theory of correspondences: "Rendered weightless, eviscerated, filled with symbols and signs, the world which envelops him in its immense totality is nothing but himself; it is himself this Narcissus wants to embrace and contemplate."[2]

It is not only "the book of nature" that the poet is capable of reading in this manner, but also that of history. With respect to the great men of the past, Emerson says in "Literary Ethics": "The youth, intoxicated with his admiration of a hero, fails to see that it is only a projection of his own soul which he admires" (W.I.162). The Plotinian background of this view is shown in an area of the journal for 1837 echoed in "History": "Let me say with Plotinus, 'Since therefore you admire soul in another thing, admire yourself'" (JN.V.384–385). The full theory is given in the essay itself. Here it is suggested that the purpose of all inquiry into literature and the past is essentially to identify with authors and heroes. It is remarkable, says Emerson, "that involuntarily we always read as superior beings"—we are not in the least astonished by the deeds of the great, but feel that we would act in the same manner under the same circumstances. The moral is that the heroes of the past are simply our proxies. The student is to learn "to read history actively and not passively; to esteem his own life the text, and books the commentary" (W.II.6–8).

One of the assumptions behind this doctrine is that one mind wrote all the books. This idea is also the basis of Emerson's conviction that the great author can safely generalize from his own experience and—as he himself so often does—simply change an "I" into "a man" or "each man" in transferring a paragraph from his journal to the essay he is working on. In "History," this point is made in various ways, but one formula is particularly noteworthy from our present point of view: "The universal nature, too strong for the petty nature of the bard, sits on his neck and writes through

his hand" (W.II.34). This image has found a more clearly "narcissistic" development in a poem called "The Park":

> I cannot shake off the god;
> On my neck he makes his seat;
> I look at my face in the glass,—
> My eyes his eyeballs meet.

In terms of the theory outlined in "History," the universal
nature that writes a text must also read it, which again means that
the great author is "born to deliver the thought of his heart from
the universe to the universe" (W.I.208). This does not necessarily
imply that the individual great writer who represents the universe
must read his own text; the statement can be seen against the
background of Emerson's theory of "creative reading" (W.I.93)—
that is, reading involving an identification with the author based
upon the idea that all men share in the same universal soul and
therefore ultimately represent the universe. However, there is
ample evidence that Emerson frequently goes beyond the idea that
the great authors write for "like-minded men" who then use their
works as mirrors in the manner he himself does in *Representative
Men* and many other places.

The theme is definitely given another turn of the screw when
he suggests that since even the greatest authors only tell us what
we know, a man might as well "read what he writes" (W.II.149).
This idea is based not only on the Platonic theory of *anamnesis,*
according to which learning is just a remembering of what we
always knew, but also on the premise that every man is closest to
himself and that Transcendentalists in particular must often pick
themselves for friends (W.I.347). Emerson was struck by Goethe's
suggestion that "We must write as we live, first for ourselves then
for related beings" (JN.V.129), and in a sense this is literally what
he did. Quite correctly, he has been characterized as essentially a
diarist and "preacher to himself."[3] He did not always enjoy com-
piling essays for publication on the basis of what he had already
told himself in the privacy of his journals. On one occasion he
speaks of this occupation as "a cold exhibition of dead thoughts"
and contrasts it with his experience in writing a letter to someone
he loves; then he is not at a loss for a word: "I am wiser than
myself and read my paper with the pleasure of one who receives
a letter" (JN.VII.405). He must often have experienced a similar

pleasure in reading old journal entries: His journals certainly contain his most spontaneous and unlabored writing. In a very real sense they are also letters to himself and he often shows his awareness of this, sometimes even addressing himself by name (e.g., JN.V.40 and 480).

Looked at from this point of view, Emerson's writing situation can thus be called the "narcissistic" or Plotinian equivalent of the dialectic situation involving Socrates and Phaedrus. In the *Phaedrus,* Plato describes how the lover projects his inner vision of ideal human beauty on his beloved and strives to mold him in that image; in Plotinus, on the other hand, this activity has become self-sculpture: The lover molds himself in the image of ideal beauty which he glimpses through introspective contemplation. In these terms, what matters is not what one writes but what the writer becomes through his work. In a sense his writing is addressed to the new self that he hopes to become and from his Transcendentalist point of view expects to be superior to his old self: "Every man sees an angel in his future self" (JN.III.186).

Although the phrase is probably inspired by the title editors have given to one of Milton's letters, "the unknown friend" to whom Emerson says the great and successful author addresses himself (JN.X.315) can be seen as an image of the ideal self which is always superior not only to the actual self but also to the self-images which at a given time are offered by the identifiable friends of real life. Ultimately this friend merges with the unknown god; at the end of an infinite chain of new selves and new friends waits "the Universal Friend" (W.IX.359). Emerson's work, one might say, is nothing but a prolonged adoration of this friend; it is Augustine's *Confessions* with a difference. In this sense, too, "He that writes to himself writes to an eternal public" (W.II.153).

A mystical aspiration à la Plotinus is of course first of all what Plato represents as the love of Penia (insufficiency) for Poros (sufficiency)—a desire to transcend one's earthly state of being both in its general and its personal aspects. It is for this reason that it can be seen as the philosophical equivalent of psychological narcissism, which has been defined as a rejection of one's actual self in favor of an ideal self that one would like to possess. Even the Ovidian Narcissus is characterized by an outrageous and paradoxical neglect of his own person. The purely philosophical side of this syndrome is expressed in the passage in Emerson's essay on "The Over-Soul" where he says: "I, the imperfect, adore my own Perfect" (W.II.296). One may think that the "I" in this case is a perfectly general one. But his works also contain some rather personal-sounding statements of this order, like the one expressing his apparent delight in his alleged discovery that "we" always are superior persons when we read. There is also a definite autobiographical background for the journal passage in which he states the reverse side of his "new Narcissus" by exclaiming: "Show me thy face, dear nature, that I may forget my own!" (JN.IX.398). Among the many early journal entries in which he complains about his own lack of "presence," there is one in which he says that he must "flee to the secretest hemlock shade in Walden Woods" to recover his equilibrium and sense of personal worth (JN.VII.315).

Emerson's transcendental aspiration is of course not always in line with the mysticism of a Plotinus. In some ways he would seem to have more in common with Paul, whose habit of contrasting his own transcendent powers with his unprepossessing physical presence is alluded to in an early poetic fragment (RW.IX.293):

> Has God on thee conferred
> A bodily presence mean as Paul's
> Yet made thee bearer of a word
> Which sleepy nations as with trumpet calls?

Paul's looking forward to his own transformation into an angelic being, though probably more literal than Emerson's, is expressed in similar terms: To achieve angelic status in his future state, a man must begin molding himself (and if possible others) in the image of his inner and spiritual ideal, Jesus Christ. In the process, the lower self must continually be killed off, sacrificed on the altar of a higher self.

Even the obvious lack of tenderness for former, transcended selves—which in Emerson's case is also reflected in the fate suffered by transcended "wives" in his theory of conversation—can be stated in Paulinian language: "Forgetting what is behind me," says the apostle, "and reaching out for that which lies ahead, I press toward the goal." So can Emerson's conviction that a man in his continual effort to "work a pitch above his last height" must ultimately measure himself not against the friends he has at a given moment but against himself alone. In this respect, Paul is also engaged in what Emerson with Plotinus sees as "the flight of the alone to the Alone."

Ultimately, of course, Emerson also parts company with Paul. The latter, just like Plotinus, postpones the consummation of the union of real and ideal to a world radically distinct from that of time and space. This can hardly be said of Emerson, especially not of the mature Emerson. After his resignation from the ministry, and more specifically after the frustration of his early hopes for some kind of apocalyptic change in human affairs that would take place in his own time, he turned more and more to the elaboration of an imaginary superman of the future representing a regeneration of mankind sometimes thought of in evolutionary terms: "He That Shall Come."

Like Nietzsche's Superman, to whom he has so often been compared, Emerson's future potentate is a kind of Antichrist. As Christ replaces Apollo in the vision of Paul, so "He That Shall Come" replaces Christ in Emerson's dream. There are even some direct comparisons. On one occasion Emerson notes that Jesus failed to give us the "victory to the senses" needed to prove complete spirituality and godmanhood; he did well, but "he that shall come shall do better" (JN.VIII.227–228). In the "Divinity School Address," so prophetic of Nietzsche, Jesus is reduced to a prophet of the "new Teacher" Emerson awaits (W.I.151).

As early as 1836, Emerson had written in his journal: "Jesus is but the harbinger and announcer of the Comforter to come, and his continual office to us is to make himself less to us by making us demand more" (JN.V.181). Here the theme of perpetual self-transcendence for the species, and for the individual as well, merges with Emerson's dream of the great and heroic friend, the greater self always yearned for and always so slow to arrive. Even earlier he had complained about the difficulty he experienced in his attempts to see a friend in Jesus. He would be willing to love him freely and in the manner of friends, he says in "The Lord's Supper," but the authoritarian image imposed by the Church was too forbidding (W.XI.20). In a letter to Aunt Mary, written not long afterwards, he bluntly says that Jesus cannot be to him what he was to John (L.I.375–376).

This does not prevent Emerson from identifying with Jesus

on occasion, but he does so mainly as a prophet of the "new Teacher" to come, as in certain journal comments on the public reaction to the "Divinity School Address," one of which makes the redeemer to come look remarkably like Christ coming on the clouds (JN.VII.126). As a rule, he prefers to find reflections of his own inner vision of divine manhood in other historical figures who to him seem more truly superhuman than the youth "hanged at the Tyburn of his nation" (W.III.114). One such figure is Zoroaster, the very man whom Nietzsche works up into an announcer of the Superman who is himself superhuman and at the same time the friend and comforter to come. Emerson does not project his own ideal self on Zoroaster as insistently as he does in the case of a much later Persian, Saadi, but he does ask himself whether a man like him cannot be considered "another Waldo" (JN.V.465); it is clear that he sees Zoroaster, too, as a poet in the high sense and as the author of a universal autobiography (W.VIII.65 and W.-VII.218), not to mention the fact that the godlike stature of men like him prove to Emerson that Apollo and Jove are not "impossible in the flesh" (W.III.108–109).

As Charles Andler has pointed out, Emerson may well have been one of the "prototypes" of Nietzsche's Zarathustra.[4] Similarly, Zoroaster was not the only nourisher of Emerson's dream about the superhuman figure whom he also refers to as "the semigod whom we await" (W.IX.273). One notes his interest in Swedenborg's definition of God as "the Grand Man" and his own suggestion in the essay on Swedenborg that "man, in his perfect form, is heaven" (W.IV.115 and 126). In the same spirit, Swedenborg's disciple Oegger, whom Emerson also read, states that the divine man is the perceptible side of God. Behind the Swedenborgian doctrine, one glimpses Boehme's heavenly Adam, in his turn derived from the Adam Kadmon of the cabala, to some extent by way of Paul's characterization of Christ as the "last" or "new" Adam. Significantly, one of Emerson's alternate names for "He That Shall Come" is "the perfect Adam" (W.IX.283).

However, to understand the intellectual context in which Emerson operates in this respect, one must also consider the neopagan thought currents of the Italian Renaissance. It seems that the dream of universal power for mankind, so important to Emerson, first arose at this time, just like the related idea of universal men of which he also makes so much. Among the more well-known prophets of man were Ficino and Pico Della Mirandola, whom Emerson mentions in *Representative Men* as two of the many great men nature allegedly keeps sending up "out of night" to be Plato's spiritual children and heirs (W.IV.40). Ficino's "Know thyself, O divine race in mortal dress" sums up Emerson's message. Yet he certainly goes beyond both Plato and Plotinus—not to mention Paul—when he speaks of the human soul as the "rival of God" (*aemula Dei*) in his *Theologia Platonica*.

As Anders Nygren has noted, Ficino's statement shows that Nietzsche was not the first philosopher to ask the enormous question: "If there were gods, how could I endure not to be a god?"[5] The remark seems even more apt if one knows that Emerson also felt that way: "Broad as God is the Personality we want, and which all great souls have or aspire to have," he says in his journal. "We stand for God" (JN.XIV.260). He also anticipates the suggestion in *Thus Spake Zarathustra* that man, far from having been created in the image of God, created him; God is simply the ultimate self-projection of man, transcending the Homeric and other naïve conceptions (cf. JN.III.182 and W.X.104). But unlike Nietzsche he shared the Renaissance man's belief that Platonism and Christianity could be married and that men's faith in his own divinity and his worship of himself actually form the essential content of the Christian religion. It is for this reason that he notes so approvingly that "Jones Very thought it an honor to wash his own face" (JN.XIV.125).

Pico suspected Ficino of "a Narcissus-like self-love through God," but this did not prevent him from suggesting in "The Dignity of Man" that man can re-create himself through self-sculpture and make of himself whatever he wants. Such ideas do not have more to do with Plotinus' self-sculpture than Ficino's "Know Thyself" has to do with the Delphic motto of Socrates. On the other hand, they are perfectly compatible with the pragmatism for which Emerson is noted and his vague evolutionary scenario for mankind. In "Art," he actually calls on man to reshape himself and his world according to his own desire and in the free manner of artists: "There is higher work for Art than the arts. Nothing less than the creation of man and nature is its end" (W.II.363).

The importance of the intellectual tradition associated with

Ficino and Pico to Emerson's work is increased by the fact that Michelangelo, his favorite artist, heard them expound their views at the court of Lorenzo Il Magnifico during his formative years. In accordance with this schooling, it was whispered already in his lifetime apropos of works like the *Creation of Adam* that they rivaled those of God, and Emerson can be said to echo this gossip when he describes Michelangelo as "largely filled with the Creator that made and makes men" (W.VIII.39), or marvels in his journal at the divine power of this artist, whose designs "teach us how near to creation we are" (JN.IX.389). His lecture on Michelangelo already testifies to his fascination with what he saw as the superhuman quality of many of his creations, which, he says, makes us "feel that we are greater than we know" (EL.I.104).

It may not be a mere coincidence that Michelangelo, like Paul —and Ficino and Plotinus—seems to have been dissatisfied with his personal presence and that we have only one self-portrait by his hand, the one which Emerson says he coveted more than anything else he saw in Florence (JN.IV.165). In the lecture which he wrote dressed in a coat that he had made in this city, Emerson explains that the artist was also rather unhappy with the appearance of other living forms and "abhorred to draw a likeness unless it were of infinite beauty" (EL.I.110). Michelangelo being the judge of what constitutes infinite beauty, this is as much as saying that he projected his inner vision of what man should look like both on his models and his material in accordance with the conception of art as self-sculpture which Emerson endorses. The individual model is of course fundamentally irrelevant in this perspective. The *Moses* as well as the *David*—to mention two of the works on which Emerson bases his view of Michelangelo as the molder of a superhuman humanity—are equally part of the artist's universal self-portrait.

The hatred which seems to be the inescapable corollary of this type of Platonistic love and aspiration does not fail to surface in this context. As Brandes notes, Michelangelo seems to have delighted in letting his Apollo-like Christ wield the scourge, and this posture is definitely related to the harsh view he took not only of his personal enemies but of all mankind to the extent that it did not meet his moral and aesthetic specifications.[6] Emerson does not explicitly comment on *The Last Judgment* in these terms, and it must be said that he rather disliked torture scenes out of hell. But he dwells with sympathy on Michelangelo's deep contempt for the vulgar, "that abject and sordid crowd of all classes and all places who obscure as much as in them lies every beam of beauty in the universe," and then relates this attitude to an "intense love of solitude" reminiscent of the "populous solitude" in which he himself found it easiest to deify mankind (EL.I.112–113). There cannot be much doubt that his fascination with Michelangelo has something to do with his own judgment of those who "discredit Adamhood" (i.e., the vast majority of humanity) in "Alfonso of Castile" (W.IX.25–28) and other places. Nor can one help thinking in this context of the already mentioned journal entry in which he apparently identifies with Christ coming on the clouds. As Lewis Mumford puts it, "This sweet man carried a lash."[7]

Yet another facet of the moral implications of Emerson's desire to be God is reflected in those lines from the year during which he resigned from the ministry: "That which myself delights in shall be Good, / That which I do not want,—indifferent; / That which I hate is Bad . . ." (JN.IV.47). This is the attitude which in due time would lead to the well-known epigram in "Self-Reliance" according to which "the only right is what is after my constitution; the only wrong what is against it" (E.I.42). Significantly, this suggestion is preceded by the provocative statement that the author does not care if he is "the devil's child" and followed by repeated attacks on the Christian idea of charity. These attacks are accompanied by a stress on the importance of going it alone: "Do not spill thy soul; do not all descend; keep thy state; stay at home in thine own heaven . . ." (E.I.59). There are few things in Emerson's thought that cannot in one way or another be related to his metaphysical narcissism.

13

THE MARRIAGE OF HEAVEN AND HELL: EMERSON'S ALTERNATIVE TO BLAKE

Even in a millennial-evolutionary perspective, Emerson often seems as eager to marry heaven and hell as to reconcile heaven and earth: One day man will be "amphibious," he notes on one occasion, "with one door down into Tartarus, and one door upward into light, belonging to both" (JN.XI.450). He is perfectly aware that this extension of man's range and affinities involves nothing less than a revaluation of all values. As early as 1840, he has this to tell Margaret Fuller about that aspect of his dream: "Certainly the votary of the true God will see that his most commended virtues are snares to his feet, fatal barriers to his progress . . . . As soon as we are more catholicly instructed we shall be helped by all vices and shall see what indispensable elements of character men of pride, libertinism and violence conceal." Significantly, he has previously suggested that the epiphany that might help us "break all conventions" is as likely to occur "in caves underground" as in "turrets under the stars" (L.II.342–343).

Apparently, Emerson does not see any kind of contradiction between this picture of the future and the marriage of heaven and earth to be brought about by the poet; rather, he views them as complementary. The instructor in the new and more "catholic" faith is the very man whose amphibious roaming on other occasions has the more limited purpose of reconciling heaven and earth:

the poet-thinker. Thus Merlin's Muse is called "Bird that from the nadir's floor / To the zenith's top can soar" (W.IX.122), and Plato is described as a man who with equal agility mounts "into heaven" and dives "into the pit" (W.IV.75–76).

The analogy between the two ways of reconciling the "extremes of nature" is reinforced through the use of hermetic-alchemic imagery with reference to the internal marriage of heaven and hell as well as to that of heaven and earth: Just as the "healthful" and fertile mind of the androgynous poet of genius is sometimes discussed in terms of the marriage of Ouranos and Gaia (EL.I.297), so the mind of the Great Doer, in which good and evil mix and marry with most productive results, is often seen as the microcosmic version of a universal marriage of heaven and hell. In "The Uses of Great Men," for instance, the wonder of intellectual liberation from the pedantic norms of every-day life is described as the ecstatic moment when "our heads are bathed with galaxies, and our feet tread the floor of the Pit" (W.IV.17).

"As I am, so I see," says Emerson in "Experience" (W.III.79); and in terms of that statement the mind of "Seyd" (one of his favorite poetic alter egos) must also be rather similar to the universe in which he sees "strong Eros struggling through, / In dens of passion and pits of woe" (W.IX.276). Love's ability to bridge these poles at both the universal and the individual level is celebrated in similar terms in "Cupido":

> His blinding light
> He flingeth white
> On God's and Satan's brood,
> And reconciles
> By mystic wiles
> The evil and the good.

Again, just as the union of heaven and earth in the mind of the androgynous man of genius has a tendency to turn monistic in what one might call the narcissistic phase, so does the union of heaven and hell in the same mind. Indeed, it is in this unity, monistic rather than bipolaric, that the tension between the two different types of "reconciliation" expected from the great man is finally resolved. As for the distinction between bipolarity and monism, Emerson's pantheism helps blur it both in the case of the marriage of good and evil and in that of the marriage of male and female, as shown in "Compensation" (W.II.96–97).

Another text of considerable importance in this context is a poem called "Spiritual Laws." It presents the universe and the mind which perceives and defines its laws as a unified field. Moreover, the alchemic language calls to mind Emerson's androgynous "heaven of invention," while the elimination of the earth and the anticipated disappearance of evil in conjunction with the stress on self-sufficient solitude reflect his preponderantly monistic orientation:

> The living Heaven thy prayers respect,
> House at once and architect,
> Quarrying man's rejected hours,
> Builds therewith eternal towers;
> Sole and self-commanded works,
> Fears not undermining days,
> Grows by decays,
> And, by the famous might that lurks
> In reaction and recoil,
> Makes flame to freeze and ice to boil;
> Forging, through swart arms of Offence,
> The silver seat of Innocence.

By no coincidence, Emerson makes lavish use of the circle to describe this spiritual milieu. A closed circuit—"puss and her tail," as he puts it in "Experience"—is a good image of the "solitary performance" of the soul which has attained its "due sphericity" (circularity) by pushing its knowledge of all things, including that of evil, to the point where it can be seen to turn into its opposite (W.III.80). It is, in fact, used archetypally (sometimes in the guise of the *ourobouros,* the snake biting its own tail) to symbolize both types of internal marriage. It is also convenient in demonstrating how the analogy between microcosm ("unit") and macrocosm ("universe") applies in this context, as shown by the statement of "Uriel" overheard by "Seyd": "Line in nature is not found; / Unit and universe are round; / In vain produced, all rays return; / Evil will bless and ice will burn" (W.IX.14).

"Uriel" is usually considered an autobiographical statement; the scornful and self-sufficient withdrawal of the archangel mirrors Emerson's own attitude when faced with the adverse reaction to

the "Divinity School Address" of 1838, in which he anticipates the
advent of a "new Teacher" destined to supersede Jesus by boldly
following the laws of the universe until they "come full circle"
(W.I.151). A journal comment on the same adverse reaction definitely suggests that he at the time saw himself as a persecuted "new
Teacher" of this kind (JN.VII.126). "Circles" (1841) indicates that
he no longer worries much about the possibility that he might be
thought a "circular philosopher" teaching that "our crimes may
be lively stones out of which we shall construct the temple of the
true God," provided we, too, are true (W.II.317).

Emerson sees himself entirely in the role of theorist, of course.
In the mentioned letter to Margaret Fuller, he says of "the votary
of the true God" that "he must be divorced and childless and
houseless and friendless a churl and a fool if he would accompany
with the Cherubim and have the Alone to his friend." But he also
tells her that he personally is not willing to go quite that far; he
has "no immediate thought of burglary or arson" and is "much
more likely to keep a safe distance from all the instructive extremes
of life and condition." In other places—as, for instance, in "Ode,
Inscribed to W. H. Channing"—he stresses the idea that the poet-
thinker cannot afford to be distracted from his work as the interpreter of the divine will even to help redress apparent wrongs,
and that he can refrain from doing so in the certitude that the
universe knows how to administrate itself: "Foolish hands may
mix and mar; / Wise and sure the issues are. / Round they roll till
dark is light, / Sex to sex, and even to odd."

On the other hand, in interpreting the will of "the overgod /
Who marries Right to Might," the poet-thinker, Emerson himself,
may justly celebrate those who carry it out. Thus the "gentlemen"
of "Manners" are seen as "the working heroes" in history whose
"personal force and love" will make them as important to the new
era as the Christians have been in the past (W.III.120–128). Among
those mentioned by name is Napoleon, who in "Experience" is
viewed as one of "the mind's ministers" in the very area where
Christian charity and the Christian fear of sin are criticized along
with "other weak emotions" (W.III.79–82).

Apparently attempting to unify his two types of great men,
Emerson sometimes comes close to seeing Napoleon as a "poet" as
well as a doer. In the case of Byron, Napoleon's chief rival for

admiration in the nineteenth century, that kind of fusion is easily managed. Byron had made a name for himself not only as a poet and hero but also as an experimenter in the area of devil worship. In "New England Reformers," included in the second series of *Essays*, Emerson mentions him as someone who is ready to "tread the floors of hell" in order to procure for himself the experience which he craves (W.III.274).

Both Napoleon and Byron must be counted among the "darlings" of nature, "the great, the strong, the beautiful," who, according to "Experience," are not "children of our law" and do not come "out of the Sunday School" (W.III.64). To underline that his target is Christianity, Emerson here adds that if we want to be strong with the strength of nature, "we must not harbor such disconsolate consciences, borrowed too from the consciences of other nations"; rather, he says, "We must set up the strong present tense against all the rumors of wrath, past or to come."

The passage about nature's darlings gives some idea of the image Emerson has in mind when he writes in the same essay: "I carry the keys of my castle in my hand, ready to throw them at the feet of my lord, whenever and in what guise soever he shall appear" (W.III.53). It is plainly a messianic idea, but there is also something satanic about this figure, just as there is something satanic about the poet-thinker who celebrates and justifies him with reference to the will of a ruling "over-god" who, like the Jehovah vindicated by Isaiah against the inroads of Zoroastrian dualism, is responsible for the bad as well as the good in this world. If a more contemporary parallel is needed, one might adduce the Lord depicted in Blake's "Songs of Experience"—the god who made the tiger as well as the lamb.

At this point a question naturally arises concerning the relation between Emerson and Blake. In a sense the essay Emerson calls "Experience" is to him what "Songs of Experience" is to Blake. In it he notes with satisfaction that he is no longer the "novice" he had been seven years earlier—that is, at the time when he published *Nature,* a book which might properly be called his "Songs of Innocence." The change actually came much earlier, of course. The "Divinity School Address," for instance, already belongs to his "Songs of Experience"; as a matter of fact, one may also appropriately compare it with *The Marriage of Heaven and Hell.* Like this work, Emerson's address is marked by attacks on institutionalized religion and more particularly on the falsely authoritarian image of Jesus allegedly imposed by the Church. Both authors hint that the history of the Church is nothing but an elaborate and concerted effort to stifle the divine and creative energies of man. Both texts suggest that the devil has been slandered.

This is not to say that Emerson was strongly influenced by Blake during his formative years. Journal passages suggesting an acquaintance with Blake's poetry only begin to appear somewhat later, and they are rather vague, like the one in which he suggests that poets "draw the Energy from hell" when they paint God (JN.XI.121), or the appearance of the lines "Foxes are so cunning / Because they are not strong" (which seem reminiscent of "the proverbs of hell") immediately after the primitive version of "Spiritual Laws" asserting that there is a living heaven which "thro' the arms of all the devils / Builds the firm seat of Innocence" (JN.IX. 442–443). The only specific mention of Blake that shows that Emerson knew about him in the forties is his statement that William Blake the artist had said quite frankly that he "never knew a bad man in whom there was not something very good" (W.VIII. 317). It is thus possible that it was only much later, in the context of the so-called Blake revival, that Emerson acquired the kind of interest in his poetry that led him to copy several "proverbs of hell" into his notebooks, including the one according to which "the tigers of wrath are wiser than the horses of instruction" (J.IX.575), and to recite again and again "The Tiger."[1]

Striking as the similarities between Emerson and Blake are in some respects, one must also say that the differences are even more so. To begin with, Emerson may occasionally seem as pleased to play the devil's attorney as Blake is, but on the whole his allegiance to the devil is less ironic and literary. Blake is rebelling against what he sees as the suppression of man's creative power, but he does not share Emerson's fascination with absolute power—power as the sign and promise of man's potential godhood: in fact, he is not even for empire, a subject which clearly thrills Emerson. Accordingly, his idea of internal heaven-hell marriage is also different from Emerson's. An image of the agony of creative desire, it seems closer to Whitman's "sweet hell within" than to the frame of mind of Emerson's gentlemen of "force and love."

Emerson's poet is also rather different from Blake's conception of the great and creative man. Blake is more like Whitman than Emerson in his insistent claim to be the poet of the body as well as of the soul because neither can be imagined without the other. There is nothing angelic about his idea of creative genius: Saying that body and soul are complementary and indissolubly joined does away with the androgynous autonomy of the man of genius. "Lust," "desire," and "sensual enjoyment"—in short, marriage—becomes the supreme purpose of life. Creative energy is closely linked to sexual potency in Blake, and yet he never suggests that the libido ought to be sublimated and used only at the level of androgynous internal marriage, or that sexual indulgence leads to loss of power, as Emerson and Plato suggest.

A fortiori, Blake does not hold that sensual indulgence is to be shunned as evil in a purely moral sense, as taught not only by Plato but also by the Puritan Church whose lingering influence is so obvious in Emerson's works. Perhaps this matter is what most clearly separates the two and makes it seem unlikely that *The Marriage of Heaven and Hell* could in any circumstances have become his favorite reading. Unlike Blake, who only associates sexual enjoyment with evil in an ironic manner, Emerson does so in a quite serious vein and in this respect sides with the established Church rather than with his fellow critic of it. Nor does it make any difference in this respect that he updates the doctrine of the Church by discussing the consequences of sin not in terms of eternal damnation but in terms of negative "compensation" manifested in a loss of self-propelling power.

As a result of this attitude, Emerson is loath to include sensual enjoyment among "evils" productive of good. The "darlings of nature," for instance, in whom she "comes eating and drinking and sinning," obviously go on to do the great things for which she sent them into the world *despite* such activities, not thanks to them. They can afford them because they are so great that they make mere means and circumstances irrelevant. Their sensual indulgence is only a sign of their "exuberance," their superabundance of energy; it cannot swerve them from their course. A similar attitude with regard to this kind of "evil" is noticeable in "Ghaselle" (P.216–217), where Hafiz need not fear hell but can indulge in his "sweet chase of the nuns" because "heaven is secure" *regard-*

less of what he does. It is secure because Hafiz is generally on the right road, as a servant of the true God; inconsequential pastimes cannot significantly interrupt his soaring.

On other occasions, it is intimated that "the divine effort," whose instruments are men like Hafiz, "is never relaxed." Goodness will prevail for that reason in spite of the *seeming* power of evil in the world (W.IV.138–139). That even sinful sex can be reconciled with Emerson's monistic eschatology in terms of this idea is easy to see in this part of the essay on Swedenborg, in spite of the alchemic imagery used at one point: "the carrion in the sun will convert itself to grass and flowers; and man, though in brothels, or jails, or on gibbets, is on his way to all that is good and true. . . . Every thing is superficial and perishes but love and truth only."

Even Emerson's critique of Swedenborg is rather different from Blake's. The author of *The Marriage of Heaven and Hell* is as gratified by Swedenborg's nuptial-alchemic approach to marriage as he is disappointed by his rigorous separation of good and evil. Emerson, on the other hand, seems to view what he sees as Swedenborg's Manichean tendencies (cf. JN.VII.103) as simply another facet of the imperfect idealism which also causes him to pin his theory of love "to a temporary form" and make man and wife eternally dependent on one another (W.IV.128). Swedenborg's doctrine of heavenly marriage, he suggests more than once, does not allow enough room for the kind of progress to which every individual is entitled. Nor is he satisfied that the sum of good will increase sufficiently, thanks to these marriages. Indeed, the whole idea of a heaven in which the volume of goodness and truth keeps increasing while evil eternally persists in another part of the universe is entirely against the monistic grain of his religious-philosophical convictions.

Emerson may seem to be quite close to Blake's position in denouncing Swedenborg's heavens and hells as dull for lack of great individuals, and saying, with respect to the latter, that he misses "the interest that attaches in nature to each man, because he is right by his wrong, and wrong by his right. . . . strong by his vices, often paralyzed by his virtues" (W.IV.134). However, it is typical of Blake's more ironic approach to the problem that he has angels turn into devils and praises Milton for his portrait of Satan, who illustrates that kind of metamorphosis: Emerson, for all his talk about liberating man by showing that he cannot afford "to waste his moments in compunctions," betrays his overriding interest in the ultimate elimination of evil (including sensual enjoyment) by the way in which he concentrates entirely on the need to grant evil spirits the right and power to convert themselves into angels, which Swedenborg denies them.

These differences between Emerson and Blake also explain the former's negative attitude to that other landmark in the literary history of the rehabilitation of the devil, Goethe's *Faust*. One might have expected Emerson to seize upon the image of Faust as a magnificent example of a man who boldly married heaven and hell in his mind in an attempt to achieve divine manhood in accordance with those lines in "The Sphinx": "The fiend that man harries / Is love of the Best; / Yawns the pit of the Dragon, / Lit by rays from the Blest." However, all that Emerson sees in *I Faust* seems to be an illustration of his own theory of negative compensation, the sad tale of a man who bartered his soul for sensual pleasure, as he incidentally strongly suspected that the author himself did, figuratively speaking. One journal criticism of the book is that it makes Priapus "an equal hero with Jove," a statement which obviously has something to do with the child Faust fathered on Margaret and his subsequent participation in the witch sabbath. In the essay on Goethe, finally, Mephistopheles, the symbol of the satanic element in Faust and in Goethe himself is more specifically said to represent "pure intellect, applied . . . to the service of the senses" (W.IV.277). But Emerson does not in this context take as positive a view of intellect as he does in "Experience," where he rather triumphantly, and with Napoleon as his example and authority, states that "there is no crime to the intellect" (W.III.79). Nor is there any suggestion that Faust is a darling of nature whose sins are irrelevant in view of the transcendent services he is going to render humanity.

It is of course possible that Emerson would have viewed Faust as at least as satisfactory a symbol of internal heaven-hell marriage as Napoleon, had he read the second part of Goethe's poem. A journal note from 1844 stating that Goethe attempted to save Satan's soul in *II Faust* indicates that he, at least at that time, was familiar only with the so-called "Helena fragment" (JN.IX.43).[2] On the other hand, it seems more likely that Faust's ultimate concentration on charitable works under the influence of Margaret's spiritual beauty—not to mention his eventual, quasi-Swedenborgian reunion with her in heaven—would have seemed anticlimactic to Emerson rather than the seal of a great life. One notes his disappointment with the story of Wilhelm Meister, a less demonic version of Faust in the tradition of the *Bildungsroman*. He dwells on the many "weaknesses and impurities" of Goethe's fornicating hero, blemishes which are not, as in the case of Sand's Count Rudolstadt, offset by a prodigious spiritual growth suggesting that he is after all a servant of the true God. It also seems significant that the end of the book is singled out as particularly "lame and immoral." This is where Meister betrays his lack of self-sufficiency by marrying a noblewoman who is also portrayed as his moral superior. In other words, Meister's salvation and "heaven" are earthly versions of Faust's (W.IV.278–279).

Thus it seems more than likely that Emerson has *Wilhelm Meister* even more than *Faust* in mind when he complains in a *Dial* article about what he sees as Goethe's way of suggesting the "equivalence of good and evil in action." This criticism is really too inconsistent with what he himself says in "Experience" and many other places unless one assumes that it is predicated on his dissatisfaction with the immoral activities of a hero whose goals and achievements are too mediocre to justify them. The concomitant suggestion that Goethe failed to be the redeemer of the human mind also fits Meister's priapic tendencies and his urgent need to get married. There is nothing angelic and self-sufficiently androgynous about him, nothing suggesting a marriage of heaven and earth in the terms dear to Emerson (W.XII.328–333).

Obviously, it is not easy to find perfect human incarnations, real or fictional, of the kind of divine completeness symbolized by Emerson's vision of internal heaven-hell marriage combined with and indeed predicated on spiritual androgyny. The problem becomes especially ticklish if the great man is to represent both of the human types which Emerson thinks fit the bill—the poet-thinker as well as the hero-doer. In the case of historical characters, their usefulness is often inversely proportionate to the amount of biographical information available about them and directly proportionate to their distance in time and space. This may be one reason why Emerson prefers to use Hafiz rather than, say, Byron in his poetic demonstrations of the good of evil.

However, the image can be fragmented, and even relatively recent authors may be used to illustrate a particular facet of Emerson's great man. Thus the retired mayor of Bordeaux is portrayed as the very image of the stand-offish poet-thinker in the essay on Montaigne. His "politics," says Emerson, are those of Krishna (the Vishnu of the adjacent essay on Swedenborg): "There is none who is worthy of my love or my hatred." Thus "he is not the champion of the operative, the pauper, the prisoner, the slave." Rather, he has learned to be "content with just and unjust, with sots and fools, with the triumph of folly and fraud," knowing that "the world-spirit is a good swimmer." Everything will be fine in the end: "Through the years and the centuries, through evil agents, through toys and atoms, a great and beneficent tendency irresistibly streams" (W.IV.172–186). The circumstance that Emerson is supposedly describing the attitude of a skeptic rather than his own hardly hides the fact that he is using Montaigne as a mirror and that self-justification is the main purpose of this portion of his argument, which is very much like that of his "Ode."

Needless to say, Emerson did not consistently act in accordance with this uncharitable part of his theory any more than he tested another portion of it by committing actual crimes. It remains that this attitude is the one that is most in line with his idealism—from a philosophical point of view he was bound to see any deviation from his theoretical position as a sign of weakness of which he ought to be somewhat ashamed, as stated so eloquently in "Self-Reliance."

How great Emerson's philosophical allegiance to the various aspects of his ideal of divine completeness actually is can be seen in his frequent references to certain classes of supernatural beings who illustrate them and can serve as images of the "lord" to whom he is willing to surrender the keys of his castle whenever he recognizes him in mortal guise (W.III.53). In this context, Krishna has to take a back seat: In the interest of immediate recognition, these potentates are familiar figures drawn from Greek mythology, to which Emerson attributes a special catholicity (JN.XIV.194), or from pagan European lore, or from some other universally known body of legends. Indeed, one may identify a group of images

(Apollo, the angel, the fairy, Dionysus) that present a number of common traits which fit Emerson's idea of divine completeness, with the added advantage that some of these traits can be left understood whenever the context might make them embarrassing or they seem irrelevant to a particular character trait he wants to focus on.

As for Apollo, the conventional image of the ideal world, one must say that Emerson paints a somewhat Orientalized, Krishna-like picture of him when he adduces his example in "Experience" to reinforce the suggestion that "A preoccupied attention is the only answer to the importunate frivolity of other people." Analyzing Flaxman's illustration of Aeschylus' *Eumenides,* which features Orestes supplicating Apollo while the Furies sleep on the threshold of the temple, Emerson notes: "The face of the god expresses a shade of regret and compassion, but is calm with the conviction of the irreconcilableness of the two spheres. He is born into other politics, into the eternal and beautiful. The man at his feet asks for his interest in turmoils of the earth, into which his nature cannot enter . . . . The god is surcharged with his divine destiny" (W.III.82).

In this particular reference to Apollo, Emerson apparently sees no need to dwell on the dark side of the god of enlightenment, although it may not be entirely unrelated to the posture there attributed to him. He was of course perfectly aware of the quality in Apollo's nature that at the beginning of the *Iliad* causes him to descend upon the Achaeans "like the night" and generally of his tendency to interfere in human affairs and destroy and save as he pleases (JN.IX.369 and JN.XI.288). The active power of the god is also the basis of Emerson's frequent use of the image of Apollo in disguise as a symbol of the potential of mortal men. As for the other aspects of Apollo's circular completeness (also symbolized by the sun disc), the androgyny and sexual ambidexterity of this god is too well known for Emerson to have ignored it. Although he does not see fit to mention it explicitly in "Experience," one cannot help noting that his analysis of Flaxman's drawing follows on the heels of the passage stressing the need for "sphericity" in dealing with the problem of evil and the use of "puss and her tail" as an image of the subject-object circuit of every man's "solitary performance."

The angel, as used by Emerson, must probably be called a

somewhat more versatile image than Apollo, and yet they are virtually interchangeable in the most fundamental respects. Thus the angel is one of his alternative symbols of the ideal, a divine state of being to which we can only aspire—in the Platonic sense. In declaring that "every man is an angel in disguise," he explicitly draws the parallel of Apollo tending the flocks of Admetus (JN. V.12). There are also many examples of the use of this image in statements about the self-sufficiency and solitude of the great soul (e.g., JN.XIV.114 and J.X.221).

As for the circular completeness on which this attitude is based, one notes, in addition to the "round" mind of Uriel (the archangelic guardian of the sun), that Emerson in "Experience" opposes the "angel-whispering" of privileged moments to the "real and angular" look things wear on ordinary days. He cannot possibly have been unaware that angels are usually considered androgynous; in fact, the angelic constitution is one of his favorite reference points in discussions of suprasexual love and friendship. He is even more outspoken concerning the angelic marriage of heaven and hell, stating not only that he early communed with "angels of darkness and of light" (W.III.189)—a dichotomy of the heavenly host which may have as much to do with the Oriental devas and asuras as with the lapsed cohorts of Lucifer—but also that the cherubim themselves inspire terror as much as they radiate beauty (EL.II.284).

Even more terrible are the warlike archangels, and it seems probable that Emerson has one of them—or else the Angel of Extermination—in mind in a passage which most forcefully brings home the fact that his angel does not limit himself to theorizing about the marriage of good and evil. I am thinking of the one in which he tells the Harvard divinity students that there are "sympathies far in advance" of charity—that we have resources "on which we have not drawn," but which we should not hesitate to tap, if need be, even if we may not in this respect be able to attain the heights scaled by the great: "There are men . . . to whom a crisis which intimidates and paralyzes the majority . . . comes graceful and beloved as a bride. Napoleon said of Massena, that he was not himself until the battle began to go against him; then, when the dead began to fall in ranks around him, awoke his powers of combination, and he put on terror and victory as a robe. So it is in rugged crises, in unweariable endurance, and in aims which put sympathy out of question, that the angel is shown" (W.I.149).

This angel may not at first seem to have much in common with the angel used as a symbol of Platonic and spiritual love. Yet there is a common denominator: Emerson's hero-gentleman, just like his angelic lover, shows great disregard for the body—his own as well as those of others (W.II.252). Another thing worth noting is Emerson's tendency to use the word "subterranean" as a synonym of "celestial" both in speaking of the communications of angelic lovers (JN.VII.512) and with reference to the divine and angelic power of some men: "Power," he says in "Experience" (immediately after the passage about "angel-whispering"), "keeps another road than the turnpikes of choice and will, namely, the subterranean and invisible tunnels and channels of life."

The word "subterranean" was of course commonly used in the sense of "secret" in Emerson's time, but his adding of the word "tunnels" suggests that the idea of heaven-hell marriage is not far from his mind and that he does not share the fear of "humeurs transcendantes" which Montaigne expresses in his own essay on experience, noting that he finds a strange "accord" between "les opinions supercelestes" and "les meurs sousterraines." His appreciation of the "subterranean" can also be seen in his rhetorical use of the third of the four images I have linked. Although the fairies are spirits associated with starlight, they spend most of their time "in caves underground," appearing on the surface of the earth only after sunset.

In spite of this life-style, fairyland often appears as a symbol of the ideal world in Emerson's works (e.g., JN.IX.24). It also vies with the angelic kingdom for the first place as his emblem of spiritual love. Nor does he fail to use the fairy as a symbol of the latently divine power of some men: "There are persons from whom we always expect fairy-tokens" (W.III.165). Thanks to the small size of the fairies, and especially of their king, they can serve to make the point that power is essentially spiritual and invisible. Indeed, in this very context Emerson relates the fairy king and Apollo: Just as "in the Greek legend, Apollo lodges with the shepherds of Admetus . . . So it was the rule of our poets, in the legends of fairy lore, that the fairies largest in power were the least in size" (W.VII.176).

The self-sufficiency of the fairies is almost as proverbial as that of their less fair cousins, the trolls; significantly, Emerson compares his stand-offish Transcendentalist friends to them in this respect: "Like fairies," he says, "they do not want to be spoken of" (W.I. 344), and the "human elf" portrayed in "Woodnotes" could hardly be more sufficient unto himself (W.IX.44). As for the circular completeness that goes with this trait as well as with the love-and-power symbolism, it is as well-documented as in the cases of Apollo and the angel. It hardly makes any difference from this point of view that there are female fairies as well as male ones. On one occasion, Emerson refers to Ellen Tucker as his "faery queen" (JN. III.162). This, on the other hand, makes him the fairy king, and it is this notoriously androgynous and ambidextrous figure, Shakespeare's Oberon, who gets most of his attention.

Emerson is also well aware of the amphibious nature of the fairy king and his subjects, their connection with hell. If there is any difference in his account of fairyland and his discussion of Apollo and the angel in this regard, it is that he is more explicit and reveals a perfect awareness of the close relation between the hellish orientation and sexual orientation which marks the popular image of the fairy king. The inversion of Oberon is integrated with the inversion of other values when he notes in his journal, "The fairie kingdom stands to men and women not as the Angelic hierarchy above our heads, and with the same direction as we, but feet to feet" (JN.IX.297). An even more explicit recognition of the relation between Oberon's androgynous ambidexterity and his hellish side appears in his recording of a neighbor's comment on listening to a performance of Goethe's ballad "Erlkoening" as set to music by Schubert: "I suppose every one thinks of their own totties" (JN.VIII.129).

There is a certain poignancy in the fact that Emerson after the death of his own five-year-old son a few months later wrote the following lines in his commemorative "Threnody": "From the window I look out / To mark thy beautiful parade, / Stately marching in cap and coat / To some tune by fairies played." On the other hand, ominous as these lines sound, they also suggest that he saw something flattering in such a relationship between his son and the fairies. One is reminded of the fact that he claims to have found some consolation in a tale in which Charles Newcomb, alluding to Waldo II, tells the story of the death of a child loved by the fairies because of its transcendent beauty (JN.VIII.178). Apparently, Emerson managed to see it as a variation on the idea that "he whom the gods love dies young," a feat facilitated by the formal dissociation of the heavenly-spiritual and the hellish aspects of the fairy king in the tale. Newcomb has the child murdered by a weird old man.

No doubt one can speak of a convenient fragmentation of the complete image of the fairy in this case, and similar phenomena occur in his rhetorical use of Apollo and the angel. Nevertheless, the persistence of the same fundamental pattern from image to image is remarkable. It is also certain that Emerson found an irresistible attraction in the manner in which the idea of the marriage of light and night is typified in the fairy-grove—witness, for instance, his frequent references to certain lines in Jonson's *The Gypsies Metamorphosed*: "The faerie beam upon you / The stars to glister on you, / A noon of light in the noon of night" (e.g., EL.I.344). By the same token, the twilight of sunset is associated with fairyland as a symbol of bodiless love and friendship (e.g., W.I.17).

In view of the close relation between such friendship and creativity in Emerson's theory, it is natural that he should also see the chiaroscuro of the fairy forest as an image of the creative mind—of the poetic imagination in which everything can be converted into "every other thing" (W.VI.304). In this sense, the scene of *A Midsummer Night's Dream*, one of the more important sources of his knowledge of fairy lore, is also the scene of its creation (cf. W.IV.207). Alternatively, it can be seen as a gift of the fairies. Fairy gold is used along with alchemic gold to signify the products of poetic power—and this power itself—in Emerson's work (W. II.35 and W.VII.249). His early journals contain passages in which he facetiously implores the fairies to inspire him (JN.I.14), and in an unpublished early poem he suggests that Shakespeare was god-fathered by them (JN.II.170).

On this side, the image of the fairy is closer to Dionysus than to Apollo and the angel, whom Emerson does not so often associate with poetic power. A passage in "May-Day" is of particular interest in that it suggests that the combined influence of Dionysus and the fairies affects poets quite early. In one stanza, he claims that

"Poets praise that hidden wine / Hid in milk we drew / At the barrier of Time / When our life was new." In the next line, the same source of nourishment is referred to as a gift of the fairies: "We had eaten fairy fruit, / We were quick from head to foot. / All the forms we looked on shone / As with diamond dews thereon" (W.IX.177). The poet then goes on to celebrate the poetic sights and sounds of boys playing in the woods, the haunt of Dionysus as well as of the fairies. A poetic fragment dealing with the same topic is noteworthy because it specifically mentions the fairy king, while the allusion to the grape calls the train of Dionysus to mind (W.IX.337):

> Every shrub and grape leaf
> Rang with fairy laughter,
> I have heard them fall
> Like the strain of all
> King Oberon's minstrelsy.

This does not mean that the fairy and Dionysus are interchangeable in Emerson's works. Dionysus, often indistinguishable from his gift, offers a way of rhetorically bridging the gap between theism and pantheism, as also demonstrated in "Ghaselle," where Hafiz is quoted as saying that his clay has been "kneaded up with wine" since his first day. Incidentally, this means that the God and the man whom he inspires are also one, a point made in "Bacchus," where Emerson speaks of "wine which is already man" (W.IX.126). In view of the fusion of the god and the cupbearer who represents—one might say incarnates—him in this poem and in the Oriental poetry which inspires it, one can also say that the poet is his own cupbearer as well as "the cheerer of men's hearts." The point that he is supposed to be intoxicated by his own poetic imagination, the true "Bacchus," is made very clearly in "The Poet" (W.III.28–29). Thus the Dionysian poet partakes both of the subject-object circuit associated with Narcissus and of the power to draw all life from himself which Emerson attributes to his man of genius.

In his theistic aspect, Bacchus definitely fits the fundamental pattern of the other images of this kind used by Emerson. He often appears in disguise, most often as a young boy, "as fair as any girl" and "like a virgin of the sky," says Ovid. This is why Emerson can address the cupbearer as "Bacchus" in his poem of that name (an unconventional directness which the reader does not fully grasp before the last section). This boyish androgyny is complemented by the more terrifying facet of the god which earned him the name "Nyktelios" (The Nocturnal) and caused him to be identified with Hades—the heaven-hell duality that enables Emerson to speak in "Bacchus" about a vine which has "ample leaves and tendrils curled / Among the silver hills of heaven," but whose grapes salute the morning from "A nocturnal root, / Which feels the acrid juice of Styx and Erebus / And turns the woe of Night, / By its own craft, to a more rich delight."

One of the aspects of this heaven-hell marriage in the makeup of Bacchus and his product is the reference to wine as liquid—that is, volcanic fire. The idea can be traced to Hafiz, who in "From the Persian of Hafiz" sees wine as a kind of *crasis* of Ormuzd and Ahriman (P.209). But it is obviously also compatible with the Greek conception of Dionysus. An especially felicitous prose elaboration of the conceit can be found in "The American Scholar," where Emerson, thinking of the divine inspiration of the human mind in a broader sense, says that "It is one central fire, which, flaming now out of the lips of Etna, lightens the capes of Sicily, and now out of the throat of Vesuvius, illuminates the towers and vineyards of Naples" (W.I.108).

In "Bacchus," where the power of the poetic imagination is in the foreground, it is suggested at the very beginning that the poet wants "wine" that "never grew / In the belly of the grape," but "grew on vine whose tap-roots, reaching through / Under the Andes to the Cape / Suffer no savor of the earth to scape." But the most striking image of "wine" as volcanic fire in this poem is the one according to which it is "shed / Like the torrents of the sun / Up the horizon walls." The difference between Dionysian "fire" and Apollinian is here only one of direction, and one is reminded that sunshine alchemically and often in Emerson (e.g., W.IX.131–132) is seen as dry wine, while wine is looked upon as liquid sunshine.

Be it noted, finally, that the horizon, which has given its name to the line which in the horizontal-vertical diagram denotes the earthly and feminine principle, in itself is of no account in terms of either kind of fire. It is simply a line passed through by the jet of divine energy. Thus it is very tempting to relate Emerson's

Apollinian-Dionysian conceit to the one passage in his writings where feminine power is spoken of in terms of volcanic fire: This passage provides some concrete evidence that he is no more eager to see a heaven-hell marriage of this kind in a woman than he is to see androgyny on a feminine basis.

By a remarkable coincidence, this passage occurs in a letter to Margaret Fuller, whose dissatisfaction with his view of horizontal, earthly, and feminine power is as well known as her androgynous aspirations. While formally a comment on something that he had just read in Ockley's *History of the Saracens,* it can thus be seen as an attempt to please her: "The terrible women of that nation," he says, "set me thinking of the *latent* and beneficent state of this wild element in woman. I suppose we are not content with bright loveliness until we discern the deep sparkle of energy which when perverted and outraged flashes up into a volcano jet, and outdares, outwits, and outworks man" (L.II.344–345).

As a compliment to Margaret Fuller's womanhood, this is of course rather backhanded: The adjective "beneficent" is qualified by "perverted," a word suggesting an abnormal and undesirable state of affairs. The journal entry on which this passage is based confirms the impression that he would rather see this sparkle remain unmanifested in women (or else converted into "endurance and overcoming love"). It also contains a reference to the prime weapon of the Maenads, or feminine followers of Bacchus, thus providing an explanation for his comparing their perverted energy to the liquid fire associated with this god. Having said that to read about women who "fought and conquered men" causes "fear, or something like it," Emerson adds, as a kind of gloss: "That is to say I am so effeminate at this moment that the staves of those women do reach unto and hit me too" (JN.VII.399).

14

EUROPE AND ASIA: EMERSON'S MYTH OF THE BALANCED SOUL

It is something of a commonplace to say that Emerson is projecting a personal ideal on Plato when he describes him as a "balanced soul" (W.IV.54–55); in fact, there are scholars in whose judgment Emerson actually became a soul of the kind described in "Plato; or, the Philosopher."[1] The connection between the concept of the "balanced soul" and Emerson's theory of internal marriage is not usually mentioned in this context, however. And yet the idea that Plato's argument and sentence are "self-poised and spherical" is easily related not only to the alchemic West-East *coniunctio* but also to the archetypal use of the sphere as an image of androgynous completeness; in the suggestion that "the excellence of Europe and Asia" are in Plato's brain and that he "came to join, and, by contact, to enhance the energies of each," we are not so far from the image of the fertile androgynous brain described in the adjacent essay on Swedenborg (W.IV.108).

One reason why this aspect of Emerson's analysis has been ignored might be the circumstance that the sexual symbolism he uses does not always fit the idea that Plato and his analyst are balanced souls. F. I. Carpenter, who does see the nuptial overtones of Emerson's discussion of "Europe and Asia," inadvertently puts his finger on one problem when he says that the author of "Plato; or, the Philosopher" sees Asia as "a stay-at-home country" embodying the feminine and passive principle, while Europe with its bustling, outward-bound activity represents the male and active principle in the world.[2] The domestic part of Carpenter's thesis admirably fits the distribution of sex roles in Emerson's early lecture on love (EL.III.62); in the essay on Plato, the domestic analogy might possibly pass along with the polarities borrowed from hermetic-alchemic doctrine, which like Emerson's theory of internal marriage usually posits some kind of balance, although not necessarily on a basis of perfect equality. But the geopolitical allusion seen by Carpenter definitely looks more like subjugation than *coniugium;* here the cross-reference is to the passage in "The Superlative" where Emerson says that "the warm sons of the Southeast have bent the necks under the yoke of the cold temperament and the exact understanding of the Northwestern races" (W.X.179) —that is no balance.

Another circumstance that no doubt lessens the usefulness of the sexual analogy to those who subscribe to the theory of the balanced soul is that neither the man-wife polarity nor its geopolitical complement is used consistently in the essay on Plato. In fact, they do not even represent the dominant tendency: Emerson is, on the whole, perfectly aware that Asia was not exactly stay-at-home country from the point of view of Plato, who after all was born in a century during which Asia in the shape of the formidable Persian empire had twice threatened to impose a political unity on Greece in which this nation, for all its culture and intelligence, would have been the junior partner; like Aeschylus in the trilogy which influenced him so deeply, Emerson tends to associate this Eastern power with fate, nature-earth, and primeval night. Thus the geopolitical balance is tipped in favor of "Asia," and there are also curious reversals in the pattern of universal polarities associated with Europe as a symbol of the "male" pole and "Asia," or the "female" pole. Most strikingly, "Asia" is made to stand for "unity" and "infinity," while the preoccupation with forms and details, which Emerson usually associates with the feminine principle, is attributed to "Europe." Indeed, the superiority of "Asia" sometimes seems so great that it inevitably calls to mind the Great Mother of Asia, supposedly expelled from Greece with the coming of the Greeks but readmitted in the guise of the androgynous Bacchus.

At one point the association of "Asia" with nature-earth and the unity of the Great Mother is obscured and replaced by something more like Emerson's Over-Soul and most likely inspired by the philosophical speculation of Asia from the Hindus to Persia's Zoroaster to Dionysus. "Europe" is in this context made to stand not only for a preoccupation with forms but for frantic activity and diversity in the sphere of generation (W.IV.51). But this bow to a philosophy for which Emerson felt a theoretical sympathy almost looks like a slip. In no way does he come out in favor of reabsorption into the Buddha womb. On the contrary, the predominant polarization immediately reasserts itself; in the very same series of opposites Asia is associated not only with "being" and "genius" but also with "necessity" (fate) and "caste" (birth). These things are closely related to nature and the earth, and at the end of the paragraph we are left with what must be called the essential distinction in the essay: Asia (fate, nature, latent power, everything that tends to inspire in man a feeling of impotence) versus Europe (freedom, mind, manifest or "executive" power, man's determination to overcome).

Such a contradiction is not easily resolved through "marriage." What sympathy could a Europe thus defined possibly muster for an Asia seen as "deaf, unimplorable, immense fate"? Emerson himself suggests a hostile relationship, noting in this very context that the genius of Europe "resists caste by culture" (W.IV.52). In another passage, he explains that the origin of caste is "in the doctrine of the organic character and disposition"—that is, in the idea that some are born to be servants (W.IV.66). Significantly, the word "organic" is also used in a passage of "Courage," where the fact that "culture" twice had to resist "caste" in a military way is referred to in terms that are not very flattering to "Asia": "The best act of the marvellous genius of Greece was its first act . . . in the instinct which, at Thermopylae, held Asia at bay, kept Asia out of Europe,—Asia with its antiquities and organic slavery,—from corrupting the hope and the new morning of the West" (W.VII.272). In the essay on Plato, too, "Asia" tends to turn into something that "Europe" needs to defend and define itself against. In the process, Plato's mind ceases to symbolize the marriage of these poles and becomes synonymous with "Europe."

Emerson does of course feel the attraction of some other aspects of "Asia," Asia as "unity," Asia as "the ocean of love and power" (W.IV.62). When he speaks of the great men which "Nature is incessantly sending up out of Night," he is clearly thinking of the Great Mother operating without help from above (W.IV.40). She is closely related to the Mother one glimpses in the area of the essay entitled "Power" where the most creative period in the history of a nation is defined as the moment when "the swarthy juices" of the "Pelasgic" era (also called "the milk from the teats of nature") are still flowing abundantly (W.VI.69–71).

To some extent the author of "Plato; or, the Philosopher" also tries to develop the idea that his hero came to join "Asia and Europe" on a bipolaric and "balanced" basis. But even when day and heaven are brought into the picture—in the passage where "the moment of adult health, the culmination of power"—the imagery he uses is not nuptial: It is not to be equated with Boehme's alchemic day-night polarities, nor with the archetypal marriage of Ouranos and Gaia. The idea of balance is definitely there, but it is the balance of a man who "with his feet still planted on the immense forces of night, converses by his eyes and brain with solar and stellar creation" (W.IV.46–47). We are forcefully reminded that Emerson's angle of vision after all is upward toward the heaven of Plato and that "begin where we will," all things "ascend and ascend" until the eye and the brain reign supreme. What is more, the wording suggests a historical struggle through which a nation rises to the position which allows it to plant its feet on the Mother from which it has emerged.

If we apply this scenario to the history of Greece (or "Europe"), as Emerson himself does, it inevitably looks like an allusion to Aeschylus' *Oresteia,* in which fate and tragedy are finally overcome through what is represented as a grand reconciliation of the strong but dark and irrational chthonian forces of a vanishing matriarchal era—subtly linked to the barbaric ways of the East— with the enlightened gods of a new, patriarchal civilization. In the outline of the early history of "Europe" leading up to the definition of "the moment of adult health," Emerson does not fail to use words like "fury," "blind force," and "weak vehemence" to describe the preceding era. Such terms perfectly fit the image of the Furies given in the earlier parts of Aeschylus' play and the circumstance that the "reconciliation" of Zeus and Fate really means the utter defeat of the Furies, who after posing a threat to Athens seemingly as great as that represented by Persia in Aeschylus' time are summarily stowed away under the Pelasgian wall.

It is of course an undeniable fact that Emerson also seems to honor Asia, where the cult of the Great Mother lingered on, by suggesting that Plato went there to import the love of unity and infinity allegedly needed by the European mind. But it is worth noting what happens in the essay when the historical perspective changes slightly to focus on what happened after that memorable trip. The thought of Plato is then hailed as a victory over barbarism: "At last comes Plato, the distributor, who needs no barbaric paint, or tattoo, or whooping; for he can define. He leaves with Asia the vast and superlative; he is the arrival of accuracy and intelligence. 'He shall be as a god to me, who can rightly divide and define'" (W.IV.47). Clearly, the moment of Asia is here left behind as not only barbaric but infantile. There is no synthesis, no balance, no marriage, here, but a passionate vindication of distribution and the definitions and boundaries of Europe, which are paradoxically seen as the true source of freedom and liberation from nature. One can say that it is this embracement of "Europe" which distinguishes Emerson's analysis from the views put forth by his reader Nietzsche in *The Birth of Tragedy*. Whereas the latter felt that Socrates and Plato ushered in the decline of Greek civilization by deemphasizing "Dionysian" unity and wholeness in favor of an "Apollinian" sharpness of vision, Emerson seems to look much more indulgently at this development.

In the final analysis, then, the marriage of "Asia and Europe" is not a marriage at all, but a divorce. What Emerson saw in Plato was above all a great rebel, the first true representative of Greece, the nation that created the patriarchal Western civilization after rebelling against the old matriarchal society associated with Asia Minor and the pre-Hellenic era. "He could prostrate himself on the earth," says Emerson, "and cover his eyes whilst he adored that which cannot be numbered, or gauged, or known, or named . . . . No man ever more fully acknowledged the Ineffable." But, he adds, "Having paid his homage, as for the human race, to the Illimitable, he then stood erect, and for the human race affirmed, 'And yet things are knowable'" (W.IV.61–62). As an alternative to this picture of Plato humbling himself before Mother Earth,

Emerson goes on to describe "the Asia" in the philosopher's mind which "was first heartily honored" as "the ocean of love and power, before form, before will, before knowledge, the Same, the Good, the One." Here, too, the mystery religion quickly yields to "the instinct of Europe, namely, culture," and Plato's final feeling is again expressed in the words: "Yet things are knowable!"

In this manner, the "final superiority" of the West, which in "The Superlative" is said to have caused empire to roll that way, receives its due. At the level of the individual, too, it is intimated that the ascendency of the Mother, be she ever so loving and strong, must ultimately be transcended if true manhood is to be attained. The very fact that Emerson suggests that a temporary immersion in Asia as "the ocean of love and power" can be refreshing and empowering tells us that this phrase must not be seen as a reference to the Buddha-womb. The possibility that Emerson might be thinking of something like Freud's "oceanic feeling" is also ruled out; it is hardly compatible with the image of Plato rising to an erect posture. Nor is it conceivable that Emerson would portray his hero as towering over the "Over-Soul," even though this essence and entity is sometimes compared to the ocean. The simplest— and indeed the only—way of making everything fall into place is to assume that we are here dealing with a special application of the horizontal-vertical diagram:[3] the opposition between a potentially sinister ocean of motherly love and power to the erect stature of the male child that is weaned and no longer crawls.

A different way of approaching the problem, and of testing the offered solution, is suggested by the way in which the announced marriage of "Europe and Asia" in Plato's brain turns into a somewhat ambivalent relation between Plato and an outside force. As mentioned, Emerson is commonly thought to have projected his own frame of mind, or the mental attitude he aspired to, on that of his representative philosopher, and it therefore seems natural to wonder whether there is not some connection between the Asia symbolism in the essay on Plato and the author's use of "Asia" as a nickname for his second wife. The insistence with which he uses this and similar nicknames also makes it seem unlikely that the two symbolic nexuses were kept entirely separate in his brain and never overlap and illuminate one another in his works.

It is sometimes suggested that Emerson began to call his wife "Asia" because of her preoccupation with "forms," an attitude that easily leads to strife and schism, as illustrated by the example of the seven quarreling churches of Asia Minor.[4] But it is questionable whether the interpretation of the nickname "Asia" as an allusion to formalistic and schismatic tendencies really does justice to his view of his wife's religious stance at the time when it was first conferred upon her. In the "Divinity School Address" of 1838 (W.I.143), she is alluded to as a "devout" person who eschews religious forms to the point of thinking it wicked to go to church on Sunday (JN.V.442).

It seems more likely that Emerson's choice of nickname for his wife has something to do with the fact that his Aunt Mary had exhorted him to become a Prometheus to men and clearly did so under the influence of Shelley's recently published *Prometheus Unbound* (cf. JN.VII.446). Shelley's "Asia" also represents unity, the healing strength of unity seen as the much-needed complement to the restless analytic intellect of Europe for which Prometheus, like Emerson's Plato, manifestly stands. Obviously, the symbolic pattern of Shelley's long poem, or for that matter of Aeschylus' *Prometheus Bound,* did not fit Emerson's position in every respect; he could hardly endorse the titan's use of Fate as an ally against Zeus and heaven (cf. W.II.30–31). But the qualities attributed to Shelley's "Asia" are rather similar to those which Emerson was looking for in his second wife, who was to make a new home for him and provide the mundane background and base for his intellectual life. Supportive strength is definitely one thing he expected from her (cf. L.I.437); one cannot help thinking of his personal arrangements when he says that his representative philosopher "substructs the religion of Asia, as the base."

The awe-inspiring qualities of "Asia" have often been commented on both by contemporaries who knew her and by later Emerson critics and biographers.[5] She was only slightly older than he was but considerably (nine years) older than his first wife, and in his letter to William announcing the engagement he chooses to stress the idea that she is a person who inspires "respect" (L.I. 436). Quite early he begins to address her as "my Queen," a phrase which later developed into another of his nicknames for her: "Queenie." One also notes that her actual name, "Lydia," which he immediately changed to "Lidian," is closely related to the part of Asia Minor which Euripides so insistently joins to Phrygia as the home of the Great Mother. Whereas the adjective "Lydia" was originally applied to female slaves from that part of the world, Emerson sometimes refers to his wife as his "Lydian Queen." As for "Asia," it is also the place where Paul was confronted with the worship of the Great Mother in the guise of the moon goddess, the Diana of the Ephesians.

This is not all. The moon goddess herself appears in Emerson's writings in a context which at least indirectly involves the motherliness of Lidian. In a journal report on a nightly excursion on the Concord River undertaken with Thoreau in 1841, he describes how the moon rose on the two of them and "sat in her triumph so maidenly and yet so queenly, so modest and yet so strong, that I wonder not that she ever represents the Feminine to men" (JN.VII.455). The passage clearly goes beyond the ordinary alchemic-archetypal equation of the moon and the feminine principle. There is a strong element of maternity in the femininity for which the moon, closely associated with the purity and strength of mother nature, is here made to stand. Emerson understandably does not mention his wife here, but Thoreau, whose admiration for the mother in Lidian was great at the time, significantly echoes the conversation about the moon he had had with his mentor in a letter in which he tells her that he sees in her "a sort of lunar influence," a "moonlight" that follows him wherever he goes: "You must know that you represent to me woman . . . . You always seemed to look down at me as from some elevation . . . one of your high humilities—and I was the better for having to look up."[6]

Scrutinizing Emerson's second marriage for signs of an emotional ambivalence paralleling the ambiguities of his discussion of "Asia" in *Representative Men,* one will find that he himself soon became disappointed in his expectations of motherly strength and support. Moreover, this disappointment matches the feeling of having been let down which one glimpses in some of his references to motherhood, like the suggestion in "Fate" that "the gate of gifts" closes as soon as the child leaves its mother's womb (W.VI.10–11). Lidian, his "fate" in a common sense of the word, also found it difficult to live up to the symbolism placed on her. References to the "dyspepsia" and "flebile tendencies" of the mother of Waldo II began to appear in the journals about the same time as the first comments on her religious conservatism, which of course became more apparent after Emerson had resolutely struck out in what he believed to be a new direction.

When this disappointment combines with the need for freedom to "roam" that Emerson opposes to the strings of marriage, or with his feeling that too much conversation with woman is dangerous to nonconformist manhood (JN.VIII.391), we have something that is not entirely unlike the ambivalent picture of "Asia" given in the essay on Plato. The most striking expression of his determination to stand up to the threat his marriage to Lidian might pose in this respect significantly comes soon after she ceased to be a mere symbol and actually became a mother. The birth of a first son is obviously an occasion which will invite most men to take stock of their situation, but Emerson must be said to muse in a remarkably somber manner about how a man is apt to lose the wife in the mother and for this reason "cannot rejoice with her in the child" (JN.V.297). Moreover, this more than ordinarily potent dose of paternal jealousy also resulted in a poem called "Holidays," in which he grimly notes that his wife is now as firmly anchored in the ground as a tree and that he must loosen his ties to her if he is to rise in the scale of being. Addressing himself as if he were a child that has not been properly weaned, he tells himself to consider his playing days over and grow up: "Now must thou be man and artist, / 'T is the turning of the tide." Sour grapes, perhaps, but also rebellion against the tendency in himself that created this particular dependence in the first place. These lines suggest a compensation along the lines of Plato's vindication of the cultural creativity of men as superior to the biological fertility of women, a theme which philosophically, and possibly also historically, is linked to man's rebellion against the Great Mother.

It must of course be observed that the deep attraction to the Great Mother which caused Emerson to make symbolic use of Lydian was not as easily transcended as his reliance on that particular symbol. The quoted journal passage about the strength and maidenliness of the full moon skirting the treetops and transfiguring nature is one example of abiding attachment. Another is the characterization of "Asia" as an "ocean of love and power" in the essay on Plato.

As for the ambivalence of the account of "Asia" given in *Representative Men,* which eventually cracks the image of Plato as a "balanced soul," it also goes well beyond his ambivalent feelings about any mortal woman. In fact, it goes beyond resistance to any threat that the Great Mother might pose to the coming of age of an individual man or a nation. Ultimately, the attitude Emerson attributes to Plato is a somewhat desperate gesture of defiance in the face of man's destiny. Although this idea is kept in the background in the essay as un-Platonic, "Asia" stands not only for the allegedly constricting and unmanning conventions of the East in association with those imposed by the procreative needs of nature, but also for old age, which Emerson defines as a loss of manhood in this very sense (e.g., W.VI.13 and W.VII.320), and the final unmanning, death, as the return to the womb which comes to all men, regardless of how high they may have risen. With this aspect of "Asia" neither Lidian nor Ruth Emerson can be associated, except by implication.

It might be objected at this point that the Great Mother is not mentioned explicitly either in the essay on Plato or apropos of Emerson's second wife. But such references could hardly be expected, given the personal dimension of his Asia symbolism. The Great Mother *was* part of his rhetorical machinery at the time in contexts where "Asia" is not mentioned. What is more, the peculiar mixture of attraction and repulsion which marks his discussion of "Asia" in *Representative Men* is also present in these instances.

One example occurs in "The Sphinx," the enigmatic piece Emerson chose to put at the head of his *Poems* of 1847. Philosophically speaking, there was definitely something in him that looked with a certain envy at the infant which is there made the symbol of the unity and wholeness that adult men have lost: "The babe by its mother / Lies bathed in joy." The Sphinx, which is contrasting the two states, at one point has "the great mother" angrily wonder who has "drugged my boy's cup"—that is, dissolved his Dionysian unity with her. The awesomeness of the Great Mother (not clearly distinguished from the Sphinx) is well brought out in the words describing the impact of her words: "Cold shuddered the sphere." Nevertheless "a poet" makes bold to answer: "The Lethe of nature / Can't trance him again, / Whose soul sees the perfect / Which his eyes seek in vain." This sounds like an allusion to the irreversible character of the dialectic ascent which leads to a glimpse of Plato's ideas. The preceding lines have a more clearly Western, not to say Faustian, ring: "The fiend that man harries / Is love of the Best; / Yawns the pit of the dragon, / Lit by rays from the blest." Moreover, the Sphinx, having heard the poet, "crouched no more in stone" but turned very genial. At the end, she is "the universal dame," nature mastered and used by the poet.

Another text worth noting is the chapter entitled "Stonehenge" in *English Traits*, a book inspired by Emerson's English lecture trip of 1847–1848 (during which the essay on Plato was one of his offerings). One gathers that Carlyle and other English friends had asked him about his house in Concord and about the American landscape. He reportedly stressed the overwhelming and "overgrowing" character of American nature, on which "man seems not able to make much impression" and which causes a certain "tristesse" in the beholder, especially at night. "There," he adds, "in that great sloven continent, in high Alleghany pastures, in the sea-wide sky-skirted prairie, still sleeps and murmurs and hides the great mother, long since driven away from the trim hedge-rows and over-cultivated garden of England" (W.V.288). Obviously, the Mother is here located in the West, not in the East. On the other hand, England, citadel of the West, is described as a country that has conquered the Great Mother and imposed culture. Moreover, the American situation is deliberately described as preliminary, archaic, and in that respect it fits the distinction between the Pelasgian era and Plato's Greece. The passage must be related to the previous paragraph in "Stonehenge" where Emerson reports that he urged upon Carlyle the idea that America was to replace the mother country as the chief home of the English race; its geography, he says, forces that prophecy on the observer: As the nature to be conquered in America is more powerful than it ever was in England, so man will be stronger in America and ensure that empire continues to roll West.

This said, it is necessary to state again that Emerson's ambivalent attitude to the Great Mother cannot be summed up as a simple oscillation between a nostalgic love of the "unity" of infancy and the rebelliousness of youth (using these phrases in a general and more or less metaphorical sense). There are "other moods," as he himself likes to put it, and occasionally he yields to the previously mentioned un-Platonic feeling that the condition of man is such that it makes final defeat a certainty regardless of individual or national achievement. One example is "Hamatreya," the "Earth-Song" in which Mother Earth is depicted as triumphing over those who would possess her. Another is provided in an earlier part of "Stonehenge."

While the Great Mother is not mentioned by name in this part of the text, the references to "mounds" and "barrows" in the accounts of his and Carlyle's visit to the prehistoric monument on Salisbury Plain does sound like an allusion to Bryant's "Thanatopsis," the poem in which nature—and the prairie with its Indian mounds—is represented as the great womb and tomb of man. The entrance is compared to "the gates of the old cavern temples" as well as to various ancient monuments of the East. Stonehenge is described as "a circular colonnade . . . enclosing a second and a third colonnade" and said to be "the old egg" out of which all the "ecclesiastical structures and history" of the English race had proceeded. On the whole, the stress is here on the immensity and futility of the past. England has had many great and good men, but they and their work seem to have been lost in "the flight of the ages and the succession of religions." Nor does the difference between English and American seem very significant to Emerson in the light of what "the old sphinx" tells him. As he leaves "this quiet house of destiny" with Carlyle in the twilight hour, it must have seemed to him that the Lethe of nature *can* trance even those whose souls have seen the perfect.

William T. Harris noted long ago that while Emerson's characterization of Plato in *Representative Men* may appropriately be applied to himself, he nevertheless "goes farther than Plato toward the Orient, and his pendulum swings farther into the Occident."[7] This statement is noteworthy because it implicitly recognizes that the marriage of "Europe and Asia" in Plato's—or rather in Emerson's—mind is not the kind of dynamic and productive tension suggested by the concept of the "balanced soul," but a passive oscillation between moods. On the other hand, the image of the pendulum still suggests a kind of balance in the idea of a swing that goes equally far in two directions, and here it is as impossible to agree with Harris as it is to agree with those who think that Emerson consistently projects the image of a "balanced soul" in the essay on Plato. Emerson definitely goes farther than Plato in the direction of the Occident—the ancient philosopher is not really interested in "executive power" over nature—but he does not go very far into the Orient. To go farther than Plato in that direction would require an extremely positive attitude to the idea of final reabsorption into the One. Harris is clearly alluding to Emerson's interest in Oriental, and especially Indian, mysticism, but not only does the essay on Plato itself suggest the limits of this interest,—quite generally speaking, navel-studying and a yearning for the Buddha womb are hard to reconcile with aggressive self-assertion, even in terms of a pendulumlike oscillation: Mournful meditations of the kind reflected in "Stonehenge," which can be considered the reverse of such self-assertion, are much more probable.

Very instructive from this point of view is Emerson's relation to the Neo-Platonists who really did what they could to import the element in search of which he says Plato traveled into Egypt and "perhaps even farther East." For good reasons they are not mentioned in the essay on Plato, unless they are included in the "Asia" which at one point is said to represent an attempt to seek liberation from nature and the sphere of generation: Neo-Platonism does not fit the predominant association of "Asia" with nature-earth-night-fate, and any emphasis on the radical monism for which this school eminently stands would entirely upset the idea of a marriage of "Europe and Asia" in Plato's mind which Emerson to some extent does want to promote.

If we look specifically at Plotinus, the Egyptian mystic whose language influenced Emerson so deeply, we might possibly see in his philosophy a facet of the rebellion against the Great Mother started by the Greeks. But it is hardly comparable to the attitude which Emerson attributes to Plato-Europe in *Representative Men.* Moreover, Plotinus' rebellion goes so far that it tends to illustrate his own dictum that "extremes meet." In a sense he stands for an escape from the dominion of the Great Mother into a unity which is either thought of as devoid of attributes or else ambiguously associated with heaven—the opposite of earth—and even with the idea of heavenly fatherhood, more specifically with Father Dionysus. Obviously, the difference between the Great Mother and Dionysus is not so great in every respect. As mentioned, what Emerson sees as self-assertion and even rebellion against the Great Mother is by

Nietzsche construed as an attack on the Dionysian unity which he feels was respected by the Greeks during the archaic period. Plotinus' "Dionysian" unity is not of the popular kind, of course. Yet one may reasonably look upon his ecstatic reunion with the One as an aristocratic and solitary version of the unity offered by the Great Mother whose cult still blends with that of Dionysus in Euripides' *Bacchae*.

Some of Plotinus' most frequently used imagery supports this thesis. Whether it is to be seen as a last metaphorical reflection of an older religion or as a lingering personal attraction—Porphyry stresses that Plotinus was not weaned until he was eight—the image of the suckling infant is hard to miss in his references to "Dionysian" drinking. Moreover, his Dionysian "intoxication" is not unlike the assimilation "by the draught" of which Emerson speaks in "Bacchus." In these terms, the reunion with "the One" is a reabsorption into the womb of Father Bacchus. Accordingly, Stephen MacKenna points out that the soul's "odyssey" back to the "Fatherland" in "three successive stages of internalization and simplification" is a process more aptly called "envelopment" than development.[8] From this point of view, too, reunion with the All is a return to a male womb.

One may be surprised at the extent to which Emerson follows Plotinus in arrogating motherly qualities and attributes to a Deity which he usually thinks of as masculine. But the resemblance is actually superficial. When he speaks of genius as "a larger imbibing of the common heart" in "The Over-Soul," or of advanced souls who find God "a sweet enveloping thought" in the same essay (W.II.288 and 295), he is not referring to a final reabsorption into the One, or even an anticipation of that event. As in other cases when he speaks in this vein, he is extolling the blessings of "unity" with God in this life. Moreover, he is as interested in power as in security. This tendency is equally obvious in the definition of genius put forward in "The Over-Soul," and in the previously cited passage in "Bacchus," not to mention the reference to a wine "hid in milk" in the Dionysian poem called "May-Day." Finally, Emerson is not exclusively concerned with the destiny of the individual soul in this context. A statement in *Nature*, for instance, specifically deals with man as a species: "As a plant upon the earth, so man rests upon the bosom of God; he is nourished by unfailing fountains, and draws at his need inexhaustible power" (W.I.64). Significantly, the passage is followed by what looks like an allusion to the "Ode to Man" in Sophocles' *Antigone* (explicitly mentioned in the previous section): "Who can set bounds to the possibilities of Man?"

Nature also illustrates another trait in Emerson's answer to "Eastern" mysticism, the fact that the power man gains by immersion in the universal womb or at the teats of God as often as not is power over nature. In the process, nature tends to be seen in a monistic perspective: She is dependent on man for any happy effect she may produce; she is an instrument which he uses to realize his own potential. At the same time, however, one cannot help noticing certain dualistic notes similar to those which so often form the reverse of Emerson's monism. He may deny that he has any hostility to nature of the kind that he here attributes to Plotinus and say: "I do not wish to fling stones at my beautiful mother, nor spoil my gentle nest." Nevertheless he comes through as a rebellious son when he adds that all he wants to do is "to indicate the true position of nature in regard to man" (W.I.59). This position obviously is under man, so far as he is concerned— the statement follows a sympathetic outline of the idealist position in the course of which he says that "the devotee 'flouts' nature" and that religion and ethics put her "under foot." The idea is given a sexual overtone in the earlier suggestion that "this feeble human being has penetrated the vast masses of nature with an informing soul."

Emerson is not entirely exempt from the death-wish. But it never takes the form of a yearning for the heavenly and fatherly womb; it is always a surrender to the Great Mother demanding her own back. Besides, the desire to be reabsorbed into the womb of Mother Nature seizes him quite rarely. What one finds in his works is hardly more than instances of a momentary acquiescence in this prospect attributable to feelings or anticipations of weakness and tiredness. A good example of his acceptance of the "common fate" of "Nature's child" is "A Mountain Grave," a poem written at a time when, significantly, he still felt threatened by tuberculosis; another is the account of the poet's destination given at the end of the first section of "Woodnotes": "Then will my mother yield / A pillow in her greenest field."

An actual desire to die is expressed in a journal report on a walk with Hawthorne in 1842 in which he notes, "The days of September are so rich that it seems natural to walk to the end of one's strength, and fall prostrate saturated with the fine floods, and cry *Nunc dimittis me"* (JN.VIII.272). Yet here, too, one senses, as the reverse side of the ecstasy, a preoccupation with the idea of ebbing power underlined by Emerson's use of the words of the old Simeon: These are the words of a man who wants to use a moment of crowning happiness as a kind of anesthesia, to quit while he is still ahead.

The essay entitled "Nature" (1844) strikes a similar and yet different note. The initial paragraph describes the refulgence of Indian summer in terms evocative of the Great Mother. It is subtly suggested that there may be something treacherous about the perfection of the sensible world on such days, which makes it seem "as if nature would indulge her offspring." On the other hand, it makes one feel ready to die: "To have lived through all its sunny hours, seems longevity enough." Moreover, when the author turns to interpreting the look of things after dark, he seems to revel in a feeling of personal insignificance and impotence flowing from a realization of the irrelevance of the "solemn trifles" that usually occupy him: "Here we find Nature to be the circumstance which dwarfs every other circumstance, and judges like a god all men that come to her. We have crept out of our close and crowded houses into the night and morning, and we see what majestic beauties daily wrap us in their bosom. . . . How easily we might walk onward into the opening landscape, absorbed by new pictures and by thoughts fast succeeding each other, until by degrees the recollection of home was crowded out of the mind, all memory obliterated by the tyranny of the present, and we were led in triumph by nature" (W.III.169–170).

In some respects this imagined triumph of nature is not unlike the surrender described in the journal note concerning the walk with Hawthorne. However, one soon realizes that the death and reabsorption Emerson is imagining in this case is not necessarily final: As one reads on, healing and recovery become important themes. Moreover—and this really introduces a new element— what the return to the womb of nature is supposed to heal him from is the disease he has contracted by yielding to the biological imperatives of life, here symbolized by the home he is walking away from. The new home that Lidian had made for him is contrasted with matter conceived of as our "old home" in accordance with the close etymological connection between "matter" and "mater" (Latin for "mother"). The way in which he speaks of making friends with this matter (rock, water, etc.) strongly suggests that he is playing with the idea of being returned to the womb of things only in order to be purified and granted a new start provided with the "new amounts of vivacity" for which one, as he points out in "Power," cannot return to one's mother's womb (W.VI.73).

One can see this passage as further proof of the lasting attraction certain aspects of the Great Mother held for Emerson in spite of the frailty of individual symbols. But it also demonstrates in a new manner the ambivalence which characterizes his approach to this female potentate. It is not enough for him to dissociate the "old home" from the new home run by his wife and his mother: Apparently self-conscious about the discrepancy between his "old home" and Plotinus' conception of it, he proceeds to remove it as much as possible from the idea of matter and motherhood. No sooner has he introduced the notion of making friends with matter before this "old home," so to speak, changes sex before our eyes and turns into "an old friend," indeed "a dear old friend," as if the author wanted to allude to his friend and guide around the "old home" on this and many other occasions—Henry Thoreau. Significantly, Emerson habitually thinks of Thoreau as Pan in disguise (L.III.44 and JN.X.344): The most striking gesture by which he signals his retreat from the worship of the Great Mother is the insistent suggestion that it is really all the elements together— those of the sky as well as those of the earth—that beguile him. Accordingly, as Emerson describes how he and his friend stole out at night to experience ecstasy on the breast of the river, his house is denounced for standing "in low land, with limited outlook."

This section of "Nature" hardly becomes less interesting because the reason we know Thoreau is involved is that the section is based in part on Emerson's experience during the very excursion with him in the course of which the feminine and motherly qualities of the moon were discussed. What strikes one most in comparing the journal entry with the corresponding portion of "Nature" is actually the way in which the symbolic importance of the stars is stressed in the latter text at the expense of the moon. This strategy obviously fits the switch from Nature-the-Mother to Pan, the companion of Dionysus. The sublunary sphere is too confined and womblike, too strongly bound up with the idea of an "over-growing" nature (also cf. JN.V.496–497), to leave sufficient room for infinite transcendental yearning. The stars do have an advantage from that point of view.

On the other hand, some of the things Emerson says in this essay call to mind the chaser of nymphs rather than the Pan he identifies with the All. After describing how he and Thoreau "with one stroke of the paddle" leave the house and the village for the bright realm of the river, he exclaims with an enthusiasm one will look in vain for in the erotic imagery of *Nature*: "We penetrate bodily this incredible beauty: We dip our hands in this painted element: our eyes are bathed in these lights and forms." No doubt this emphasis is made possible by the reduced role of the moon, associated with Emerson's wife in both his mind and Thoreau's. But the opposition of the "old home" to the new home does seem relevant in this respect, too. One can see how Emerson's thirst for beauty, not satisfied at home any more than his need for strength and purity, would make him turn to nature for certain forms of sensual enjoyment—in slightly ironic fashion, one might add, since the wording seems to contradict his habitual assertions that beauty cannot be "possessed and handled."

Considerations of space make it impossible to follow in any detail the fascinating contortions Emerson goes through to reconcile his desire to enjoy nature with his duty as a worshiper and priest of Pan, "the most continent of gods" (W.III.177). However, it needs to be said that the aggressiveness expressed in the passage in *Nature* where he also uses the verb "penetrate" is by no means absent in "Nature." Somewhat later in this essay, the idea of a romantic conquest acquires clearly dualistic overtones, incidentally of a kind that one will look in vain for in Thoreau, who, for all his "walking" away from a worn-out "East," is much less representative of the peculiarly Western spirit in this respect.[9] One notes in particular the image of a boy who falls to dreaming about "the possessors of nature" as he listens to a military band playing "on the field at night." In the end, the conclusion is not so different from the position outlined in *Nature,* although possibly somewhat less sanguine: When we are "convalescent"—i.e., when we have attained adult health—we will not look up to nature, she will "look up to us." In fact, "the necessity of being beautiful under which every landscape lies" is even now the mind of man.

Toward the end of "Nature," the conflict between man and nature becomes more difficult to bridge, as the author turns his attention to her less lovable, "secular" aspect, of which one only catches a glimpse in the earlier essay. The introduction to this part of Emerson's argument in a sense is a reference to the scholastic distinction between *natura naturata* (nature passive, nature as effect) and *natura naturans* (nature active, "the quick cause"). Nature in her feminine aspect is nature beautiful, of course, challenging us to know and possess it as a mirror of the beauty of man's mind. But she is also secular nature, not so easy to know and possess, considering her vastness. Emerson uses the feminine pronoun when he notes: "Her mighty orbit vaults like the fresh rainbow into the deep, but no archangel's wing was yet strong enough to follow it, and report of the return of the curve." The same pronoun appears a few sentences later: "If we measure our individual forces against hers, we may feel as if we were the sport of an insuperable destiny" (W.III.194).

An entirely new idea is introduced when Emerson says that we nevertheless do not have to feel discouraged because we do not have to identify with the part of us that suffers and dies, the self that seems to be subject to the rule of the Great Mother and part and parcel of *natura naturata*—that we will be saved if "instead of identifying ourselves with the work, we feel that the soul of the workman streams through us." The pantheistic conception of the womb of the All is here overlaid by a polarization of the world in analogy with the sexual dichotomy. But that is not all: One is tempted to see a reflection of the author's old theistic beliefs in the suggested possibility of identification with one's Maker, accompanied as it is by references to spirit escorts and "a beneficent purpose" awaiting man as the species for whose sake the universe presumably exists. Indeed, the suggestion that we may allow ourselves to be "enveloped" in the universal stream by an act of free choice, as it were, paints shades of the baptism and the *uterus ecclesiae,* another name for the male womb of Christ. In spite of

Emerson's way of dissociating himself from "popular" ideas about personal immortality, the promise of victory and power, along with security through identification with the race as well as with the spirit that guides it, may well have a Christian connection. Paul, Roman citizen and enemy of the Great Mother, has much to say about the power and glory which we will inherit if we agree to be reborn as the children of God.

For this portion of "Nature," the appropriate gloss is a journal note from 1839 inspired by another walk with Thoreau, late in the fall while the leaves were turning. Old age and death were on the conversational agenda: It is "a sad riddle" read to us by a "Stony Sphinx," the stark image of the womb-tomb of postlapsarian nature, says Emerson, only to reverse himself and suggest that we ought not to feel threatened by things like the Fall and old age, "lying as we do in this eternal soul originating benefit forevermore." His belief in the fatherly benevolence of the universe is here based on the observation that "the Power that deals with us" reveals itself only partially and gradually. It is "dazzling terrific inaccessible," but it is also a power "which we study and which we are to inherit as fast as we learn to use it" (JN.VII.249–252).

At the end of "Nature," we are far from any kind of balance of "Europe and Asia," in spite of the quasi-sexual polarization of *natura naturans* and *natura naturata*. Emerson says that we are aware "that we traverse the whole scale of being, from the centre to the poles of nature," and that it therefore does not make any difference what happens to us personally in the end: "Let the victory fall where it will, we are on that side." But his tone makes it as clear on which side the victory will fall as that we will be there. This vaguely optimistic statement hardly represents a real attempt to face the problem posed by nature-fate as a cause of despair, pain, and final defeat. As in the quoted journal passage, the problem is on the whole disposed of by looking the other way.

The difficulty of looking this Medusa in the eye is shown by what happens in "Fate" (1860), the only place where Emerson tries to do this in a sustained manner. This text is nevertheless worth examining as his final statement on this issue and because it in a sense resumes the discussion begun in 1844 and carries it to its logical end. One can also say that it returns us to the problem of "Plato; or, the Philosopher," simplified and stripped of the ambiguities flowing from the symbolic use of the name "Asia." The opposition of Europe and Asia is present, as is the association of Asia with feminine qualities and motherhood, but the name "Asia" does not appear. Nor are any of the attractive aspects of nature—like, say, her beneficent motherly strength—allowed to confuse the issue. What we have is the stark conflict between the East (associated with fate, matter, circumstance, servitude) and the West (associated with freedom, mind, power, progress).

Doubtless the author of "Fate" does make certain gestures that seem calculated to bring about something like the "coincidence of the Eastern and Western speculation" which Emerson here attributes to Schelling (W.VI.12–13). He specifically suggests that "a just balance" is needed; indeed, even the ideal of the "balanced soul" tends to reappear, thanks to his focus, which is "the conduct of life," and his decision to obey his own "polarity" in the hope that it will prove in line with the universal spirit of the time (and that of all times). In accordance with these principles, a good deal is initially conceded to nature, fate, and the East (which here also stands for ancient times). The Eastern and early races are given credit for a healthy respect for fate. There are references to the leading role given to fate in Greek tragedy, including what looks like an allusion to Aeschylus' use of the ferocious inhabitants of the ocean as a reflection of the savagery of fate–earth–night–the East (W.VI.5–8).

However, already the circumstance that the arguing on the other side is reserved for the second part of the essay, where the emphasis naturally falls, tends to tip the balance in favor of freedom. In this part we are moreover soon reminded that the pains and defeats of individuals must be balanced against "the ascending effort of the universe" (which of course is associated with "the imperial Saxon race" and Western technology). In this context, Emerson makes some attempts to suggest an almost nuptial relation between freedom and fate; he even resorts to his usual alchemic language in order to show how the world spirit transmutes individual pain into universal benefit (W.VI.35–40). But the idea of a nuptial relation is superseded by that of the rider and the ridden, the victor and "the vanquished enemy." Fate, we are told, is really only causes which are yet "unpenetrated" (W.VI.32–33). It is also clear that the ultimate result of "amelioration" will be a rather different "unity," the kind which swallows one of the poles. In any time, "Intellect annuls fate." All we have to do is place ourselves in the stream of thought, conceived of as a kind of womb ("It is not in us so much as we are in it") and we will be "born again" immortal, as it were, and heirs to final victory and universal power (W.VI.23–25).

It is true that Emerson says at the end of "Fate" that we ought to "build altars to the beautiful Necessity." But the acquiescence and even embracement of the inevitable that he recommends here is quite different from the "instinctive" acceptance of fate which he at the beginning attributes to the Eastern and ancient nations. In fact, the "necessity" which he speaks of here is not fate at all, but the laws of the universe as defined by Western man. Some of them may be tough on him but are yet acceptable as "dictation which knows itself." We can and must accept what we ourselves in a sense have legislated for nature.

Emerson's most balanced solution to the problem posed by "the terrific benefactor" who secures universal benefit through individual pain is that of "the double consciousness": "A man must ride alternately on the horses of his private and his public nature, as the equestrians in the circus throw themselves nimbly from horse to horse, or plant one foot on the back of one and the other foot on the back of the other." This definitely goes beyond what he says at the end of "Nature," and no doubt taking sides with the universe against oneself may in some circumstances offer a kind of bitter consolation; Spinoza certainly believed so. On the other hand, the image suggests certain difficulties. Not least in these terms, the balancing of "Europe and Asia" is precarious at best.

NOTES

CHAPTER ONE

1. Cf. Stephen Whicher, *Freedom and Fate: An Inner Life of Ralph Waldo Emerson* (Philadelphia: Univ. of Pennsylvania Press, 1953), p. 47.

2. Charles Feidelson discusses this problem, although from a rather different point of view, in *Symbolism and American Literature* (Chicago: Univ. of Chicago Press, 1953), pp. 119–161.

3. Not surprisingly, Emerson figures prominently in R. W. B. Lewis' *The American Adam* (Chicago: Univ. of Chicago Press, 1955).

4. For Emerson's use of Oegger's *The True Messiah,* also see K. W. Cameron, *Emerson the Essayist,* 2 vols. (Raleigh, N. C.: Thistle Press, 1944), 1: 295–302.

5. Cf. G. R. Elliott, "Emerson as Diarist," *The University of Toronto Quarterly* 6 (April, 1937): 299–308.

6. Walter Harding, *Emerson's Library* (Charlottesville, Va.: Univ. Press of Virginia, 1967), pp. 133–134, and Vivian Hopkins, "Emerson and Cudworth," *American Literature* 23 (March, 1951): 80–98.

7. Emerson's use of the sun-earth *coniunctio* is conspicuous enough for Carl Jung to refer to it in *Psychology and Alchemy,* vol. 12 of the *Collected Works,* ed. William McGuire, trans. R. F. C. Hull, 2nd rev. ed. (Princeton: Princeton Univ. Press, 1968), p. 343 n.

8. Cf. John Harrison, *The Teachers of Emerson* (New York: Sturgis and Walton, 1910), p. 70.

9. See Ronald Gray, *Goethe, the Alchemist* (Cambridge, England: Cambridge Univ. Press, 1952), especially the chapter "Male and Female."

10. Désirée Hirst, *Hidden Riches: Traditional Symbolism from the Renaissance to Blake* (London: Eyre and Spottiswoode, 1964), p. 306.

CHAPTER TWO

1. Kate Millet, *Sexual Politics* (New York: Doubleday, 1970).
2. Margaret Fuller, *Woman in the Nineteenth Century, and Kindred Papers Relating to the Sphere, Condition and Duties of Women,* ed. Arthur B. Fuller (1874; rpt. New York: Greenwood Press, 1968).
3. Fuller, *Woman,* p. 102.
4. D. H. Lawrence, *Studies in Classic American Literature* (1923; rpt. New York: Viking Press, 1964), passim.

CHAPTER THREE

1. Cf. Léon Robin, *La théorie platonicienne de l'amour* (Paris: F. Alcan, 1908), pp. 191–193.
2. James Elliot Cabot, *A Memoir of Ralph Waldo Emerson,* 2 vols. (Boston: Houghton Mifflin, 1887), I: 61–62.
3. René Wellek, *A History of Modern Criticism: 1750–1950,* 4 vols. (New Haven: Yale Univ. Press, 1965), 1: 150.
4. Robert Clements, *The Poetry of Michelangelo* (New York: New York Univ. Press, 1966), pp. 144 ff. and 211 ff.
5. Emerson used Giambattista Biagiolo's edition of the *Rime* (Parigi: Dondey-Dupré, 1831) for the translations discussed by F. B. Newman in "Emerson and Buonarroti," *The New England Quarterly* 25 (1952): 524–535. For the history of the bowdlerization of Michelangelo's verse, see, besides Clements, E. N. Girardi's edition of the *Rime* (Bari: G. Laterza, 1960).
6. Girardi, *Rime,* no. 260.
7. John Addington Symonds, *The Life of Michelangelo Buonarroti* (1892; rpt. New York: Capricorn, 1962), p. 171.
8. Vivian Hopkins, *Spires of Form: A Study of Emerson's Aesthetic Theory* (1951; rpt. New York: Russell and Russell, 1965), pp. 63 ff. ("The Work of Art").
9. Charles Seymour Jr., *Michelangelo's David: A Search for Identity* (Pittsburgh: Univ. of Pittsburgh Press, 1967).

CHAPTER FOUR

1. Sherman Paul, *Emerson's Angle of Vision* (Cambridge, Mass.: Harvard Univ. Press, 1952), p. 239 n. 9.
2. Newton Arvin, "The House of Pain: Emerson and the Tragic Sense," *The Hudson Review* 12 (April, 1959): 37–53.
3. G. Wilson Knight, *The Wheel of Fire,* 4th rev. ed. (London: Methuen, 1949), pp. 298–325 ("Hamlet Reconsidered").
4. Cf. Richard Chase, *Whitman Reconsidered* (New York: William Sloane, 1955), p. 35.

CHAPTER FIVE

1. S. G. Brown, "Emerson's Platonism," *New England Quarterly* 18 (Sept., 1945): 325–345.
2. See, for instance, pp. 222, 83–86, and 157 in the edition of Taylor's translation of the *Timaeus* and *Critias* published by the Princeton University Press in 1944.
3. Ralph William Inge, *The Philosophy of Plotinus,* 2 vols. (London: Longmans, Green, 1918), 1: 77 and 1: 177.
4. Arthur Lovejoy, *The Great Chain of Being* (1936; rpt. Cambridge, Mass.: Harvard Univ. Press, 1966), p. 319 ff.
5. Lewis Mumford, *The Golden Day* (1926; rpt. New York: Dover, 1968), p. 49.
6. L. E. Emerson, "Emerson and Freud: A Study in Contrasts," *Psychoanalytic Review* 20 (1933): 208–209.

CHAPTER SIX

1. John Albee, *Remembrances of Emerson* (New York: R. G. Cooke, 1901), p. 27.
2. Perry Miller, *Consciousness in Concord* (Boston: Houghton Mifflin, 1958), p. 95.
3. Carl Strauch, "Hatred's Swift Repulsions: Emerson, Margaret Fuller, and Others," *Studies in Romanticism* 7 (Winter, 1968): 87.
4. Paul, *Angle of Vision,* p. 182.
5. Ralph L. Rusk, *The Life of Ralph Waldo Emerson* (New York: Columbia Univ. Press, 1964), p. 281.
6. Edmund Berry, *Emerson's Plutarch* (Cambridge, Mass.: Harvard Univ. Press, 1961), pp. 174 and 184.
7. See *Dante's Vita Nuova Translated by Ralph Waldo Emerson,* ed. J. Chesley Mathews (*Harvard Library Bulletin* no. 11, Spring and Autumn, 1957; rpt.), The Ralph Waldo Emerson Memorial Association, 1957, p. i.
8. Rusk, *Life of Emerson,* p. 145.
9. This is the file edited by E. W. Gregg in *One First Love: The Letters of Ellen Louisa Tucker to Ralph Waldo Emerson* (Cambridge, Mass.: Harvard Univ. Press, 1962).

CHAPTER SEVEN

1. Henry Nash Smith, "Emerson's Problem of Vocation," *The New England Quarterly* 12 (March–December, 1939): 52–67.
2. M. C. Conway, *Emerson at Home and Abroad* (Boston: J. R. Osgood, 1882), pp. 32 ff.
3. Rusk, *Life of Emerson,* p. 31.

4. Régis Michaud, *The Enraptured Yankee,* trans. George Boas (New York: Harper, 1964), p. 19.

5. Rusk, *Life of Emerson,* p. 4.

6. T. S. Eliot, "Hamlet and His Problems," *The Sacred Wood,* 7th ed. (London: Methuen, 1966), pp. 95–103.

7. Sigmund Freud, *The Interpretation of Dreams,* trans. and ed. James Strachey (New York: Avon, 1968), pp. 298–299. Cf. Ernest Jones, *Hamlet and Oedipus* (Garden City, N.Y.: Doubleday, 1954).

8. *The Journals of Charles King Newcomb,* ed. Judith Kennedy Johnson (Providence, R.I.: Brown Univ. Press, 1946), p. 262.

9. See, for instance, Knight, *Wheel of Fire,* p. 315, and John Dover Wilson, *What Happens in Hamlet* (1935; Cambridge, England: Cambridge Univ. Press, 1964), p. 306.

10. *The Parnassus,* Ralph Waldo Emerson, ed. (Boston: J. R. Osgood, 1874).

CHAPTER EIGHT

1. Frank Sanborn, *The Personality of Emerson* (Boston: Charles E. Goodspeed, 1903), p. 99.

2. *The Journals of Bronson Alcott,* ed. Odell Shepard (Boston: Little Brown, 1938), pp. 284, 336, and 173.

3. C. G. Shaw, "Emerson the Nihilist," *International Journal of Ethics* 25 (October, 1914): 68–86.

4. Cf. the discussion of Philip L. Nicoloff in *Emerson on Race and History: An Examination of English Traits* (New York: Columbia Univ. Press, 1961).

5. Cf. Michele Schiavone, *Il problema dell' amore nel mondo greco* (Milano: Marzorati, 1965), 1: 192 (so far as I know, no other volumes have appeared).

6. See Rudolf Hirzel, *Plutarch* (Leipzig: Dieterich, 1912), pp. 22 and 28.

7. F. I. Carpenter, *Emerson Handbook* (New York: Hendricks House, 1953), p. 10.

CHAPTER NINE

1. Rusk, *Life of Emerson,* p. 311, and Townsend Scudder, *The Lonely Wayfaring Man* (London and New York: Oxford Univ. Press, 1936).

2. For Wilkinson, see Emanuel Swedenborg, *The Economy of the Animal Kingdom,* trans. A. Clissold, with Introductory Notes by James John Garth Wilkinson (London: W. Newberry, 1846).

3. See Kenneth Cameron, "Emerson, Thoreau, and the Town and Country Club," *The Emerson Society Quarterly* 8 (1957): 2 ff.

4. Wellek, *Modern Criticism,* 3: 169.

5. Denis de Rougemont, *Love Declared,* trans. Richard Howard (New York: Pantheon, 1963), pp. 101–107.

CHAPTER TEN

1. E. W. Emerson, *Emerson in Concord: A Memoir* (Boston: Houghton Mifflin, 1916), p. 35; Rusk, *Life of Emerson,* p. 121.
2. *The Letters of Ralph Waldo Emerson,* ed. Ralph L. Rusk, 6 vols. (New York: Columbia Univ. Press, 1939), 2: 341 n.
3. *Select Works of Plotinus,* ed. and trans. Thomas Taylor (London: The Author, 1817), p. 506.

CHAPTER ELEVEN

1. *The Journals of Bronson Alcott,* p. 221.
2. See Miller, *Concord,* pp. 32, 94, and 96.
3. Margaret Fuller, "The Great Lawsuit—Man Versus Men; Woman Versus Women," in *The Dial: A Magazine for Literature, Philosophy and Religion* 4, i (July, 1843): 1–11.
4. Harding, *Library,* pp. 133–134.
5. Mario Praz, *The Romantic Agony,* trans. Angus Davidson (Cleveland and New York: Meridian Books, 1956).
6. Mark Rose, "Sidney's Womanish Man," *Review of English Studies* 15 (1964): 353–354.
7. Paul, *Angle of Vision,* p. 171.
8. Robert Langbaum, *The Poetry of Experience* (New York: Norton, 1957).
9. Henry James (the elder), *The Literary Remains* (Boston: Osgood, 1885), p. 296.
10. Cabot, *Memoir,* 1: 353–354 and 1: 358.
11. For this whole syndrome, see Knight, *Wheel of Fire,* p. 312 ff.
12. Fuller, *Woman,* p. 116.
13. Fuller, *Woman,* p. 233.
14. Fuller, *Woman,* p. 63.
15. See the letter to Elizabeth Hoar reprinted in *Margaret Fuller, American Romantic: A Selection from Her Writings and Correspondence,* ed. Perry Miller (Garden City, N.Y.: Doubleday, 1963), pp. 261–265.
16. Fuller, *Woman,* p. 129.
17. Gray, *Goethe,* p. 223.

CHAPTER TWELVE

1. Michaud, *Enraptured Yankee,* pp. 216–217.
2. Jean-Paul Sartre, *Baudelaire* (Paris: Gallimard, 1968), pp. 227–228 (my translation). For Emerson's influence on Baudelaire, cf. Margaret

Gilman, "Baudelaire and Emerson," *Romanic Review* 24 (October, 1943): 211–222.

3. Austin Warren, *New England Saints* (Ann Arbor, Mich.: Univ. of Michigan Press, 1956), p. 46.

4. Charles Andler, *Nietzsche, sa vie et sa pensée,* 3 vols. (Paris: Bossard, 1920), 1: 342.

5. Anders Nygren, *Agape and Eros,* trans. Philip S. Watson (London: S.P.C.K., 1953), vol. 2, pt. 1, p. 458.

6. Georg Brandes, *Michelangelo: His Life, His Times, His Era,* trans. Heinz Norden (New York: Ungar, 1963), p. 379.

7. Mumford, *Golden Day,* p. 45.

CHAPTER THIRTEEN

1. Charles Woodbury, *Talks with Emerson* (1890; rpt. New York: Horizon Press, 1970), p. 53.

2. This is also the conclusion of F. W. Wahr in *Emerson and Goethe* (Ann Arbor, Mich.: G. Wahr, 1915), p. 117.

CHAPTER FOURTEEN

1. See, for instance, Edward Wagenknecht, *Ralph Waldo Emerson: Portrait of a Balanced Soul* (New York: Oxford Univ. Press, 1974). The classic example of course is John Jay Chapman's analysis in *Emerson and Other Essays* (1899; rpt. New York: AMS, 1969), pp. 36–37.

2. F. I. Carpenter, *Emerson and Asia* (Cambridge, Mass.: Harvard Univ. Press, 1930), p. 38.

3. Paul, *Angle of Vision,* p. 239.

4. Cf. Rusk, *Life of Emerson,* p. 226.

5. E. g., Jonathan Bishop, *Emerson on the Soul* (Cambridge, Mass.: Harvard Univ. Press, 1964), p. 182.

6. Here quoted from *Familiar Letters of Thoreau,* vol. 11 of *The Writings of Henry David Thoreau,* ed. Frank Sanborn (Boston: Riverside, 1894), p. 89 ff. Cf. the discussion in Henry Seidel Canby's *Thoreau* (1939; rpt. Gloucester, Mass.: P. Smith, 1965), pp. 162–163.

7. William T. Harris, "Emerson's Orientalism" in *The Genius and Character of Emerson* (Boston: J. R. Osgood, 1885), p. 372.

8. Paul Henry, Introduction to the *Enneads,* by Plotinus, trans. Stephen MacKenna, rev. B. G. Page (London: Faber and Faber, 1962), pp. lx–lxi.

9. Cf. Joel Porte, *Emerson and Thoreau: Transcendentalists in Conflict* (Middletown, Conn.: Wesleyan Univ. Press, 1966). Although Porte does not stress the point, I think there is a relation between this difference in attitude and the circumstance that it is Emerson, not Thoreau, he has chosen to portray as a truly representative American in his recent work, *Representative Man: Ralph Waldo Emerson in His Time* (New York: Oxford Univ. Press, 1979).

BIBLIOGRAPHY

Albee, John. *Remembrances of Emerson.* New York: R. G. Cooke, 1901.
Alcott, Amos Bronson. *The Journals of Bronson Alcott.* Edited by Odell Shephard. Boston: Little, Brown, 1938.
Andler, Charles. *Nietzsche, sa vie et sa pensée.* 3 vols. Paris: Bossard, 1920.
Arvin, Newton. "The House of Pain: Emerson and the Tragic Sense." *The Hudson Review* 12 (April, 1959): 37–53.
Berry, Edmund. *Emerson's Plutarch.* Cambridge, Mass.: Harvard Univ. Press, 1961.
Bishop, Jonathan. *Emerson on the Soul.* Cambridge, Mass.: Harvard Univ. Press, 1964.
Brandes, Georg. *Michelangelo: His Life, His Times, His Era.* Translated by Heinz Norden. New York: Ungar, 1963.
Brown, S. G. "Emerson's Platonism." *The New England Quarterly* 18 (Sept., 1945): 325–345.
Buonarroti, Michelangelo. *Le rime di Michelangelo Buonarroti il vecchio.* With commentary by Giambattista Biagiolo. Parigi: Dondey-Dupré, 1831.
———. *Le rime di Michelangelo Buonarroti.* Edited by E. N. Girardi. Bari: G. Laterza, 1960.
Cabot, James Elliot. *A Memoir of Ralph Waldo Emerson.* 2 vols. Boston: Houghton Mifflin, 1887.
Cameron, Kenneth W. *Emerson the Essayist.* 2 vols. Raleigh, N.C.: Thistle Press, 1944.
———. "Emerson, Thoreau, and the Town and Country Club." *Emerson Society Quarterly* 8 (1957): 2–17.
Canby, Henry Seidel. *Thoreau.* 1939. Reprint. Gloucester, Mass.: P. Smith, 1965.

Carpenter, F. I. *Emerson and Asia.* Cambridge, Mass.: Harvard Univ. Press, 1930.

———. *Emerson Handbook.* New York: Hendricks House, 1953.

Chapman, John Jay. *Emerson and Other Essays.* 1899. Reprint. New York: AMS, 1969.

Chase, Richard. *Whitman Reconsidered.* New York: William Sloane, 1955.

Clements, Robert. *The Poetry of Michelangelo.* New York: New York Univ. Press, 1966.

Conway, M. C. *Emerson at Home and Abroad.* Boston: James R. Osgood, 1882.

A Correspondence between John Sterling and Ralph Waldo Emerson. Edited by E. W. Emerson. Boston: Houghton Mifflin, 1897.

The Correspondence between Ralph Waldo Emerson and Hermann Grimm. Edited by F. W. Holls. Boston: Houghton Mifflin, 1903.

The Correspondence of Carlyle and Emerson. Edited by Joseph Slater. New York: Columbia Univ. Press, 1965.

Eliot, T. S. "Hamlet and His Problems." *The Sacred Wood.* 7th ed. London: Methuen, 1950.

Elliott, G. R. "Emerson as Diarist." *The University of Toronto Quarterly* 6 (April, 1937): 299–308.

Emerson, E. W. *Emerson in Concord: A Memoir.* Boston: Houghton Mifflin, 1916.

Emerson, L. E. "Emerson and Freud: A Study in Contrasts." *Psychoanalytic Review* 20 (1933): 208–214.

Emerson, Ralph Waldo. *The Complete Works of Ralph Waldo Emerson.* Edited by E. W. Emerson. Centenary Edition. 12 vols. Boston: Houghton Mifflin, 1903–1904.

———, trans. *Dante's Vita Nuova.* Edited by J. Chesley Mathews. *Harvard Library Bulletin* no. 11 (Spring and Autumn, 1957). Reprint. The Ralph Waldo Emerson Memorial Association, 1957.

———. *The Early Lectures of Ralph Waldo Emerson.* Edited by S. E. Whicher, R. E. Spiller, and W. E. Williams. 3 vols. Cambridge, Mass.: Belknap Press, 1961–1972.

———. *Essays* and *Essays: Second Series.* 1841–1844. Facsimile reprint. Columbus, Ohio: Charles E. Merrill, 1969.

———. *The Journals and Miscellaneous Notebooks of Ralph Waldo Emerson.* Edited by W. G. Gilman et al. 14 vols. to date. Cambridge, Mass.: Belknap Press, 1960–1978.

———. *The Journals of Ralph Waldo Emerson.* Edited by E. W. Emerson and W. E. Forbes. 10 vols. Boston: Houghton Mifflin, 1909–1914.

———. *Letters from Ralph Waldo Emerson to a Friend.* Edited by Charles Eliot Norton. Boston: Houghton Mifflin, 1899.

———. *The Letters of Ralph Waldo Emerson.* Edited by Ralph L. Rusk. 6 vols. New York: Columbia Univ. Press, 1939.

BIBLIOGRAPHY

————, ed. *The Parnassus*. Boston: J. R. Osgood, 1874.

————. *Poems*. 1847. Boston: Ticknor and Fields, 1860.

————. Preface to *The Gulistan or Rose-Garden*, by Saadi. Translated by Francis Gladwin. Boston: Ticknor and Fields, 1865.

————. *The Works of Ralph Waldo Emerson*. Edited by J. E. Cabot. 14 vols. Boston: Houghton Mifflin, 1883–1887.

————. *Uncollected Writings: Essays, Addresses, Poems, Reviews and Letters by Ralph Waldo Emerson*. Edited by Charles Bigelow. New York: The Lamb, 1912.

————. "Visits to Concord." In *Memoirs of Margaret Fuller Ossoli*. 2 vols. Boston: Phillips and Sampson, 1852. 1: 199–316.

Feidelson, Charles. *Symbolism and American Literature*. Chicago: Univ. of Chicago Press, 1953.

Freud, Sigmund. *The Interpretations of Dreams*. Translated and edited by James Strachey. New York: Avon, 1968.

Fuller, Margaret. "The Great Lawsuit: Man Versus Men; Woman Versus Women." *The Dial: A Magazine for Literature, Philosophy and Religion* 4, i (July, 1843): 1–11.

————. *Woman in the Nineteenth Century, and Kindred Papers Relating to the Sphere, Conditions and Duties of Women*. Edited by Arthur B. Fuller. 1874. Reprint. New York: Greenwood Press, 1968.

Gilman, Margaret. "Baudelaire and Emerson." *Romantic Review* 24 (October, 1943): 211–222.

Gray, Ronald. *Goethe, the Alchemist*. Cambridge, England: Cambridge Univ. Press, 1952.

Gregg, E. W., ed. *One First Love: The Letters of Ellen Louisa Tucker to Ralph Waldo Emerson*. Cambridge, Mass.: Harvard Univ. Press, 1962.

Harding, Walter. *Emerson's Library*. Charlottesville, Va.: Univ. Press of Virginia, 1967.

Harris, William T. "Emerson's Orientalism." In *The Genius and Character of Emerson*. Edited by Frank Sanborn. Boston: J. R. Osgood, 1885.

Harrison, John. *The Teachers of Emerson*. New York: Sturgis and Walton, 1910.

Henry, Paul. Introduction to *The Enneads*, by Plotinus. Translated by Stephen MacKenna. 3rd ed., revised by B. G. Page. London: Faber and Faber, 1962.

Hirst, Désirée. *Hidden Riches: Traditional Symbolism from the Renaissance to Blake*. London: Eyre and Spottiswoode, 1964.

Hirzel, Rudolf. *Plutarch*. Leipzig: Dieterich, 1912.

Hopkins, Vivian. "Emerson and Cudworth." *American Literature* 23 (March, 1951): 80–98.

————. *Spires of Form: A Study of Emerson's Aesthetic Theory*. 1951. Reprint. New York: Russell and Russell, 1965.

Inge, William Ralph. *The Philosophy of Plotinus*. 2 vols. London: Longmans, Green, 1918.

James, Henry (the elder). *The Literary Remains*. Boston: J. R. Osgood, 1885.

Jones, Ernest. *Hamlet and Oedipus*. Garden City, N.Y.: Doubleday, 1954.

Jung, Carl. *Psychology and Alchemy*. Vol. 12 of the *Collected Works*. Edited by William McGuire. Translated by R. F. C. Hull. 2nd rev. ed. Princeton: Princeton Univ. Press, 1968.

Knight, G. Wilson. *The Wheel of Fire*. 4th rev. ed. London: Methuen, 1949.

Langbaum, Robert. *The Poetry of Experience*. New York: Norton, 1957.

Lawrence, D. H. *Studies in Classic American Literature*. 1923. Reprint. New York: Viking Press, 1964.

Lewis, R. W. B. *The American Adam*. Chicago: Univ. of Chicago Press, 1955.

Lovejoy, Arthur. *The Great Chain of Being*. 1936. Reprint. Cambridge, Mass.: Harvard Univ. Press, 1966.

Michaud, Régis. *The Enraptured Yankee*. Translated by George Boas. New York: Harper, 1964.

Miller, Perry. *Consciousness in Concord*. Boston: Houghton Mifflin, 1958.

Miller, Perry, ed. *Margaret Fuller, American Romantic: A Selection from Her Writings and Correspondence*. Garden City, N.Y. Doubleday, 1963.

Millet, Kate. *Sexual Politics*. Garden City, N.Y.: Doubleday, 1970.

Mumford, Lewis. *The Golden Day*. 1926. Reprint. New York: Dover, 1968.

Newcomb, Charles King. *The Journals of Charles Newcomb*. Edited by Judith Kennedy Johnson. Providence, R.I.: Brown Univ. Press, 1946.

Newman, F. B. "Emerson and Buonarroti." *The New England Quarterly* 25 (1952): 524–535.

Nicoloff, Philip L. *Emerson on Race and History: An Examination of English Traits*. New York: Columbia Univ. Press, 1961.

Nygren, Anders. *Agape and Eros*. Translated by Philip S. Watson. London: S. P. C. K., 1953.

Paul, Sherman. *Emerson's Angle of Vision*. Cambridge, Mass.: Harvard Univ. Press, 1952.

Porte, Joel. *Emerson and Thoreau: Transcendentalists in Conflict*. Middletown, Conn.: Wesleyan Univ. Press, 1966.

———. *Representative Man: Ralph Waldo Emerson in His Time*. New York: Oxford Univ. Press, 1979.

Praz, Mario. *The Romantic Agony*. Translated by Angus Davidson. 2nd ed. New York: Meridian Books, 1956.

Robin, Léon. *La théorie platonicienne de l'amour*. Paris: F. Alcan, 1908.

Rose, Mark. "Sidney's Womanish Man." *Review of English Studies* 15 (1964): 353–363.

Rougemont, Denis de. *Love Declared*. Translated by Richard Howard. New York: Pantheon Books, 1963.

Rusk, Ralph L. *The Life of Ralph Waldo Emerson*. New York: Columbia Univ. Press, 1964.

Sanborn, Frank, ed. *The Personality of Emerson*. Boston: Charles E. Goodspeed, 1903.

Sartre, Jean-Paul. *Baudelaire*. Paris: Gallimard, 1968.

Schiavone, Michele. *Il problema dell' amore nel mondo greco*. Milano: Marzorati, 1965.

Scudder, Townsend. *The Lonely Wayfaring Man*. London and New York: Oxford Univ. Press, 1936.

Seymour, Charles, Jr. *Michelangelo's David: A Search for Identity*. Pittsburgh: Univ. of Pittsburgh Press, 1967.

Shaw, C. G. "Emerson the Nihilist." *International Journal of Ethics* 25 (October, 1914): 68–86.

Smith, Henry Nash. "Emerson's Problem of Vocation." *The New England Quarterly* 20 (March–September, 1939): 52–67.

Strauch, Carl. "Hatred's Swift Repulsions: Emerson, Margaret Fuller, and Others." *Studies in Romanticism* 7 (Winter, 1968): 65–103.

Symonds, John Addington. *The Life of Michelangelo Buonarroti*. 1892. Reprint. New York: Capricorn, 1962.

Taylor, Thomas, ed. *Select Works of Plotinus*. London: The Author, 1817.

——, trans. *The Timaeus and the Critias,* by Plato. Introduction and notes by the translator. 1804. Reprint. Princeton: Princeton Univ. Press, 1944.

Thoreau, H. D. *Familiar Letters of Henry David Thoreau*. Vol. 11 of *The Writings of Henry David Thoreau*. Edited by Frank Sanborn. Boston: Riverside, 1894.

Wagenknecht, Edward. *Ralph Waldo Emerson: Portrait of a Balanced Soul*. New York: Oxford Univ. Press, 1974.

Wahr, F. W. *Emerson and Goethe*. Ann Arbor, Mich.: G. Wahr, 1915.

Warren, Austin. *New England Saints*. Ann Arbor, Mich.: Univ. of Michigan Press, 1956.

Wellek, René. *A History of Modern Criticism: 1750–1950*. 4 vols. New Haven: Yale Univ. Press, 1955–1965.

Whicher, Stephen. *Freedom and Fate: An Inner Life of Ralph Waldo Emerson*. Philadelphia: Univ. of Pennsylvania Press, 1953.

Wilkinson, James John Garth. Introduction to *The Economy of the Animal Kingdom,* by Emanuel Swedenborg. Translated by A. Clissold. London: W. Newberry, 1846.

Wilson, John Dover. *What Happens in Hamlet*. 1935. Reprint. Cambridge, England: Cambridge Univ. Press, 1964.

Woodbury, Charles. *Talks with Emerson*. 1890. Reprint. New York: Horizon Press, 1970.

INDEX

Abd-el-Kadir, 186
Abolitionist movement: E's attitude to, 73–74; women's participation in, 39
Achilles, 186; Greenough's sculpture of, 190
Active/passive (hermetic-alchemic polarity), 23, 65, 70
Acts of the Apostles, 147
Adam: Christ as "the last," 189, 217; as image of the poet, 7; the "original," 24, 68, 74–75, 132, 189, 217; the "perfect," 63, 189, 217; as simile in E's account of a childhood experience, 119
Adultery, 123–124
Aeschylus: the *Eumenides*, 232; the *Oresteia*, 242, 244–245, 261; *Prometheus Bound*, 247
Affections: comparable to mists, 37, 63–64; opposed to intellect, 23–24, 27–28, 63–64, 66–67; women ruled by, 37–38, 63–64
Ahriman, 238
Ajax, 184
Albee, John, 95, 96
Alchemy: *coniunctiones* of, x, 13, 16, 241, 244; and science, 13–14
Alcmaeons's decade, 14, 18
Alcott, Abba May (wife of Bronson Alcott), 133

Alcott, Bronson: and androgyny, 187–188, 196; and "angelic" type of man, 142; conversation of, 172–173, 175–176, 180; journals of, 142, 187; and Plato's State, 133, 134
Alexander (of Macedonia), 193. *See also* Hosmer, Edmund
Alleghany (mountains), as home of Great Mother, 251
Allston Gallery, 143
Ambiguity: in essay on "Love," 103; ironic, 53, 55, 170; in E's Platonistic sources, 78; in E's thought, x–xi; in "Woman," 33
America: future center of the English race, 251; place where the blue-eyed people gravitate, 142
Amore Greco, the, 53
Amphibiousness: heaven-earth, 136, 138, 144, 149, 151, 210; heaven-hell, 221–222
Andler, Charles, 217
Androgyny: and "balanced soul," 241–243; divine, 24, 30, 232, 237–238; and English mind, 193; and friendship, 194–197; and hero-gentleman, 192–194; and man of genius, 71, 189–192; and marriage, 198; in women, 24, 189, 191, 198–203. *See also* Hermaphroditus
Angels: androgyny of, 135, 233; and

275

children, 141, 142; and the English, 141–142; and love, 135, 145–146, 233–234; and power, 233–234; silence of, 145

Anima mundi, 11, 174. *See also* Nature

Antichrist, 216

Aphrodite (Venus): the heavenly, 45, 167; the vulgar, 46, 47, 48, 106. *See also* Venus

Apocalyptic expectations, 5, 216. *See also* Millennial hopes

Apollo: and Dionysus, 238, 245; as image of ideal masculine beauty, 53, 57; as image of the ideal world, 195; as image of internal heaven-hell marriage, 232–236, 238–239; as image of male adrogyny, 24, 30, 195

Appalachia, symbol of masculine American strength, 178

Apuleius, 106

Arabs, 159–161. *See also* Intellectual nomadism

Archetypes: in E's dichotomy of the world in terms of sex and polarity, x, 13, 16, 30, 50–57, 65; in E's imagery, 89–93, 177, 223; Plato's, 164

Aristophanes, 35, 39; in Plato's *Symposium,* 18

Aristotle: on catharsis, 93; on difference between love and friendship, 209

Arrian, 86, 139

Ars chymica, 13

Art, role of in regeneration of mankind, 218. *See also* Sculpture; names of individual artists and works

Arvin, Newton, 70–72

Asia: and Europe, 241–262; as nickname for E's wife, 246–250. *See also* Great Mother

Asia Minor: as home of the Great Mother, 245, 247–248; quarreling churches of, 247

Augustine (Saint): on biological hermaphrodites, 189; on charity, 147; development and attitudes of, compared with E's, 83, 85, 214. *See also* City of God

Baader, Franz von, 188

Bacchus, *See* Dionysus

Bacon, Sir Francis, 173

Balance: in Plato's mind, 241–246, 252–253; in E's thought, xi, xii, 33, 261–262

Balzac, Honoré de, *Le livre mystique* (*Louis Lambert* and *Séraphita*), 188, 201

Barker, Anna: beauty and charm of, discussed by E, 32–33, 40, 44, 45, 46–47; friendship with Margaret Fuller, 32, 44, 45, 101, 201; marriage to Samuel Ward, and E's reaction to it, 100–101

Barron, Nancy (the madwoman), 92

Baudelaire, Pierre Charles, 212

Beatrice (Dante's), 109–113; possible association with Ellen Tucker Emerson, 110–111

Beautiful enemies, 181–186. *See also* Friendship

Beautiful souls, 102, 120

Beauty: feminine, 1, 43–48, 50–52, 56–57, 86–87, 100, 107, 108, 110; intellectual, 46–47, 57; man of (the poet), 43; masculine, 48–50, 56–59; of nature, 1, 43–44, 49, 211, 258; in E's philosophical authorities, 43, 45–46, 55–58, 95, 102; of the Soul, 102, 207; universality of, 45, 47

Being and Seeming, 69

Berry, Edmund, 105–106

Beyle, Marie Henri (Stendhal), 51

Biagiolo, Giambattista, 264 n

Bible, the, 11, 49. *See also* specific texts

Bigendians and Littleendians, 175

Bipolarity: defined, x, xii; E's deviations from, x, xiii, 4–6; and hermetic-alchemic doctrine, 13; and pantheism, 10

Bishop, Jonathan, 268 n

Blacks, 72–75

Blake, William: and Emerson, 20, 225–229; *Marriage of Heaven and Hell, The,* 20, 225–227; *Songs of Innocence and of Experience,* 225; "The Tyger," 226

Boccaccio, Giovanni: the *Decameron,* 88

Body: beauty of, 103; and charity,

"Conventional Devil," the, 86

Conversation, E's theory of: as the practice and consummation of friendship, 171, 175–176; and Swedenborg's doctrine of heavenly marriage, 157–158; symbolic sex changes in, 157; women in, 37, 158–159

Conway, Moncure, 120

Corrine (in Madame de Staël's novel), 70

Courtly tradition, 108–109. See also Troubadours

Crashaw, Richard, "Satan," 129

Cudworth, Ralph, 12, 65

Cupid (in Apuleius' "Cupid and Psyche"), 106. See also RWE's poem "Cupido"

Custom, 95–96, 153. See also Society; Home and family

Cuvier, Georges, 7

D'Abrantes, Duchesse, 47

Dante (Alighieri): Il Convivio, 111; the Divine Comedy, 38, 124; life of, compared with E's, 109–113; E's translation of the Vita Nuova, 110; on the Virgin Mother, 38, 124; the Vita Nuova, 109–113, 182

Daumas, M. J. E. (French general), 186

Day/night (archetypal polaric opposition), 244

Dead, the: seek the living among, 144, 149

Delphic: sibyls (Pythia), 28, 32, 191; motto of Socrates, 211, 218

Descartes, René, 6, 13

Desert, the: and feminine principle, 159. See also Intellectual nomadism; Nihilism

Devil, the (the Serpent, the Snake, Satan); E as attorney of, 226; E as child of, 220; and Eve, 86–87; equated with intellect, 129, 229; in matter, 82; as multitude, 144; rights and rehabilitation of, 229; and witchcraft, 92; worship of, 225. See also Blake, William; Conventional Devil, Mephistopheles

Dial, the, 31, 112, 187, 203, 230. See also Fuller, Margaret; Emerson,

Ellen Tucker; RWE's prose works

Diana of the Ephesians, 248

Dido (in "The Tale of Good Women"), 46

Dionysus: androgyny of, 237–238; and Apollo, 238, 245; and Great Mother, 253–254, 258; an internal heaven-hell marriage, 232, 236–239. See also Nietzsche

Doer/sufferer (hermetic-alchemic polarity), 65–66, 70–71. See also Suffering

Donati, Gemma (estranged wife of Dante), 111

Don Juan (Byron's), 65, 165

Donne, John, 13

Double consciousness, 262

Dream: one of E's, 92–93; the poet's world as, 17

Dualism (E's): defined, x; as an inconsistent "squint" in E's thought, 77–130 (general focus of chapters 5–7); radical (in science), 6

Duality. See Bipolarity

Dudevant, Baronne (George Sand), 202–203, 230

Earth: archetypally opposed to heaven, x, 13, and passim; associated with woman, x, 38, 46; E's monistic view of, 4; Plato and, 245–246. See also Nature; Great Mother

Eden: "of God" (as image of impersonal love), 157; as image of state of innocence to which man must return, 3; as symbol of perfect beauty, 51. See also Adam; Eve

Egypt: "fleshpots of," 80; native country of Plotinus, 253; Plato's trip to, 253

Eliot, T. S., 126

Elliott, G. R., 263 n

Elysium, as image of heroic friendship, 183

Emancipation. See Abolitionist movement; Women's rights movement

Emerson, Bulkley (brother of RWE), 122

Emerson, Charles (brother of RWE): RWE's attachment to, 149; early death of, 122; engaged to Elizabeth

Hoar, 135; and lady-ghoul, 89; on male androgyny, 200; and Shakespeare's *Sonnets*, 170

Emerson, Edith (RWE's daughter), 98

Emerson, Edward (RWE's brother), 122

Emerson, Edward Waldo (RWE's son), 98, 267 n

Emerson, Ellen (RWE's daughter), 98

Emerson, Ellen Tucker. *See* Tucker, Ellen

Emerson, L. E., "Emerson and Freud," 92

Emerson, Lidian: "Asia" as RWE's nickname for, 246–250, 257; and Ellen's letters, 112; "flebile tendencies," 248; and RWE's theory of impersonal love, 99; Thoreau's admiration for, 248; yearning for a love letter, 112–113. *See also* Jackson, Lydia

Emerson, Mary Caroline (RWE's sister), 122

Emerson, Mary Moody: called "Amita," 121; as RWE's confidante, 149, 216; intellectual brilliance of, 47; role in RWE's spiritual formation, 116, 120–121, 247; virginity of, celebrated in "The Nun's Aspiration," 121

Emerson, Ralph Waldo: friendships with men, 98, 100–101, 111, 171, 176, 180–181, 185; friendships with women, 97–98, 100–101, 135, 136, 158–159, 183; health of (physical and mental), 81–83, 92, 111, 121–123; marriages, 1, 27, 45, 83, 84–86, 98–99, 111–113, 154, 161–162, 246–249, 257–258; Platonic aspirations of, xiv, xv; practical deviations from theories, xiv, 21, 85, 149, 161–162; problem of vocation, 116–117; relations with father, 115–119, 122–123; relations with mother, 119–121, 123–130

—Journals and notebooks, *passim*

—Letters to: Thomas Carlyle, 119; Lidian Emerson, 45, 112, 113, 135, 145; Mary Moody Emerson, 111, 149, 216; William Emerson, 115–125 *passim*, 247; Margaret Fuller, 45, 100–101, 136, 158, 188, 221, 224, 239; Hermann Grimm, 56; John Boynton

Hill, 121; Elizabeth Hoar, 194; Lydia Jackson, 3, 57, 99, 194, 257; Charles Newcomb, 257; John Sterling, 139, 209; Caroline Sturgis, 98, 143, 144; Anna and Samuel Ward, 45; Samuel Ward, 97, 98, 137

—Poems: "Alphonso of Castile," 220, "Bacchus," 166, 237, 238, 254; "Beauty," 12, 222; "Blight," 7–8; "The Bohemian Hymn," 214; "Boston Hymn," 74; "Brahma," 18; "The Celestial Love," 100, 101, 137–138, 144, 145, 164; "Culture," 217; "Cupido," 12, 222; "The Daemonic Love," 86; "Dirge," 120, 122; Epigraph to "The Poet," 19; "Eros," 145; "Etienne de la Boéce," 96, 183; "Eva," 207; "From the Persian of Hafiz," 238; "Ghaselle," 227–228, 237; "Give All to Love," 160; "Hamatreya," 252; "The Harp," 19, 65, 96; "Has God on thee conferred" (fragment), 215; "Holidays," 249; "The Humble-Bee," 163; "I bear in youth . . ." (fragment), 83; "If thou go in thine own likeness" (fragment), 118; "Illusions," 9, 162–163; "The Initial, Daemonic and Celestial Love," 101; "A Letter," 112; "May-Day," 236–237, 254; "Merlin," 19–21, 222; "A Mountain Grave," 255; "Nature" (fragment), 237; "The Nun's Aspiration," 121; "Ode to Beauty," 195; "Ode Inscribed to W. H. Channing," 224, 231; "Pan," 19, 164, 166–167; "The Park," 213; "Philosopher," 128–130; "The Poet," 153, 194; (fragments on) "The Poet and the Poetic Gift," 160; "The Problem," 58, 71, 116, 174, 191; "Promise," 217; "Romany Girl," 50–51, 123; "Saadi," 123, 144, 159, 197, 238; "The Song of Nature," 72; "A Sonnet by Michelangelo Buonarotti," 58; "The Sphinx," 72, 229, 250; "Spiritual Laws," 223, 226; "Terminus," 122; "Thine Eyes Still Shined," 1; "Threnody," 235; "Uriel," 223–224; "The Waterfall," 178; "Woodnotes," 3, 18, 19, 53, 119, 163, 166, 235, 255; "Written at Naples," 179–180; "Written at

INDEX

213, 235; "Uses of Great Men," 16, 156–157, 177, 180, 222; "The Uses of Natural History," 1, 5, 19; "Woman," 15–16, 26, 33–41, 46, 62, 63, 64, 191; "Works and Days," 17, 210, 234; "Worship," 46, 121–122
—Translations, 110, 166, 238

Emerson, Ruth (RWE's mother). *See* Emerson, Ralph Waldo

Emerson, Waldo (RWE's son): RWE's reaction to birth of, 249; RWE's reaction to death of, 78, 235

Emerson, William (RWE's brother), 115, 247

Emerson, William (RWE's father). *See* Emerson, Ralph Waldo, relations with father

Emotions, weak, 224. *See also* Affections; Women

Empedocles, 121

Empire, 226, 246, 261

England: best of actual nations, 141; tender-hearted, 173; yielding to America as the chief home of the English race, 251

Epaminondas, 49, 193

Ephebes, 50, 53

Equality between the sexes. *See* Sexes

Eros, 222. *See also* Cupid

Eugenics, 121–123, 141

Euripides, *Bacchae,* 248

Europe: light/dark complexions of, 142; opposed to "Asia," symbol of the East–Nature–Fate–the Great Mother, 241–262

Eve: and Anna Barker, 32; creation of, 34; dangerous physical charms of, 107; eliminated from Milton's picture of first couple, 75; and Fall of Man, 86–87; humility of, 38; "vagina dentata" of, 92. *See also* RWE's poem "Eva"

Everett, Edward, 52–53, 97

Evil: and sex, x, 224, 227–228. *See also* Devil; Dualism

Experience (personal): as basis for generalization, 89, 212–213; irrational, 77, 81; irrelevant, 78; painful, 77–78, 84–85, 149

Eyes: in free love and friendship, 55; in hero worship and heroic friendship, 177–179; "more womanly" (of

man of genius), 191–192; in Plotinian contemplation, 206; in quest for self-knowledge, 207

Fairies: circular completeness of, 235; image of ideal world, 102, 234; power of, 234; of true love, 102, 234. *See also* Androgyny; Internal marriage

Falkland, Lord, 140

Fall of Man: as man's coming of age, 128, 130; perpetual, 84, 86–87; as sexual differentiation, 25; woman's role in, 86–87

Family, the. *See* Home and family

Fate: associated with mortal mothers, 120, 248, 260–262; and nature-matter, the Great Mother, Earth, Night, the East, 243–262

Fatherland, the: the soul's journey back to, 90

Fathers, and self-transcendence, 117

Feidelson, Charles, 263 n

Feminine principle, the: associated with the earth, x, 44, 46; bipolaric view of, 1–3, 15, 23; and the irrational, 89–93; and old age, 62–63, 86; voided of content, 4, 16. *See also* Alchemy; Archetypes; Polarization (sexual); Women

Feminists, 23–24; E's attitude to, 26–27, 31–32, 39–40. *See also* Women's rights movement

Feudal-heroic view of woman, 33–34, 35

Fichte, Johann Gottlieb, 16

Ficino, Marsilio, 218, 219; *Theologia Platonica,* 218

Flaxman, John, 232

Florence, E's early visit to, 44, 219

Florida, E's convalescence trip to, 176

Fourier, F. M. C., 87

Freud, Sigmund, 126, 246

Friendship: and androgyny, 171, 175–179, 194–198; angelic, 135–136, 140–142, 144–146; as conversation, 157–159, 172–176; discussed in mystical terms, 170–171; equated with love, 169–170, 209; erotic language in discussions of, 98, 169–172; heroic, 181–187; as "intellectual nomadism,"

281

159–160; and marriage, 96–98, 100–
101, 140, 156–159; as a means to
self-acquaintance, 206–209; between
men and women, 158–159, 183;
paradoxical, 188–189; as redemption,
169, 179–180; transcends time and
space, 137–139, 144. *See also* Universal friend; Unknown friend; City
of God
Fugitive Slave Law, the, 73, 178
Fuller, Margaret: and Anna Barker,
32, 45, 47, 100–101; feminist views
of, 40, 65, 67, 68, 200–203; "The
Great Lawsuit: Man Versus Men;
Woman Versus Women," 31, 187,
200; intellectual relations with E,
183, 187, 188, 221, 239; journals of,
65; letters to Caroline Sturgis, 68;
"Nuovissimi Vita," 110; personal
relationship with E, 136, 147, 158,
198, 200–201; E's varying assessment
of, 40, 65, 67, 68, 200–203; *Woman
in the Nineteenth Century*, 26, 31,
200, 202, 267 n, 268 n
Furies, the, 91, 232, 244–245

Gaia, Ouranos' marriage with, x, 3, 11,
222, 244
Garrison, William Lloyd, 190
Gay, Martin, 97
Genesis, 73, 86, 181. *See also* Adam;
Devil; Eve; Fall of Man; Ham
Genius. *See* Man of genius
Gentleman. *See* Hero
German Romantics, 13, 24, 188. *See
also* individual authors
Gilman, Margaret, 267–268 n
Gypsies, 51, 123
Girardi, E. N., 264 n
God: as all in all, 64; man as heir of,
260; in matter, 82; means of com-
municating with man, 8, 10, 17; and
metamorphosis, 163; security in, 254;
source of inexhaustible power, 254–
255. *See also* Jehovah; One; Over-
Soul; Pan; Universal friend
Goethe, Johann Wolfgang von: as
E's "Bigendian," 175; distrust of,
192; *Elective Affinities*, 15, 182;
"Erlkoenig," 235; *Faust*, 229–230;
Italienische Reise, 57; knowledge of,

149, 183, 188; not redeemer of man's
mind, 4, 9, 203; E's spiritual inter-
course with, 173; *West-Oestliche
Diwan*, 110; *Wilhelm Meister*, 67,
202–203
Good of evil, the, 221–223, 228, 231
"Gorgon of Convention," the, 140
Gray, Ronald D., 203, 263 n
Great Daemon Love, the, ix, 10
Great Mother, the 242–262
Greece, creator of a patriarchal
civilization, 242–246
Greek mythology, 231. *See also*
individual names
Greek philosophy, 10. *See also*
individual representatives
Greek tragedy, 261. *See also* individual
authors
Greenough, Horatio, 190, 205–206
Gregg, E. W., 265 n
Gregory I (Pope), 141
Grimm, Hermann, 56
Griselda (in Chaucer's tale), 38

Hades, and Dionysus, 238. *See also*
Hell
Hafiz: and free love/friendship, 110;
influence on E's "Bacchus," 166;
intellectual and artistic freedom of,
165; moral emancipation of, 228–
229, 237, 238
Ham, 73
Hamlet, 193–194, 197
Hammer-Purgstall, Joseph von, 160
Hardenberg, Baron Friedrich von
(Novalis), 2, 8, 18, 154
Harding, Walter, 263 n, 267 n
Harris, William T., 252–253
Harrison, John, 263 n
Harvard Divinity School, 233. *See
also* RWE's "Divinity School
Address"
Hawthorne, Nathaniel, 162, 256
Heart, the. *See* Affections
Heaven: associated with male prin-
ciple, x, 61; equated with inner
world, 205; hour of, 180; of inven-
tion, 223; kingdom of, 135–136,
140–141; of letters, 138–139, 149;
"living," 223; as prison, 165
Heaven and earth: dualistic tendency

INDEX

Manicheism, 80, 83, 228
Man of genius: androgyny of, 71,
189–192; does not need a wife as
much as other men do, 198, 230;
enjoys angelic relations with other
men, 197–198; marries heaven and
hell in his mind, 222–223, 226–228
Manual of Artistic Anatomy (Robert
Knox), 48
Margaret (in Goethe's *Faust*), 229–230
Mark (gospel of), 147
Marriage: E's attempt to rehabilitate,
101–109; E's critique of Swedenborg's doctrine of, 157–159; harmful
to the soul's progress, 83–86, 99–
101, 157; merely empirical and
without ideal basis, 85; place of
children in, 104, 107; "the real
marriage," 15, 30, 104–105; symbol
of male friendship, 77–78. *See
also* Alchemy
Martineau, Harriet, 199
Masséna, André, 233–234
Mathews, J. Chesley, 265 n
Matriarchal era, 242. *See also* Great
Mother
Matter: associated with fate, 261; as
dead mind, 11; evil of, 80; not of
the devil, 82; our "old home," 257.
See also Dualism; Nature; Man-
icheism; Pantheism
Matthew (gospel of), 123
Maya, 16–17
Medora, the, 190
Medusa, 57
Melville, Herman: *Battle-Pieces*, 72;
Billy Budd, 141; *Moby Dick*, 53;
Pierre, 125–126
Mémorial de Sainte-Hélène (by Las
Cases, Emmanuel, Comte de), 192
Mephistopheles, 229
Merlin, 20, 222
Messiah: the friend as, 179; of
nature, 2
Metamorphosis. *See* Change
Method of composition (E's), xi-xii,
30–31, 34, 54, 103, 162
Mezentius, 85
Michaud, Régis, 121, 207, 267 n
Michelangelo (Buonarroti): the *David*,
58, 219; ideal self-portraiture, 219;
idea of Man, 57–58, 220; the *Last*

Judgment, 57, 219; and the masculine form, 56; the *Moses*, 219; as
"passive master," 71, 174; as rival
of God, 219; and Socrates, 132–133;
and the *Sonnets (Rime)*, 56, 58, 108,
133, 198; as teacher of true love,
108, 109; and Vittoria Colonna, 56,
108, 198; on woman, 56, 207
Mill, John Stuart, *On the Subjection
of Women*, 24
Millennial hopes: early, 4–5; possibility of symbolic fulfillment of,
135; revised, 9, 131. *See also* Apocalyptic expectations
Miller, Perry, 265 n, 267 n
Millet, Kate, 264 n
Milton, John: as an "angelic soul,"
75; as an authority on marriage,
106–107; and *Doctrine and Discipline of Divorce*, 106–107; and
hermetic-alchemic doctrine, 13, 16;
and E's ideas about angelic love,
157, 201; "letter to an unknown
friend," 214; *Paradise Lost*, 16, 32–
33, 38, 75, 86, 107, 108, 155, 228;
E's view of woman, 16, 32–33, 38–
39, 86, 156
Minerva; symbol of female androgyny,
24, 30
Mohammed, 35, 47, 133
Molière, 120
Monism: as defense against dualistic
fears, 77–78, 93, 148; defined, x, xiii;
as deviation from E's bipolaric-
nuptial approach, 4–5; as one per-
vasive strain in E's thought, 23–75
(chapters 2–4). *See also* Pantheism
Montaigne, Michel de: "De l'art de
conferer," 158, 183; as authority on
friendship, 96, 183; "Considération
sur Cicéron," 183, "De l'experience,"
234; *Les Essais*, 138; as guarantor of
E's "heaven of letters," 138; and
La Boétie, 183; on marriage, 96, 99;
E and skepticism, xi, 96; "spermatic" author, 174; and Vishnu, 231
Moon, the: as symbol of nature and
the Great Mother, 248, 249. *See
also* Sun
More, Henry, 12
More, Sir Thomas, 91
Mothers: chastity in, 124–130; and

285

INDEX

Optimism (philosophical). *See* Monism

Orientalism: limits of Emerson's, 241–262 *passim*. *See also* Buddha womb; Mysticism

Ormuzd, 238

Orpheus, 120

Ossoli. *See* Fuller, Margaret

Ouranos, and Gaia, x, 3, 11, 222, 244

Ourobouros, 223. *See also* Circle; Sphere

Outdoors/indoors (archetypal polarity), 13, 23, 30, 50–51

Over-Soul, the: and the passive master, 174; rivers and waterfalls as images for, 178–179; the sun as image for, 191; uncertain sex of (breast and womb imagery), 254–255; union with, 254. *See also* One

Ovid (Publius Ovidius Naso): *Metamorphoses*, 206, 237; *Remedia amoris*, 68

Pan: chaser of nymphs, ix, 258; choregus of the universe, 19, 166–167; equated with the All, 19, 163; the poet as priest of, ix, 2, 11–12, 258. *See also* Pantheism

Pantheism: and bipolarity, 12; and hermetic-alchemic thought, 12; and Pythagoreanism, 19; as a Romantic simplification of the doctrines of Plotinus and Proclus, 11; and theism, 237

Paradise. *See* Eden

Parmenides, 16

Pascal, Blaise, 147, 174

Passion, as a disastrous element in the lives of women, 37–38, 64, 65–66. *See also* Affections; Suffering; Women

Passive Master, the, 71, 174–175. *See also* Androgyny; Man of genius

Past, the, 160–167

Patmore, Coventry, *The Angel in the House*, 34–35

Patriarchal civilization, 35, 244, 245

Paul (Apostle): E's admiration for, 133–134; on charity, 147; I Corinthians, 147; and E's idea of self-transcendence, 215–216; and the Great Mother, 248, 260; on marriage,

106–107; on the "new" Adam, 189

Paul, Sherman, 61–62, 100, 194, 268 n

Pausanias (in Plato's *Symposium*), 45, 95

Peabody, Elizabeth, 27

Penia. *See* Poros and Penia

Pericles, 30, 178, 193

Persian: empire, 242; Lilla, 32–33, 37; poets, 32–33, 159–160. *See also* Hafiz; Khayyám, Omar; Saadi

Petrarch, Francesco, 108–109, 182; *Rime in vita e morte della mia donna Laura*, 108

Phidias, *Jove*, 58

Philanthropy, 146. *See also* Charity

Philosophers' Stone. *See* Rebis

Phocion, 193

Phosphorus, 58–59

Phrygia, as home of the Great Mother, 148

Pico della Mirandola, 218, 219; "The Dignity of Man," 218

Pindar, 138

Plato: as "the balanced soul," 241–252; E's early adoption of viewpoint of, 52, 95–98, 138; E's fascination with the *Phaedrus* and the *Symposium*, 95–98; the *Laws*, 80; E's limited endorsement of the *Republic*, 131–134; the *Phaedrus*, ix, 41, 52, 53, 57, 95, 96, 98, 101, 102, 107, 131, 132, 158, 170, 214; E's reading of the *Timaeus*, 78–80; the *Republic*, 10, 24, 25, 41, 64, 79–80, 81, 131–135, 141, 142, 189; the *Symposium*, ix, 20, 37, 41, 45, 53, 95, 96, 98, 101, 102, 111, 153, 158; and E's theory of amphibious life, 151; the *Timaeus*, 18, 25, 60, 79, 81, 131, 132, 147, 156, 189

Platonic aspiration (E's), xiv–xv. *See also* Self-transcendence

Platonists, 6, 16, 43, 80, 103. *See also* Neo-Platonists

Pleasure and pain, union of, 185

Plotinus: and E's dualistic squint, 5, 80; the *Enneads*, 80; and E's ideas about amphibious life, 138–139; "The Intellectual Beauty," 58; and E's "metaphysical narcissism," 206–216; E and mysticism of, 253–255, 257; and E's philosophical objec-

INDEX

131–149. *See also* Apocalyptic
expectations; Millennial hopes
Revelation, 131, 136
Rhymes, polaric correspondences as,
9, 14, 20
Richard I, 186
Richter, J. P. F. (Jean-Paul), 8
Ripley, Sarah Alden Bradford, 47, 120
Rob (one of E's pseudonyms), 197
Robin, Léon, 264 n
Robin Hood, 193
Rodney, George Brydges, 140, 193
Rome, 138, 179–180
Rose, Mark, 267 n
Rougemont, Denis de, 165
Rusk, Ralph, 102, 265 n, 266 n, 267 n,
268 n
Ruskin, John, 190

Saadi: as a historic phenomenon, 162,
197; as E's ideal poet, 159–160, 197,
222, 223
Saint-Simonians, the, 188
Saladin, 186
Sanborn, Frank, 98, 266 n, 268 n
Sand, George. *See* Dudevant, Baronne
Sappho, 65, 201
Sartre, Jean-Paul: *Baudelaire,* 212;
Nausea, 128
Satan. *See* Devil
Saxon, as male element in English, 193
Scandinavians. *See* Nordic race; Race
Schelling, F. W. J. von, 8, 81; influ-
ence on E's thought, 20, 65, 66, 188,
261
Schiavone, Michele, 266 n
Schopenhauer, Arthur, 81
Schubert, Franz, 235
Science, E's relation to, 1–21. *See also*
Naturalists
Scudder, Townsend, 154
Sculpture, 214, 218, 219. *See also* Art
Self-knowledge: equated with solitude,
208; and friendship, 176, 180, 206–
207, 208; and love, 207; and reading,
175; and study of nature, 211
Self-projection: the "balanced soul"
(Plato) as, 241, 246; the poet as, 53
and *passim*; in reading, 212; in
Representative Men, Saadi as,
159–160, 197

Self-transcendence: for the individual,
117, 214–216; for species, 216–220
Self-union, 205–206, 208
Sensuality: effect on offspring, 123;
mortal, 124; after thirty, 84, 86
Sex: emasculating effect of indulgence,
87, 122–123, 227; and the irrational,
77–78, 79–81; nausea (E's), 127–128;
and polarity, ix–x, 15; in relation
to evil, x, 77–83, 222–228; universal,
14–17. *See also* Bipolarity; Puritan
heritage; Sexual intercourse
Sexes, the: division of man into, 81,
86, 189; equality between, 23–41;
love in, 97; sun and moon as symbols of, 13, 16; unification of, 24,
74–75. *See also* Adam; Alchemy;
Archetypes; Feminine principle;
Male principle; Man II; Polarization
(sexual); Women
Sexual intercourse: as an image in
E's discussion of friendship, 169–
172; as an image of the reader-
author relationship, 172–174; and
E's theory of conversation, 157,
171–172, 175–176. *See also* Sex;
Alchemy
Seyd, 222, 223. *See also* Saadi
Seymour, Charles, Jr., 58
Shakers, the, 39, 87
Shakespeare: "Bigendian" of Charles
Newcomb, 119; goddess-born, 119;
Hamlet, 125–129, 193–194, 197; love
and identification with, 181; *A
Midsummer Night's Dream,* 236;
Newcomb as E's "best key" to, 126;
Sonnets, 170, 184–185; E's spiritual
intercourse with, 173
Shaw, C. G., 143
Shelley, Percy Bysshe, *Prometheus
Unbound,* 247
Shepard, Odell, 266 n
Shih Ching (Sheking), 62
Shiraz, 159
Sidney, Sir Philip, 194
Simeon (in Luke 2:25–35), 256
Sirens, 89
Skepticism: E's compared with Mon-
taigne's, x; E's on Montaigne's, 96;
the poet's dream world and, 17
Smith, Henry Nash, 116
Snake (s), 86–87, 91–92. *See also* Devil

289

INDEX

oracular, 28, 38, 191, 199; strong
by humility, 38–39. *See also*
Feminine principle; Wives
Women's rights movement, the, 26–27,
31, 33–41
Woodbury, Charles, 268 n
Wordsworth, William: "Intimations
of Immortality," 4; on Plato's State,

141; "The Recluse," 2; "Tintern
Abbey," 11–12

Zarathustra, E and Nietzsche's, 217
Zeno, 86, 139
Zeus (Jove), 53, 57, 58, 210, 217, 229
Zoroaster, 217. *See also* Zarathustra